Thank you for purchasing the 3rd Supplement to the [barcode]

CW00515425

☑ **Don't miss important updates**

So that you have all the latest information, **McGregor on Damages** [...]
Order to ensure you receive the updating copies / supplements as [...]
Sweet & Maxwell is hassle-free, simply tick, complete and return th[...]

You may cancel your Standing Order at any time by writing to us at [...] PO Box 2000, Andover, SP10 9AH
stating the Standing Order you wish to cancel.

Alternatively, if you have purchased your copy of **McGregor on Damages** from a bookshop or other trade supplier,
please ask your supplier to ensure that you are registered to receive the new supplements.

All goods are subject to our 30 day Satisfaction Guarantee (applicable to EU customers only)

Yes, please send me new supplements and /or new editions of **McGregor on Damages**
to be invoiced on publication, until I cancel the standing order in writing.

☐ [All new editions]

☐ [All new supplements to the 18th edition]

☐ [All new supplements and editions]

Title   Name

Organisation

Job title

Address

Postcode

Telephone

Email

S&M account number (if known)

PO number

All orders are accepted subject to the terms of this order form and our Terms of Trading (see www.sweetandmaxwell.co.uk). By submitting this order
form I confirm that I accept these terms and I am authorised to sign on behalf of the customer.

Signed   Job Title

Print Name   Date

UK VAT Number: GB 900 5487 43. Irish VAT Number: IE 9513874E. For customers in an EU member state (except UK & Ireland) please supply your VAT
Number. VAT No [   ]

Delivery charges are not made for titles supplied to mainland
UK. Non-mainland UK please add £4/€5 per delivery.
Europe – please add £10/€13 for first item, £2.50/€3 for each
additional item. Rest of World – please add £30/€38 for first
item, £15/€19 for each additional item.

Thomson Reuters (Professional) UK Limited – Legal
Business (Company No. 1679046). 100 Avenue Road,
Swiss Cottage, London NW3 3PF. Registered in England
and Wales. Registered office: Aldgate House, 33 Aldgate
High Street, London EC3N 1DL. Trades using various
trading names, a list of which is posted on its website at
sweetandmaxwell.co.uk
Thomson Reuters (Professional) UK Limited is a registered
data controller under number 27602050.

Your information will be added to the marketing database
and will not be given to third parties without your prior
consent. Your information will be used to send you relevant
marketing and informational material on our products
and services.

If you do not wish to receive information about products
and services from the following please tick the relevant
box[es] Sweet & Maxwell ☐ W Green ☐ Incomes Data
Services ☐ Round Hall ☐
For a detailed privacy statement, a copy, or correction of
your information please write to Marketing Information, 100
Avenue Road, London NW3 3PF or call 0207 393 7000.
UK VAT is charged on all applicable sales at the prevailing
rate except in the case of sales to Ireland where Irish VAT
will be charged on all applicable sales at the prevailing

rate. Customers outside of the EU will not be charged
UK VAT.
The price charged to customers, irrespective of any prices
quoted, will be the price specified in our price list current
at the time of despatch of the goods, as published on our
website unless the order is subject to a specific offer or
discount in which case special terms may apply.

Rates, prices, delivery charges, discounts, dates and other
information are subject to change at anytime without prior
notice. Goods will normally be despatched within 3-5
working days of availability.

"Thomson Reuters" and the Thomson Reuters logo
are trademarks of Thomson Reuters and its affiliated
companies.

(BC003) V9 (11.2012) ES / KS

SWEET & MAXWELL

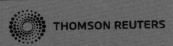

THOMSON REUTERS

SWEET & MAXWELL

FREEPOST

PO BOX 2000

ANDOVER

SP10 9AH

UNITED KINGDOM

THE COMMON LAW LIBRARY

McGREGOR
ON
DAMAGES

Third Supplement
to the
Eighteenth Edition

Up-to-date to September 1, 2012

BY

HARVEY McGREGOR
Q.C., D.C.L., S.J.D.

CHAPTER 43 ON THE HUMAN RIGHTS ACT
BY MARTIN SPENCER Q.C.

CHAPTERS 44–46 ON PROCEDURE
BY JULIAN PICTON Q.C.

SWEET & MAXWELL

THOMSON REUTERS

Published in 2012 by Sweet & Maxwell, 100 Avenue Road, London, NW3 3PF
Part of Thomson Reuters (Professional) UK Limited
(Registered in England & Wales, Company No 1679046.
Registered Office and address for service:
Aldgate House, 33 Aldgate High Street, London EC3N 1DL)

For further information on our products and services, visit:
http://www.sweetandmaxwell.co.uk

Typeset by Interactive Sciences Ltd, Gloucester
Printed and bound in Great Britain by CPI Group (UK) Ltd,
Croydon, CR0 4YY

No natural forests were destroyed to make this product.
Only farmed timber was used and replanted.

British Library Cataloguing in Publication Data

A CIP catalogue record for this book
is available from the British Library
ISBN 978–0–41–402–442–7

HOW TO USE THIS SUPPLEMENT

This is the Third Supplement to the Eighteenth Edition of
McGregor on Damages, and has been compiled according to the
structure of the main volume.

At the beginning of each chapter of this Supplement is an abbreviated table
of contents from the main volume. Where a heading in this table of
contents has been marked with a square pointer, this indicates that there is
relevant information in the Supplement to which the reader should refer. Material
that is new to the Cumulative Supplement is indicated by the symbol ■.
Material that has been included from the previous Supplements is indicated
by the symbol □.

Within each chapter, updating information is referenced to
the relevant paragraph in the main volume.

CONTENTS

	Page
Table of Cases	vii
Table of Statutes	xxi
Table of Statutory Instruments	xxii
Table of Civil Procedure Rules	xxii

BOOK ONE
GENERAL PRINCIPLES

Chapter 1—Definition, Scope, Object and Terminology	3
Chapter 2—Pecuniary Losses	9
Chapter 3—Non-Pecuniary Losses	12
Chapter 4—The General Problem of Limits	19
Chapter 5—Reduction of Damages for Contributory Negligence	21
Chapter 6—Remoteness of Damage	23
Chapter 7—Mitigation of Damage	33
Chapter 8—Certainty of Damage	43
Chapter 9—Past and Prospective Damage	59
Chapter 10—Nominal Damages	63
Chapter 11—Exemplary Damages	65
Chapter 12—Restitutionary Damages	71
Chapter 13—Liquidated Damages	74
Chapter 14—The Incidence of Taxation	79
Chapter 15—The Awarding of Interest	81
Chapter 16—The Effect of Changes in Value	89
Chapter 17—The Recovery of Costs, Damages and Fines Incurred in Previous Proceedings	91

BOOK TWO
PARTICULAR CONTRACTS AND TORTS

Chapter 19—The Measure of Damages in Contract and Tort Compared 95

Chapter 20—Sale of Goods 99

Chapter 21—Hire and Hire-purchase of Goods 103

Chapter 22—Sale of Land 104

Chapter 23—Lease of Land 106

Chapter 24—Sale of Shares and Loan of Stock 109

Chapter 25—Contracts to Pay or to Lend Money 110

Chapter 26—Building Contracts 111

Chapter 27—Contracts of Carriage 113

Chapter 28—Contracts of Employment 115

Chapter 29—Contracts for Professional and Other Services 116

Chapter 30—Contracts Concerning Principal and Agent 121

Chapter 31—Contracts of Warranty of Authority by Agent 122

Chapter 32—Torts Affecting Goods: Damage and Destruction 125

Chapter 33—Torts Affecting Goods: Misappropriation 130

Chapter 34—Torts Affecting Land 135

Chapter 35—Torts Causing Personal Injury 148

Chapter 36—Torts Causing Death 158

Chapter 37—Assault and False Imprisonment 163

Chapter 38—Malicious Institution of Legal Proceedings 168

Chapter 39—Defamation 170

Chapter 40—Economic Torts 174

Chapter 41—Misrepresentation 182

Chapter 42—Invasion of Privacy and Misfeasance in Public Office 186

BOOK THREE
HUMAN RIGHTS

Chapter 43—Damages Under the Human Rights Act 191

BOOK FOUR
PROCEDURE

Chapter 44—The Statement of Case 203

Chapter 45—The Trial 204

Chapter 46—Appeals 211

TABLE OF CASES

2 Travel Group Plc (In Liquidation) v Cardiff City Transport Services Ltd [2012] CAT 19;
[2012] Comp. A.R. 211 ....11–014, 11–020, 11–043

A Nelson & Co Ltd v Guna SpA [2011] EWHC 1202 (Comm); [2011] E.C.C. 23 7–087

AAA v Associated Newspapers Ltd [2012] EWHC 2103 (QB) 42–009C

AB v Nugent Care Society (formerly Catholic Social Services (Liverpool)); sub nom. AB
v Nugent Care Society [2010] EWHC 1005 (QB); (2010) 116 B.M.L.R. 84 37–006

ABB v Milton Keynes Council [2011] EWHC 2745 (QB); [2012] 1 F.L.R. 1157; [2012]
Fam. Law 28 35–280

AM v Secretary of State for the Home Department Unreported March 13, 2012 Cty Ct 37–018

ASM Shipping Ltd of India v TTMI Ltd of England, The Amer Energy [2009] 1 Lloyd's
Rep. 293 QBD (Comm) 6–173A, 6–173I, 27–032

AT v Dulghieru [2009] EWHC 225 (QB) 11–028, 11–043, 37–001, 37–003, 37–006, 37–010,
37–012, 37–018, 37–019

Abrahams v Herbert Reiach Ltd [1922] 1 K.B. 477 CA 8–095B, 8–095C

Achilleas, The. See Transfield Shipping Inc v Mercator Shipping Inc (The Achilleas)

Acre 1127 Ltd (In Liquidation) (formerly Castle Galleries Ltd) v De Montfort Fine Art
Ltd [2011] EWCA Civ 87 20–112

Activa DPS Europe Sarl v Pressure Seal Solutions Ltd (t/a Welltec System (UK) [2012]
EWCA Civ 943; [2012] T.C.L.R. 7; [2012] 3 C.M.L.R. 33 7–049

Adan v Securicor Custodial Services Ltd [2004] EWHC 394 (QB); [2004] C.P. Rep. 33;
[2005] P.I.Q.R. P6 .... 8–025, 45–039

AerCap Partners 1 Ltd v Avia Asset Management AB [2010] EWHC 2431 (Comm);
[2010] 2 C.L.C. 578; [2011] Bus. L.R. D85 ....8–038, 20–112, 20–116, 20–117

Aerospace Publishing Ltd v Thames Water Utilities Ltd [2007] EWCA Civ 3; [2007] Bus.
L.R. 726; 110 Con. L.R. 1; [2007] 3 Costs L.R. 389; (2009) 25 Const. L.J. 121;
[2007] C.I.L.L. 2429; (2007) 104(4) L.S.G. 32; (2007) 151 S.J.L.B. 123; [2007]
N.P.C. 5 15–081

Ahmed v Shafique [2009] EWHC 618 (QB) 37–018

Alan Nuttall Ltd v Fri-Jado UK Ltd [2010] EWHC 1966 (Pat) 7–004

Albion Water Ltd v Dwr Cymru Cyfyngedig [2010] CAT 30; [2011] Comp. A.R. 25 CAT 11–014,
11–043

Alexander v Rolls Royce Motor Cars Ltd [1996] R.T.R. 95 CA (Civ Div) 32–044B

Amalgamated Metal Corp Plc v Wragge & Co (A Firm) [2011] EWHC 887 (Comm);
[2011] P.N.L.R. 24 8–041

Amer Energy, The. See ASM Shipping Ltd of India v TTMI Ltd of England, The Amer
Energy

Amin v Imran Khan & Partners [2011] EWHC 2958 (QB) 36–100, 36–126, 42–022

Ampurius Nu Homes Holdings Ltd v Telford Homes (Creekside) Ltd [2012] EWHC 1820
(Ch) 2–041D

Amstrad Plc v Seagate Technology Inc 61632, 86 B.L.R. 34; [1998] Masons C.L.R. Rep.
1 QBD 14–021A, 15–140

Andrew Weir & Co v Dobell & Co [1916] 1 K.B. 722 KBD 7–084A

Andrews v Aylott [2010] EWHC 597 (QB); [2010] 4 Costs L.R. 568; [2010] P.I.Q.R.
P13 45–037

Aneco Reinsurance Underwriting Ltd (In Liquidation) v Johnson & Higgins Ltd; sub nom.
Aneco Reinsurance Underwriting Ltd v Johnson & Higgs Ltd [2001] UKHL 51;
[2001] 2 All E.R. (Comm) 929; [2002] 1 Lloyd's Rep. 157; [2002] C.L.C. 181;
[2002] Lloyd's Rep. I.R. 91; [2002] P.N.L.R. 8 6–132

Anglia Television Ltd v Reed [1972] 1 Q.B. 60; [1971] 3 W.L.R. 528; [1971] 3 All E.R.
690; (1971) 115 S.J. 723 CA (Civ Div) 2–041C

[vii]

TABLE OF CASES

Anglo Continental Educational Group (GB) Ltd v ASN Capital Investments Ltd (formerly) Capital Homes (Southern) Ltd [2010] EWHC 2649 (Ch) 22–031
Anthracite Rated Investments (Jersey) Ltd v Lehman Brothers Finance SA (In Liquidation); Fondazione Enasarco v Lehman Brothers Finance SA [2011] EWHC 1822 (Ch); [2011] 2 Lloyd's Rep. 538 .... 7–125C
Appleton v El Safty [2007] EWHC 631 (QB) 35–078
Aquilina v Malta (28040/08) June 14, 2011 43–093
Armory v Delamirie, 93 E.R. 664; (1722) 1 Str. 505 KB 8–002D, 33–049A, 40–031
Att Gen of Ghana v Texaco Overseas Tankships Ltd (The Texaco Melbourne) [1994] 1 Lloyd's Rep. 473; [1994] C.L.C. 155 HL 16–044
Attrill v Dresdner Kleinwort Ltd [2012] EWHC 1468 (QB) 15–117
Azimut-Benetti SpA v Henley [2011] 1 Lloyd's Rep. 473 .... 13–014, 13–020A
BJM v Eyre [2010] EWHC 2856, QB 35–277
Bailey & Co v Balholm Securities. See E Bailey & Co v Balholm Securities
Barr v Biffa Waste Services Ltd [2011] EWHC 1003 (TCC); [2011] 4 All E.R. 1065; 137 Con. L.R. 125 34–019
Beechwood Birmingham Ltd v Hoyer Group UK Ltd [2010] EWCA Civ 647; [2011] Q.B. 357; [2010] 3 W.L.R. 1677; [2010] Bus. L.R. 1562; [2011] 1 All E.R. (Comm) 460; [2010] R.T.R. 33 .... 3–009, 3–011, 7–019, 7–062A, 7–062B, 32–044A, 32–044B, 32–048A, 32–051A, 46–027B
Bennett v Stephens [2012] EWHC 58 (QB); [2012] R.T.R. 27 45–035
Bent v Highways and Utilities [2012] EWCA Civ 961; [2012] C.I.L.L. 3213 34–019
Berezovsky v Russian Television and Radio Broadcasting Company [2010] EWHC 476 (QB) 45–057A
Berry v Laytons [2009] EWHC 1591 (QB); [2009] E.C.C. 34 .... 8–063, 8–066, 29–008
Best v Smyth [2010] EWHC 1541 (QB) 5–006
Birmingham Corp v Sowsbery [1970] R.T.R. 84; (1969) 113 S.J. 877 QBD 32–044A
Blue Sky One Ltd v Mahan [2010] EWHC 631 (Comm) 33–065
Bocardo SA v Star Energy UK Onshore Ltd [2010] UKSC 35; [2010] 3 W.L.R. 654; [2010] 3 All E.R. 975; [2010] 31 E.G. 63 (C.S.); [2010] N.P.C. 88 .... 12–010, 34–051A
Bole v Huntsbuild Ltd (2009) 127 Con.L.R.154, CA 34–005
Borders (UK) Ltd v Commissioner of Police of the Metropolis [2005] EWCA Civ 197; [2005] Po. L.R. 1; (2005) 149 S.J.L.B. 301 11–028
Borealis AB v Geogas Trading SA [2010] EWHC 2789 (Comm); [2011] 1 Lloyd's Rep. 482 .... 2–051, 6–147A, 6–185, 7–043, 20–076, 20–103A
Boreham v Burton [2012] EWHC 930 (QB) 45–035
Boston Deep Sea Fishing & Ice Co v Ansell (1888) L.R. 39 Ch. D. 339 .... 8–103, 8–106
Botham v Ministry of Defence [2010] EWHC 646 (QB) 28–023A
Bowman v MGN Ltd [2010] EWHC 895 (QB) 39–055
Brewer v Mann [2010] EWHC 2444 (QB) 21–007
Brightlingsea Haven Ltd v Morris [2009] EWHC 3061 (QB); [2009] 48 E.G. 103 (C.S.) ... 1–009
Brit Inns Ltd (In Liquidation) v BDW Trading Ltd; Barber v BDW Trading Ltd [2012] EWHC 2143 (TCC) 26–011
British Racing Drivers Club Ltd v Hextall Erskine & Co [1996] 3 All E.R. 667; [1996] B.C.C. 727; [1997] 1 B.C.L.C. 182; [1996] P.N.L.R. 523 Ch D 17–005, 17–019
British Westinghouse Electric & Manufacturing Co Ltd v Underground Electric Railways Co of London Ltd (No.2) [1912] A.C. 673 HL 2–041D, 2–041E
Broome v Cassell & Co Ltd (No.1) [1972] A.C. 1027; [1972] 2 W.L.R. 645; [1972] 1 All E.R. 801; (1972) 116 S.J. 199 HL 45–057A
BSkyB Ltd v HP Enterprise Services UK Ltd (formerly t/a Electronic Data Systems Ltd) [2010] EWHC 86 (TCC); [2010] B.L.R. 267; 129 Con. L.R. 147; (2010) 26 Const. L.J. 289; [2010] C.I.L.L. 2841 .... 7–070, 14–021A, 15–140
Bullimore v Pothecary Witham Weld [2011] I.R.L.R. 18; [2010] Eq. L.R. 26 EAT ... 3–011, 6–056
Bungay v Saini [2011] Eq. L.R. 1130 3–011
Butler-Creagh v Hersham; Cherrilow Ltd v Butler-Creagh [2011] EWHC 2525 (QB) 41–026, 41–028
C&P Haulage v Middleton [1983] 1 W.L.R. 1461; [1983] 3 All E.R. 94; (1983) 127 S.J. 730 CA (Civ Div) 2–041C
Cairns v Modi [2012] EWHC 756 (QB) 39–046
Cambridge v Makin [2011] EWHC 12 (QB) 1–031, 39–034, 39–068

Cantor Fitzgerald LP v Drummond Unreported August 4, 2009 .... 13–018, 13–123
Capita Alternative Fund Services (Guernsey Ltd) (formerly Royal & SunAlliance Trust
(Channel Islands) Ltd) v Drivers Jonas (A Firm) [2011] EWHC 2336 (Comm); 139
Con. L.R. 125 ....6–132, 14–049, 29–052
Carroll v Kynaston [2010] EWCA Civ 1404; [2011] Q.B. 959; [2011] 2 W.L.R. 1346   17–038
Carter v Cole [2009] EWCA Civ 410; [2009] 33 E.G. 66; [2009] 21 E.G. 103 (C.S.) ...   22–002
Checkprice (UK) Ltd v Revenue and Customs Commissioners [2010] EWHC 682
(Admin); [2010] S.T.C. 1153; [2010] A.C.D. 679 .. 8–041, 8–082, 10–006, 15–048, 33–009A,
33–066
Choil Trading SA v Sahara Energy Resources Ltd [2010] EWHC 374 (Comm) 1–037, 7–096A,
20–059A, 20–061, 20–062, 20–087A
Chubb Fire Ltd v Vicar of Spalding [2010] EWCA Civ 981; [2010] 2 C.L.C. 277; (2010)
154(33) S.J.L.B. 29; [2010] N.P.C. 92   6–059
Ciorap v Moldova (No.3) (AG0003622)   43–045
Clarke v Maltby [2010] EWHC 1201 (QB) 8–033, 8–040, 8–047, 8–074A, 35–078
Cleveland Bridge UK Ltd v Multiple Constructions (UK) Ltd [2010] EWCA Civ 139 8–102,
26–013
Clifford v Chief Constable of Hertfordshire [2011] EWHC 815 (QB) 38–004, 38–005, 38–012,
38–014, 42–022
Clynes v O'Connor [2011] EWHC 1201 (QB)   39–031
Coles v Hetherton [2012] EWHC 1599 (Comm); [2012] R.T.R. 33; (2012) 162 N.L.J. 873 32–007,
32–021B
Collett v Smith; sub nom. Smith v Collett [2009] EWCA Civ 583; (2009) 106(26) L.S.G.
18; (2009) 153(24) S.J.L.B. 34 CA (Civ Div) 8–081, 35–078
Collins Stewart Ltd v Financial Times Ltd (No.1) [2004] EWHC 2337 (QB); [2005]
E.M.L.R. 5; (2004) 101(43) L.S.G. 33   40–051
Colour Quest Ltd v Total Downstream UK Plc; sub nom. Shell UK Ltd v Total UK Ltd
[2010] EWCA Civ 180; [2010] 3 All E.R. 793; [2010] 2 Lloyd's Rep. 467; [2010]
1 C.L.C. 343; 129 Con. L.R. 104; [2010] 10 E.G. 117 (C.S.)   4–004
Commissioner of Police of the Metropolis v Shaw [2012] I.C.R. 464; [2012] I.R.L.R. 291 3–011,
37–018, 37–013, 39–039, 42–013
Conner v Bradman & Co Ltd [2007] EWHC 2789 (QB) 35–099, 35–139
Connery v PHS Group Ltd [2011] EWHC 1685 (QB) 35–139
Cook v Cook [2011] EWHC 1638 (QB) 8–025, 9–033, 45–039
Cooper v National Westminster Bank Plc [2009] EWHC 3035 (QB); [2010] 1 Lloyd's
Rep. 490 .... 15–098, 25–010A
Cooper v Turrell [2011] EWHC 3269 (QB) 3–011, 39–043, 42–013
Co-operative Group (CWS) Ltd v Pritchard; sub nom. Pritchard v Co-operative Group
(CWS) Ltd [2011] EWCA Civ 329; [2012] Q.B. 320; [2011] 3 W.L.R. 1272; [2012]
1 All E.R. 205 .... 5–005A, 37–009A
Copley v Lawn; Maden v Haller [2009] EWCA Civ 580; [2010] Bus. L.R. 83; [2010] 1
All E.R. (Comm) 890; [2009] R.T.R. 24; [2009] Lloyd's Rep. I.R. 496; [2009]
P.I.Q.R. P21 .... 7–068, 32–019
Costain Ltd v Charles Haswell & Partners Ltd [2009] EWHC 3140 (TCC); [2010]
T.C.L.R. 1; [2010] 128 Con.L.R. 154 .... 15–098, 17–062
County Ltd v Girozentrale Securities [1996] 3 All E.R. 834; [1996] 1 B.C.L.C. 653 CA
(Civ Div)   6–059
Cowden v British Airways Plc [2009] 2 Lloyd's Rep. 653   3–021
Crehan v Inntrepreneur Pub Co (CPC) [2004] EWCA Civ 637; [2004] 2 C.L.C. 803;
[2004] U.K.C.L.R. 1500; [2004] E.C.C. 28; [2004] Eu. L.R. 693; [2004] 3 E.G.L.R.
128; [2004] 23 E.G. 120 (C.S.); (2004) 148 S.J.L.B. 662; [2004] N.P.C. 83   2–026
Crofts v Murton (2008) 152(35) S.J.L.B. 31 QBD   35–223
Da'Bell v National Society for the Prevention of Cruelty to Children (NSPCC) [2010]
I.R.L.R. 19 EAT   3–011
Dadourian Group International Inc v Simms (Damages) [2009] EWCA Civ 169; [2009] 1
Lloyd's Rep. 601 ....17–005, 17–006, 41–029
Dalwood Marine Co v Nordana Line SA [2009] EWHC 3394 (Comm) 7–118, 27–067A
Dampskibsselskabet Norden A/S v Andre & Cie SA [2003] EWHC 84 (Comm); [2003]
1 Lloyd's Rep. 287 ....   7–125B

De Beers UK Ltd (formerly Diamond Trading Co Ltd) v Atos Origin IT Services UK Ltd
[2010] EWHC 3276 (TCC); [2011] B.L.R. 274; 134 Con. L.R. 151 .... 26–006A, 29–005
Deeny v Gooda Walker Ltd (No.2); Albert v Gooda Walker Ltd; Brownrigg v Gooda
Walker Ltd [1996] 1 W.L.R. 426; [1996] 1 All E.R. 933; [1996] L.R.L.R. 109; [1996]
S.T.C. 299; [1996] 5 Re. L.R. 43; (1996) 93(15) L.S.G. 32; (1996) 146 N.L.J. 369;
(1996) 140 S.J.L.B. 92 HL 14–021A
Deeny v Gooda Walker Ltd (No.3) [1995] 1 W.L.R. 1206; [1995] 4 All E.R. 289; [1996]
L.R.L.R. 176; [1995] C.L.C. 623; [1995] 4 Re. L.R. 117 QBD (Comm) 15–140
Degainis v Secretary of State for Justice [2010] EWHC 137 (Admin); [2010] A.C.D. 46 .... 43–027A
Dennard v PricewaterhouseCoopers LLP [2010] EWHC 812 15–070
Deutsche Bank AG v Total Global Steel Ltd [2012] EWHC 1201 (Comm) 7–087, 20–001,
20–059A, 20–062
Devoy v William Doxford & Sons Ltd [2009] EWHC 1598 (QB) 36–083, 36–083
Dexter v Courtaulds [1984] 1 W.L.R. 372; [1984] 1 All E.R. 70; (1984) 81 L.S.G. 510;
(1984) 128 S.J. 81 .... 15–087A
Di Matteo v Marcus Lee & Co [2010] EWHC 312 (QB) 8–066, 8–091
Dimond v Lovell [2002] 1 A.C. 384; [2000] 2 W.L.R. 1121; [2000] 2 All E.R. 897; [2000]
R.T.R. 243; [2000] C.C.L.R. 57; 2000 Rep. L.R. 62; (2000) 97(22) L.S.G. 47; (2000)
150 N.L.J. 740 HL 32–021, 32–021A, 32–021C
Dinchev v Bulgaria (AG0003337) 43–045
Dobson v Thames Water Utilities Ltd [2009] EWCA Civ 28; [2009] 3 All E.R. 319;
[2009] B.L.R. 287; 122 Con. L.R. 32; [2009] H.R.L.R. 19; [2009] U.K.H.R.R. 617;
[2010] H.L.R. 9; [2009] 1 E.G.L.R. 167; [2009] A.C.D. 21; [2009] 5 E.G. 106 (C.S.);
[2009] N.P.C. 18 .... 34–020A, 34–020B, 34–022A, 43–027B
Dobson v Thames Water Utilities Ltd [2011] EWHC 3253 (TCC); 140 Con. L.R. 135 34–016,
34–020B
Dobson v Thames Water Utilities Ltd [2012] EWHC 986 (TCC) 15–049, 15–134A, 34–020B
Double G Communications Ltd v News Group International Ltd [2011] EWHC 961 (QB) 8–002D,
40–031
Douglas v Hello! Ltd (No.1) [2001] Q.B. 967; [2001] 2 W.L.R. 992; [2001] 2 All E.R.
289; [2001] E.M.L.R. 9; [2001] 1 F.L.R. 982; [2002] 1 F.C.R. 289; [2001] H.R.L.R.
26; [2001] U.K.H.R.R. 223; 9 B.H.R.C. 543; [2001] F.S.R. 40 40–027
Downs v Chappell; Downs v Stephenson Smart [1997] 1 W.L.R. 426; [1996] 3 All E.R.
344; [1996] C.L.C. 1492 CA (Civ Div) 41–028
Doyle v Olby (Ironmongers) Ltd [1969] 2 Q.B. 158; [1969] 2 W.L.R. 673; [1969] 2 All
E.R. 119; (1969) 113 S.J. 128 CA (Civ Div) 41–028
Drake v Foster Wheeler Ltd [2010] EWHC 2004 (QB); [2011] P.T.S.R. 1178; [2011] 1 All
E.R. 63; [2010] P.I.Q.R. P19; (2010) 116 B.M.L.R. 186; [2010] W.T.L.R. 1715;
(2010) 154(32) S.J.L.B. 29 ....35–232A, 36–084, 36–085, 36–125
Driver v Air India Ltd [2011] EWCA Civ 986; [2011] I.R.L.R. 992 .... 15–087A, 15–115
Durham Tees Valley Airport Ltd v bmibaby Ltd [2010] EWCA Civ 485; [2011] 1 All E.R.
(Comm) 731; [2011] 1 Lloyd's Rep. 68; (2010) 154(18) S.J.L.B. 28 ....8–0915A, 8–095C,
8–095D, 8–095E
E Bailey & Co v Balholm Securities [1973] 2 Lloyd's Rep. 404 QBD (Comm) 8–029A
Earlrose Golf & Leisure Ltd v Fair Acre Investments Ltd [2009] EWCA Civ 1295; [2009]
N.P.C. 139 34–044
East v Maurer [1991] 1 W.L.R. 461; [1991] 2 All E.R. 733 CA (Civ Div) 41–033A
Edwards v Chesterfield Royal Hospital NHS Foundation Trust; Botham v Ministry of
Defence [2011] UKSC 58; [2012] 2 A.C. 22; [2012] 2 W.L.R. 55; [2012] 2 All E.R.
278; [2012] I.C.R. 201; [2012] I.R.L.R. 129; [2012] Med. L.R. 93; (2012) 124
B.M.L.R. 51; (2012) 162 N.L.J. 30; (2011) 155(48) S.J.L.B. 31 .... 3–029, 28–023A
Edwards v United Kingdom (46477/99) (2002) 35 E.H.R.R. 19; 12 B.H.R.C. 190; [2002]
M.H.L.R. 220; [2002] Po. L.R. 161 43–014
Eeles v Cobham Hire Services Ltd [2009] EWCA Civ 204; [2010] 1 W.L.R. 409; [2009]
C.P. Rep. 29; [2009] P.I.Q.R. P15; [2009] LS Law Medical 274; (2009) 106(13)
L.S.G. 17; (2009) 153(11) S.J.L.B. 30 35–005
Elena d'Amico, The. See Koch Marine Inc v d'Amica Societa di Navigazione arl (The
Elena d'Amico)
Enfield LBC v Outdoor Plus Ltd [2012] EWCA Civ 608; [2012] C.P. Rep. 35; [2012] 29
E.G. 86 .... 12–010, 34–051

Environmental Systems Pty Ltd v Peerless Holdings Pty Ltd [2008] VSCA 26 ...1–036, 1–038, 1–039
Eribo v Odinaiya [2010] EWHC 301 (TCC) 26–020
Essex v Daniell; Daniell v Essex (1874–75) L.R. 10 C.P. 538 CCP 22–039
Experience Hendrix LLC v Times Newspapers Ltd [2010] EWHC 1986 (Ch) 8–002B, 8–008,
　　　　　　　　　　　　　　　　　40–032A, 40–032B, 40–032D, 40–044, 40–050
Exportadora Valle de Collina SA v AP Moller-Maersk A/S [2010] EWHC 3224 (Comm) ...1–037,
　　　　　　　　　　　　　　　　　　　　　　　　　　　　　　　　　　27–004
Fabio Perini SpA v LPC Group Plc [2012] EWHC 911 (Ch) 40–038
Fairchild v Glenhaven Funeral Services Ltd (t/a GH Dovener & Son); Pendleton v Stone
　　& Webster Engineering Ltd; Dyson v Leeds City Council (No.2); Matthews v
　　Associated Portland Cement Manufacturers (1978) Ltd; Fox v Spousal (Midlands)
　　Ltd; Babcock International Ltd v National Grid Co Plc; Matthews v British Uralite
　　Plc [2002] UKHL 22; [2003] 1 A.C. 32; [2002] 3 W.L.R. 89; [2002] 3 All E.R. 305;
　　[2002] I.C.R. 798; [2002] I.R.L.R. 533; [2002] P.I.Q.R. P28; [2002] Lloyd's Rep.
　　Med. 361; (2002) 67 B.M.L.R. 90; (2002) 152 N.L.J. 998 .... 8–020A
Fanti, The. See Firma C-Trade SA v Newcastle Protection and Indemnity Association
　　(The Fanti)
Farley v Skinner (No.2); sub nom. Skinner v Farley [2001] UKHL 49; [2002] 2 A.C. 732;
　　[2001] 3 W.L.R. 899; [2001] 4 All E.R. 801; [2002] B.L.R. 1; [2002] T.C.L.R. 6; 79
　　Con. L.R. 1; [2002] H.L.R. 5; [2002] P.N.L.R. 2; [2001] 3 E.G.L.R. 57; [2001] 48
　　E.G. 131; [2001] 49 E.G. 120; [2001] 42 E.G. 139 (C.S.); (2001) 98(40) L.S.G. 41;
　　(2001) 145 S.J.L.B. 230; [2001] N.P.C. 146 3–025
Farrall v Kordowski [2011] EWHC 2140 (QB) 39–032
Fearns (Gary) (t/a Autopaint International) v Anglo-Dutch Paint & Chemical Co Ltd
　　[2010] EWHC 2366 (Ch); [2011] 1 W.L.R. 366 16–034
Fearns v Anglo-Dutch Paint & Chemical Co Ltd [2010] EWHC 1708, Ch 8–002D, 16–034,
　　　　　　　　　　　　　　　　　40–019, 40–021, 40–033, 40–034
Feay v Barnwell [1938] 1 All E.R. 31 KBD 36–083
Fiddes v Channel Four Television Corporation [2010] EWCA Civ 730; [2010] 1 W.L.R.
　　2245; [2011] E.M.L.R. 3; (2010) 160 N.L.J. 974; (2010) 154(26) S.J.L.B. 29 45–015
Fiona Trust & Holding Corp v Privalov; Nikitin v H Clarkson & Co Ltd; Intrigue Shipping
　　Inc v H Clarkson & Co Ltd; Fiona Trust & Holding Corp v Skarga [2011] EWHC
　　664 (Comm) 15–112, 15–113, 15–118, 15–121
Firma C-Trade SA v Newcastle Protection and Indemnity Association (The Fanti);
　　Socony Mobil Oil Co Inc v West of England Shipowners Mutual Insurance Associa-
　　tion (London) Ltd (The Padre Island) (No.2) [1991] 2 A.C. 1; [1990] 3 W.L.R. 78;
　　[1990] 2 All E.R. 705; [1990] 2 Lloyd's Rep. 191; [1990] B.C.L.C. 625; 1991
　　A.M.C. 607; (1990) 134 S.J. 833 HL 1–005
Fitzroy Robinson Ltd v Mentmore Towers Ltd (No.3); Fitzroy Robinson Ltd v Good Start
　　Ltd (No.3) [2009] EWHC 3365 (TCC); [2010] B.L.R. 165; 128 Con. L.R. 103 15–038
Force India Formula One Team Ltd v 1 Malaysia Racing Team Sdn Bhd [2012] EWHC
　　616 (Ch) 40–027, 40–030B
Fox v British Airways Plc Unreported July 30, 2012 EAT 36–121
GB Gas Holdings Ltd v Accenture (UK) Ltd [2010] EWCA Civ 912 1–037
Galoo Ltd v Bright Grahame Murray [1994] 1 W.L.R. 1360; [1995] 1 All E.R. 16; [1994]
　　B.C.C. 319 CA (Civ Div) 6–150
George v Eagle Air Services Ltd (Damages) [2009] UKPC 35; 27 B.H.R.C. 498 ....36–121, 36–123
Glencore Energy UK Ltd v Transworld Oil Ltd [2010] EWHC 141 (Comm); [2010] 1
　　C.L.C. 284 7–110
Glory Wealth Shipping PTE Ltd v Korea Line Corp (The Wren) [2011] EWHC 1819
　　(Comm); [2012] 1 All E.R. (Comm) 402; [2011] 2 Lloyd's Rep. 370 .... 27–067A
Glory Wealth Shipping Pte Ltd v North China Shipping Ltd; North Prince, The [2010]
　　EWHC 1692 (Comm); 2011] 1 All E.R. (Comm) 641; [2010] 2 C.L.C. 64 ....7–084A, 7–125A
Gold v Essex CC [1942] 2 K.B. 293; [1942] 2 All E.R. 237; 40 L.G.R. 249 CA 6–173D
Golden Strait Corp v Nippon Yusen Kubishika Kaisha (The Golden Victory) [2007]
　　UKHL 12; [2007] 2 A.C. 353; [2007] Bus. L.R. 997; [2007] 2 W.L.R. 691; [2007]
　　3 All E.R. 1; [2007] 2 All E.R. (Comm) 97; [2007] 2 Lloyd's Rep. 164; [2007] 1
　　C.L.C. 352; (2007) 157 N.L.J. 518; (2007) 151 S.J.L.B. 468 HL 8–105
Golden Victory, The. See Golden Strait Corp v Nippon Yusen Kubishika Kaisha (The
　　Golden Victory)

Goldsmith v Patchcott [2012] EWCA Civ 183; [2012] P.I.Q.R. P11; (2012) 156(9)
S.J.L.B. 31 4–011
Graham v Police Service Commission [2011] UKPC 46 11–027
Grand v Gill [2011] EWCA Civ 554; [2011] 1 W.L.R. 2253; [2011] 3 All E.R. 1043;
[2011] H.L.R. 37; [2011] 2 P. & C.R. 20; [2011] L. & T.R. 26; [2011] 2 E.G.L.R. 7;
[2011] 27 E.G. 78; [2011] 21 E.G. 95 (C.S.); (2011) 108(22) L.S.G. 18; [2011]
N.P.C. 50; [2011] 2 P. & C.R. DG16 46–028
Gray v Thames Trains Ltd [2009] UKHL 33; [2009] 1 A.C. 1339; [2009] 3 W.L.R. 167;
[2009] 4 All E.R. 81; [2009] P.I.Q.R. P22; [2009] LS Law Medical 409; (2009) 108
B.M.L.R. 205; (2009) 159 N.L.J. 925; (2009) 153(24) S.J.L.B. 33 6–063
Greenglade Estates Ltd v Chana [2012] EWHC 1913 (Ch); [2012] 29 E.G. 85 (C.S.) ... 31–007
Gregg v Scott [2005] UKHL 2; [2005] 2 A.C. 176; [2005] 2 W.L.R. 268; [2005] 4 All E.R.
812; [2005] P.I.Q.R. P24; [2005] Lloyd's Rep. Med. 130; (2005) 82 B.M.L.R. 52;
(2005) 149 S.J.L.B. 145 8–044
Greta Holme, The. *See* Owners of No.7 Steam Sand Pump Dredger v Owners of
Steamship Greta Holme
Griffin v UHY Hacker Young & Partners (A Firm) [2010] EWHC 146 (Ch); [2010]
P.N.L.R. 20 6–063
HKRUK II (CHC) Ltd v Heaney [2010] EWHC 2245 (Ch); [2010] 3 E.G.L.R. 15; [2010]
44 E.G. 126 ....12–013, 12–053, 34–055
Hadley v Baxendale, 156 E.R. 145; (1854) 9 Ex. 341 Ex Ct 1–037, 1–038, 6–164D, 6–173B,
6–173H
Haithwaite v Thomson Snell & Passmore [2009] EWHC 647 (QB); [2010] Lloyd's Rep.
P.N. 98; [2009] P.N.L.R. 27; [2009] 15 E.G. 99 (C.S.) 8–066, 8–091
Hall v Harris [2012] EWCA Civ 671 10–002
Hall v Van der Heiden [2010] EWHC 586 (TCC) 13–029, 13–079, 26–011, 26–020
Harrison v Harrison [2010] EWPCC 3; [2010] E.C.D.R. 12; [2010] F.S.R. 25 40–050
Harrison v Shepherd Homes Ltd [2012] EWCA Civ 904; [2012] 28 E.G. 80 (C.S.) 34–006
Haugesund Kommune v Depfa ACS Bank [2011] EWCA Civ 33; [2012] Bus. L.R. 230;
[2011] 3 All E.R. 655; [2012] 1 All E.R. (Comm) 65; [2011] 1 C.L.C. 166; 134 Con.
L.R. 51; [2011] P.N.L.R. 14; (2011) 108(6) L.S.G. 19 ....6–135, 6–156, 7–085, 29–008A
Hayes v James & Charles Dodd (A Firm) [1990] 2 All E.R. 815; [1988] E.G. 107 (C.S.);
(1988) 138 N.L.J. Rep. 259 CA (Civ Div) 29–022A
Hays plc v Hartley [2010] EWHC 1068 (QB) 3–011, 39–032
Hayward v Thompson [1982] Q.B. 47; [1981] 3 W.L.R. 470; [1981] 3 All E.R. 450;
(1981) 125 S.J. 625 CA (Civ Div) 45–057A
Hebridean Coast, The. *See* Owners of the Lord Citrine v Owners of the Hebridean
Coast
Herrmann v Withers LLP [2012] EWHC 1492 (Ch); [2012] 4 Costs L.R. 712 ...... 3–026, 7–091A,
7–091B, 17–019, 29–042
Hillyer v Governors of St Bartholomew's Hospital [1909] 2 K.B. 820; [1909] W.N. 189
CA 6–173D
Hodge Jones & Allen LLP v McLaughlin [2011] EWHC 2402 (QB) 10–006
Holtham v Commissioner of Police for the Metropolis [1987] C.L.Y. 1154, CA 15–049
Home Office v Dorset Yacht Co Ltd [1970] A.C. 1004; [1970] 2 W.L.R. 1140; [1970] 2
All E.R. 294; [1970] 1 Lloyd's Rep. 453; (1970) 114 S.J. 375 HL 6–056
Horsford v Bird [2006] UKPC 3; [2006] 1 E.G.L.R. 75; [2006] 15 E.G. 136; (2006) 22
Const. L.J. 187; (2006) 103(6) L.S.G. 34 ....34–044, 34–058D
Howard-Jones v Tate [2011] EWCA Civ 1330; [2012] 2 All E.R. 369; [2012] 1 All E.R.
(Comm) 1136; [2012] 1 P. & C.R. 11; [2011] N.P.C. 121 .... 1–023, 22–030
Huntley v Simmons [2010] RECA Civ 54; [2010] Med LR 83, CA 46–041
IRT Oil and Gas Ltd v Fiber Optic Systems Technology (Canada) Inc [2009] EWHC
3091, (QB) 8–002C, 8–008, 8–041, 30–003
Invertec Ltd v De Mol Holding BV [2009] EWHC 2471 (Ch) 41–014
Iqbal v The Prison Officers' Association [2009] EWCA Civ 1312; [2010] Q.B. 732;
[2010] 2 W.L.R. 1054; [2010] 2 All E.R. 663; (2010) 107(1) L.S.G. 14 37–012
Isabella Shipowner SA v Shagang Shipping Co Ltd (The Aquafaith); Aquafaith, The
[2012] EWHC 1077 (Comm); [2012] 2 All E.R. (Comm) 461; [2012] 2 Lloyd's Rep.
61 .... 7–028A
Islam v Yap [2009] EWHC 3606 (QB) 34–063

Italia Express, The. *See* Ventouris v Mountain (The Italia Express) (No.3)
JN Dairies Ltd v Johal Dairies Ltd [2010] EWHC 1689 (Ch) 40–030A
Jabir v HA Jordan & Co Ltd [2011] EWCA Civ 816 .... 33–009A, 33–049
Jackson v Horizon Holidays Ltd [1975] 1 W.L.R. 1468; [1975] 3 All E.R. 92; (1975) 119
    S.J. 759 CA (Civ Div) 19–008
James v Attorney General of Trinidad and Tobago [2010] UKPC 23 11–018
Jarvis v Swans Tours Ltd [1973] Q.B. 233; [1972] 3 W.L.R. 954; [1973] 1 All E.R. 71;
    (1972) 116 S.J. 822 CA (Civ Div) 19–008
Jefford v Gee [1970] 2 Q.B. 130; [1970] 2 W.L.R. 702; [1970] 1 All E.R. 1202; [1970]
    1 Lloyd's Rep. 107; (1970) 114 S.J. 206 CA (Civ Div) 15–087A
Johnson v Fourie [2011] EWHC 1062 (QB); (2011) 155(21) S.J.L.B. 31 .... 14–060, 15–094
Johnson v Unisys Ltd [2001] UKHL 13; [2003] 1 A.C. 518; [2001] 2 W.L.R. 1076; [2001]
    2 All E.R. 801; [2001] I.C.R. 480; [2001] I.R.L.R. 279; [2001] Emp. L.R. 469 ..... 28–023A
Jones v Environcom Ltd; sub nom. Woodbrook v Environcom Ltd [2011] EWCA Civ
    1152; [2012] Lloyd's Rep. I.R. 277; [2012] P.N.L.R. 5 44–004
— v Ricoh UK Ltd [2010] EWHC 1743 (Ch); [2010] U.K.C.L.R. 1335 ....8–095E, 8–095G
— v Ruth [2011] EWCA Civ 804; [2012] 1 W.L.R. 1495; [2012] 1 All E.R. 490; [2011]
    C.I.L.L. 3085 ....1–010, 34–020B, 34–051F
Joyce v Bowman Law [2010] EWHC 251 (Ch); [2010] P.N.L.R. 22; [2010] 1 E.G.L.R. 129 8–091,
    29–012
Joyner v Weeks [1891] 2 Q.B. 31; 60 L.J.Q.B. 510; 65 L.T. 61; 39 W.R. 583; 55 J.P. 725
    CA 7–168, 23–056A
KC v MGN Ltd [2012] EWHC 483 (QB) 39–027, 39–055
Kalas v Farmer [2010] EWCA Civ 108; [2010] H.L.R. 25 34–071
Kani v Barnet LBC; sub nom. Barnet LBC v Kani [2010] EWCA Civ 818; [2011] R.T.R.
    17 33–074
Karafarin Bank v Mansoury-Dara [2009] EWHC 3265 (Comm); [2010] 1 Lloyd's Rep.
    236 ....25–013, 25–014
Kats v Ukraine (29971/04) (2010) 51 E.H.R.R. 44 43–014
Keegan v Newcastle United Football Club Ltd [2010] I.R.L.R. 94 13–035
Kennedy v KB Van Emden & Co [1996] P.N.L.R. 409; (1997) 74 P. & C.R. 19; [1997] 2
    E.G.L.R. 137; [1997] 44 E.G. 201; (1996) 93(16) L.S.G. 31; (1996) 140 S.J.L.B. 99;
    [1996] N.P.C. 56 CA (Civ Div) 7–105
Kenth v Heimdale Hotel Investments Ltd [2001] EWCA Civ 1283 8–043
Kettel v Bloomfold Ltd [2012] EWHC 1422 (Ch) 12–033, 23–019
Khan v Malik [2011] EWHC 1319 (Ch) 2–020, 2–032
Kinch v Rosling [2009] EWHC 286 (QB) 15–106, 15–119, 41–028, 41–039
Kitechnology BV v Unicor GmbH Plastmaschinen [1994] I.L.Pr. 568; [1995] F.S.R.
    765 40–027
Koch Marine Inc v d'Amica Societa di Navigazione arl (The Elena d'Amico) [1980] 1
    Lloyd's Rep. 75 QBD (Comm) 7–125A, 7–125B
Kotula v EDF Energy Networks (EPN) Plc [2011] EWHC 1546 (QB) 35–006, 35–030, 45–036
Kuvalehdet v Finland (AG0003352) 43–045
Kuwait Airways Corp v Iraqi Airways Co (No.6); Kuwait Airways Corp v Iraqi Airways
    Co (No.5); sub nom. Kuwait Airways Corp v Iraq Airways Co (No.6) [2002] UKHL
    19; [2002] 2 A.C. 883; [2002] 2 W.L.R. 1353; [2002] 3 All E.R. 209; [2002] 1 All
    E.R. (Comm) 843; [2003] 1 C.L.C. 183 33–067
Kwei Tek Chao (t/a Zung Fu Co) v British Traders & Shippers Ltd [1954] 2 Q.B. 459;
    [1954] 2 W.L.R. 365; [1954] 1 All E.R. 779; [1954] 1 Lloyd's Rep. 16; (1954) 98 S.J.
    163 QBD 20–087A
Lane v Holloway [1968] 1 Q.B. 379; [1967] 3 W.L.R. 1003; [1967] 3 All E.R. 129; (1967)
    111 S.J. 655 CA (Civ Div) 37–009A
Langford v Hebran [2001] EWCA Civ 361; [2001] P.I.Q.R. Q13 .... 8–074A
Lansat Shipping Co Ltd v Glencore Grain BV (The Paragon) [2009] EWCA Civ 855;
    [2010] 1 All E.R. (Comm) 459; [2009] 2 Lloyd's Rep. 688; [2009] 2 C.L.C. 465; 126
    Con. L.R. 1 ....13–034, 13–052, 13–071
Lavarack v Woods of Colchester [1967] 1 Q.B. 278; [1966] 3 W.L.R. 706; [1966] 3 All
    E.R. 683; 1 K.I.R. 312; (1966) 110 S.J. 770 CA 7–116, 8–095C
Law Debenture Trust Corp Plc v Elektrim SA [2009] EWHC 1801 (Ch) 8–041, 8–075, 8–081

Lawrence v Fen Tigers Ltd [2011] EWHC 360 (QB); [2011] Env. L.R. D13 .....34–020B, 34–040, 34–041

Leigh & Sillivan Ltd v Aliakmon Shipping Co Ltd (The Aliakmon); sub nom. Leigh & Sillavan Ltd v Aliakmon Shipping Co Ltd (The Aliakmon) [1986] A.C. 785; [1986] 2 W.L.R. 902; [1986] 2 All E.R. 145; [1986] 2 Lloyd's Rep. 1; (1986) 136 N.L.J. 415; (1986) 130 S.J. 357 HL 4–004

Leofelis SA v Lonsdale Sports Ltd; Trademark Licensing Co Ltd v Leofelis SA [2012] EWHC 485 (Ch) 8–103

Levicom International Holdings BV v Linklaters [2010] EWCA Civ 494; [2010] P.N.L.R. 29; (2010) 107(21) L.S.G. 14 29–008

Lightning Bolt Ltd v Elite Performance Cars Ltd Unreported November 2, 2011 33–008

Linklaters Business Services v Sir Robert McAlpine Ltd [2010] EWHC 2931 (TCC); 133 Con. L.R. 211 ....7–118, 7–145, 26–011, 34–006

Lips v Older [2004] EWHC 1686 (QB); [2005] P.I.Q.R. P14 16–034

Liverpool (No.2), The. See Owners of Steamship Enterprises of Panama Inc v Owners of SS Ousel (The Liverpool) (No.2)

Lobster Group Ltd v Heidelberg Graphic Equipment Ltd [2009] EWHC 1191 (TCC) ... 21–004

London Chatham & Dover Railway Co v South Eastern Railway Co [1893] A.C. 429 15–049

London Development Agency v Nidai; London Development Agency v Muir [2009] EWHC 1730 (Ch); [2009] 2 P. & C.R. DG23 34–044

Lordsvale Finance Plc v Bank of Zambia [1996] Q.B. 752; [1996] 3 W.L.R. 688; [1996] 3 All E.R. 156; [1996] C.L.C. 1849 QBD 13–123

Luxe Holding Ltd v Midland Resources Holding Ltd [2010] EWHC 1908 (Ch) 20–009, 24–005A

M&J Marine Engineering Services Co Ltd v Shipshore Ltd [2009] EWHC 2031 (Comm) ...7–110, 20–006, 20–029A

MMP GmbH (formerly Antal International Network GmbH) v Antal International Network Ltd [2011] EWHC 1120 (Comm) 2–026, 23–011

Mabirizi v HSBC Insurance (UK) Ltd [2011] EWCA Civ 1280 (QB) 35–004

McLaren v Hastings Direct Unreported July 1, 2009 CC 32–019

Magic Seeder Co Ltd v Hamble Distribution Ltd [2012] EWPCC 9 .... 40–044A

Maher v Groupama Grand Est [2009] EWCA Civ 1191; [2010] 1 W.L.R. 1564; [2010] 2 All E.R. 455; [2009] 2 C.L.C. 852; [2010] R.T.R. 10; [2010] Lloyd's Rep. I.R. 5438 15–067

Manning v King's College Hospital NHS Trust [2008] EWHC 3008 (QB) ..15–095, 35–236, 36–090, 36–125, 36–126

Mariapori v Finland (AG0003587) 43–045

Martin v Triggs Turner Bartons (A Firm) [2009] EWHC 1920 (Ch); [2010] P.N.L.R. 3; [2009] W.T.L.R. 1339 ....4–004, 8–063, 29–038

Martin v Triggs Turner Bartons [2009] EWHC 1920 (Ch); [2010] P.N.L.R. 3; [2009] W.T.L.R. 1339 .... 8–063, 29–038

Maud v Saundars [1943] 2 All E.R. 783 KBD 23–070

Mediana, The. See Owners of the Steamship Mediana v Owners of the Lightship Comet

Metropolitan International Schools Ltd (t/a Skillstrain and/or Train2game) v Designtechnica Corp (t/a Digital Trends) [2010] EWHC 2411 (QB) 3–011, 39–031, 39–032, 39–034

Migon v Poland (24244/94) 43–024A

Milan Nigeria Ltd v Angeliki B Maritime Co; Angeliki B Maritime Co v Milan Nigeria Ltd; Angeliki B, The [2011] EWHC 892 (Comm); [2011] Arb. L.R. 24 16–044

Milner v Carnival Plc (t/a Cunard) [2010] EWCA Civ 389; [2010] 3 All E.R. 701; [2010] 2 All E.R. (Comm) 397; [2010] P.I.Q.R. Q3; (2010) 154(16) S.J.L.B. 29 ....3–021, 19–008, 29–086A, 46–041

Ministry of Defence v Ashman (1993) 25 H.L.R. 513; (1993) 66 P. & C.R. 195; [1993] 40 E.G. 144; [1993] N.P.C. 70 CA (Civ Div) 34–051D

Ministry of Defence v Fletcher [2010] I.R.L.R. 25 .... 3–011, 11–019, 11–041, 46–027A, 46–041

Ministry of Defence v Thompson (1993) 25 H.L.R. 552; [1993] 40 E.G. 148 CA (Civ Div) 34–051D

Mitchell v Glasgow City Council [2009] UKHL 11; [2009] 1 A.C. 874; [2009] 2 W.L.R. 481; [2009] P.T.S.R. 778; [2009] 3 All E.R. 205; 2009 S.C. (H.L.) 21; 2009 S.L.T. 247; 2009 S.C.L.R. 270; [2009] H.R.L.R. 18; [2009] H.L.R. 37; [2009] P.I.Q.R. P13; 2009 Hous. L.R. 2; (2009) 153(7) S.J.L.B. 33; [2009] N.P.C. 27; 2009 G.W.D. 7–122 4–002

Morton v Portal Ltd [2010] EWHC 1804 (QB) 35–015, 45–025A

Mosley v News Group Newspapers Ltd [2008] EWHC 1777 (QB); [2008] E.M.L.R. 20; (2008) 158 N.L.J. 1112 QBD 42–009C, 42–013

Multi Veste 226 BV v NI Summer Row Unitholder BV [2011] EWHC 2026 (Ch); 139 Con. L.R. 23; [2011] 33 E.G. 63 (C.S.) 10–006

Mulvenna v Royal Bank of Scotland Plc [2003] EWCA Civ 1112; [2004] C.P. Rep. 8 ..... 8–095E, 8–095F

Murfin v Campbell [2011] EWHC 1475 (Ch); [2011] P.N.L.R. 28 7–105

Muuse v Secretary of State for the Home Department [2010] EWCA Civ 453; (2010) 107(19) L.S.G. 24 .... 11–018, 11–019A, 11–037, 42–026

Nahome v Last Cawthra Feather [2010] EWHC 76 (Ch); [2010] P.N.L.R. 19; (2010) 160 N.L.J. 766 29–028

National Coal Board v Galley [1958] 1 W.L.R. 16; [1958] 1 All E.R. 91; (1958) 102 S.J. 31 CA 1–036C

National Grid Electricity Transmission plc v McKenzie [2009] EWHC 1817 (Ch) 40–024

National Guild of Removers and Storers Ltd v Jones (t/a ATR removals) [2011] EWPCC 4 40–034

National Westminster Bank Plc v Rabobank Nederland [2007] EWHC 3163 (Comm); [2008] 1 All E.R. (Comm) 266; [2008] 1 Lloyd's Rep. 16; [2008] 6 Costs L.R. 839 ... 17–005

Nationwide Building Society v Dunlop Haywards (DHL) Ltd [2009] EWHC 254 (Comm); [2010] 1 W.L.R. 258; [2009] 2 All E.R. (Comm) 715; [2009] 1 Lloyd's Rep. 447; [2010] Lloyd's Rep. P.N. 68; [2009] P.N.L.R. 20 .... 2–051, 41–028

Needler Financial Services Ltd v Taber [2002] 3 All E.R. 501; [2002] Lloyd's Rep. P.N. 32; [2001] Pens. L.R. 253; (2001) 98(37) L.S.G. 39; (2001) 151 N.L.J. 1283; (2001) 145 S.J.L.B. 219 .... 7–146A

Network Rail Infrastructure Ltd v Conarken Group Ltd; Network Rail Infrastructure Ltd v Farrell Transport Ltd; sub nom. Conarken Group Ltd v Network Rail Infrastructure Ltd [2011] EWCA Civ 644; [2012] 1 All E.R. (Comm) 692; [2011] 2 C.L.C. 1; [2011] B.L.R. 462; 136 Con. L.R. 1; (2011) 108(24) L.S.G. 19 ..4–010, 6–104, 34–001, 34–005, 34–023A

Newcastle upon Tyne Hospitals NHS Foundation Trust v Bagley Employment Appeal Tribunal [2012] Eq. L.R. 634 EAT 3–011

Newman v Framewood Manor Management Co Ltd [2012] EWCA Civ 159; [2012] 23 E.G. 98; [2012] 1 P. & C.R. DG20 .... 3–018A, 23–010

Ng v Ashley King (Developments) Ltd [2010] EWHC 456 (Ch); [2011] Ch. 115; [2010] 3 W.L.R. 911; [2010] 4 All E.R. 914; [2011] 1 P. & C.R. 4 .... 15–043, 22–039

Nicholas Prestige Homes v Neal (2010) 107(48) L.S.G. 14 CA (Civ Div) ...8–081, 8–082, 30–003

Niedbala v Poland (27915/95) (2001) 33 E.H.R.R. 48; [2000] Prison L.R. 361 .... 43–024A

Niekrash v South London Healthcare NHS Trust Unreported March 7, 2012 3–011

Nikolova v Bulgaria [1999] ECHR 16; (2001) 31 E.H.R.R. 3 .... 43–024A, 43–027A

Noble Resources SA v Gross [2009] EWHC 1435 (Comm) 28–036, 40–024, 41–007

Norder v Andre. See Dampskibsselskabet Norden A/S v Andre & Cie SA

Ockenden v Henly (1858) E.B.& E. 485 22–039

Okoro v Commissioner of the Police of the Metropolis [2011] EWHC 3 (QB) 37–012

Olafsson v Foreign and Commonwealth Office [2009] EWHC 2608 (QB) 7–082

Omak Maritime Ltd v Mamola Challenger Shipping Co; Mamola Challenger Shipping Co v Omak Maritime Ltd; Mamola Challenger, The [2010] EWHC 2026 (Comm); [2011] Bus. L.R. 212; [2011] 2 All E.R. (Comm) 155; [2011] 1 Lloyd's Rep. 47; [2010] 2 C.L.C. 194; 132 Con. L.R. 196 ....2–041A, 2–041D, 2–014E, 7–118, 27–063

O'Sullivan v Management Agency and Music Ltd [1985] Q.B. 428; [1984] 3 W.L.R. 448; [1985] 3 All E.R. 351 CA (Civ Div) 15–140

Owners of No.7 Steam Sand Pump Dredger v Owners of Steamship Greta Holme; sub nom. Emerald, The [1897] A.C. 596 HL 32–044A, 32–044B

Owners of Steamship Enterprises of Panama Inc v Owners of SS Ousel (The Liverpool)
(No.2) [1963] P. 64; [1960] 3 W.L.R. 597; [1960] 3 All E.R. 307; [1960] 2 Lloyd's
Rep. 66; (1960) 104 S.J. 824 CA 7–085
Owners of the Lord Citrine v Owners of the Hebridean Coast [1961] A.C. 545; [1961] 2
W.L.R. 48; [1961] 1 All E.R. 82; [1960] 2 Lloyd's Rep. 423; (1961) 105 S.J. 37
HL 32–044A
Owners of the Steamship Mediana v Owners of the Lightship Comet [1900] A.C. 113 HL ...32–044A,
32–044B
Oxborrow v West Suffolk Hospitals NHS Trust [2012] EWHC 1010 (QB); [2012] Med.
L.R. 297 .... 35–206, 35–211
Page v Newman (1829) 9 B. & C. 378 15–065
Pankhurst v White [2010] EWHC 311(QB); [2010] 3 Costs L.R. 402 45–037
Parabola Investments Ltd v Browallia Cal Ltd (formerly Union Cal Ltd) [2010] EWCA
Civ 486; [2011] Q.B. 477; [2010] 3 W.L.R. 1266; [2010] Bus. L.R. 1446; [2011] 1
All E.R. (Comm) 210; [2011] 1 B.C.L.C. 26; [2010] 19 E.G. 108 (C.S.); (2010)
107(20) L.S.G. 20 ....2–046, 8–029, 8–038, 8–058, 15–065, 41–033A, 45–014A
Park Lane BMW v Whipp Unreported May 20, 2009 ....7–019, 7–062B
Patel v Anandsing Beenessreesingh [2012] UKPC 18 35–055
Pattni v First Leicester Buses Ltd; sub nom. Bent v Highways and Utilities Construction
[2011] EWCA Civ 1384; [2012] R.T.R. 17; [2012] P.I.Q.R. Q1 .... 15–047, 32–019, 32–021C,
32–021D
Paula Lee Ltd v Zehil & Co Ltd [1983] 2 All E.R. 390 QBD 8–095B
Pell Frischmann Engineering Ltd v Bow Valley Iran Ltd [2009] UKPC 45; [2011] 1
W.L.R. 2370; [2010] B.L.R. 73; [2011] Bus. L.R. D1 .... 12–010, 12–023
Peters v East Midlands SHA; East Midlands SHA v Nottingham [2009] EWCA Civ 145;
[2010] Q.B. 48; [2009] 3 W.L.R. 737; (2009) 12 C.C.L. Rep. 299; [2009] P.I.Q.R.
Q1; [2009] LS Law Medical 229; (2009) 153(9) S.J.L.B. 30 .... 7–085, 35–197
Pgf II SA v Royal & Sun Alliance Insurance plc [2010] EWHC 1459 (TCC) ; [2011] 1
P. & C.R. 11 ......7–168, 15–118, 23–055, 23–056, 23–056A, 23–062, 23–067, 23–069A, 23–070
Pindell Ltd v AirAsia Bhd [2010] EWHC 2516 (Comm); [2011] 2 All E.R. (Comm)
396 .... 6–173I
Plumbly v BeatthatQuote.com Ltd [2010] EWHC 321 (QB) 24–005A
Porton Capital Technology Funds v 3M UK Holdings Ltd [2011] EWHC 2895 (Comm) ... 8–002D
R. (on the application of Abdollahi) v Secretary of State for the Home Department [2012]
EWHC 878 (Admin) 10–002
R. (on the application of Booker) v NHS Oldham [2010] EWHC 2593 (Admin); (2011)
14 C.C.L. Rep. 315; [2011] Med. L.R. 10 35–188
R. (on the application of Degainis) v Secretary of State for Justice [2010] EWHC 137
(Admin); [2010] A.C.D. 46 .... 43–027A
R. (on the application of Greenfield) v Secretary of State for the Home Department [2005]
UKHL 14; [2005] 1 W.L.R. 673; [2005] 2 All E.R. 240; [2005] H.R.L.R. 13; [2005]
U.K.H.R.R. 323; 18 B.H.R.C. 252; [2005] 2 Prison L.R. 129; (2005) 102(16) L.S.G.
30; (2005) 155 N.L.J. 298 .... 43–024A
R. (on the application of J) v Secretary of State for Home Department [2011] EWHC 3073
(Admin) 37–018
R. (on the application of Lumba) v. Secretary of State for the Home Department; R. (on
the application of Mighty) v. Secretary of State for the Home Department, sub nom.
Abdi v. Secretary of State for the Home Department; Ashori v. Secretary of State for
the Home Department; Madami v. Secretary of State for the Home Department;
Mighty v. Secretary of State for the Home Department; Lumba v. Secretary of State
for the Home Department; R. (on the application of WL (Congo)) v. Secretary of
State for the Home Department; R. (on the application of KM (Jamaica)) v. Secretary
of State for the Home Department [2011] UKSC 12; [2012] 1 A.C. 245; [2011] 2
W.L.R. 671; [2011] 4 All E.R. 1; [2011] U.K.H.R.R. 437; (2011) 108(14) L.S.G. 20;
(2011) 155(12) S.J.L.B. 30 .....1–002, 10–002, 10–008, 11–019, 11–046, 37–013A, 42–009A,
42–009B, 42–009C, 45–061
R. (on the application of M) v Secretary of State for the Home Department [2011] EWHC
3667 (Admin); [2012] A.C.D. 34 37–018
R. (on the application of Mehari) v Secretary of State for the Home Department [2010]
EWHC 636 (Admin) 37–012

R. (on the application of MK (Algeria)) v Secretary of State for the Home Department [2010] EWCA Civ 980 .... 37–012, 37–018

R. (on the application of Moussaoui) v Secretary of State for the Home Department [2012] EWHC 126 (Admin); [2012] A.C.D. 55 .... 10–002, 10–006

R. (on the application of N) v Secretary of State for the Home Department [2012] EWHC 1031 (Admin) 37–018

R. (on the application of NAB) v Secretary of State for the Home Department [2011] EWHC 1191 (Admin) 37–013A

R. (on the application of OM) v Secretary of State for the Home Department [2011] EWCA Civ 909 .... 10–002, 10–006

R. (on the application of Pennington) v Parole Board [2010] EWHC 78 (Admin) 43–020

R. (on the application of Sturnham) v Parole Board; sub nom. Sturnham v Secretary of State for Justice [2012] EWCA Civ 452; [2012] 3 W.L.R. 476 .. 43–006, 43–024A, 43–024B, 43–027A, 43–029, 43–069A

RAR v GGC [2012] EWHC 2338 (QB) 35–277, 45–041

Rabone v Pennine Care NHS Trust [2012] UKSC 2; [2012] 2 A.C. 72; [2012] 2 W.L.R. 381; [2012] P.T.S.R. 497; [2012] 2 All E.R. 381; [2012] H.R.L.R. 10; (2012) 15 C.C.L. Rep. 13; [2012] Med. L.R. 221; (2012) 124 B.M.L.R. 148; [2012] M.H.L.R. 66; (2012) 162 N.L.J. 261; (2012) 156(6) S.J.L.B. 31 ....43–014, 43–019, 43–027C, 43–059A

Ramzan v Brookwide Ltd [2011] EWCA Civ 985; [2012] 1 All E.R. 903; [2012] 1 All E.R. (Comm) 979; [2011] 2 P. & C.R. 22; [2011] N.P.C. 95 .... 11–033A, 11–038, 11–039, 11–040, 11–042A, 11–051, 15–087A, 15–115, 15–119, 34–042, 34–044, 34–052, 34–058A, 34–058D, 46–027C

Rayment v Ministry of Defence [2010] EWHC 218 (QB); [2010] I.R.L.R. 768 3–011

Red River UK Ltd v Sheikh [2010] EWHC 1100 (Ch) 7–116

Reeves v Commissioner of Police of the Metropolis [2000] 1 A.C. 360; [1999] 3 W.L.R. 363; [1999] 3 All E.R. 897; (2000) 51 B.M.L.R. 155; [1999] Prison L.R. 99; (1999) 96(31) L.S.G. 41; (1999) 143 S.J.L.B. 213 HL 5–005A

Rehill v Rider Holdings Ltd [2012] EWCA Civ 628 5–007

Renolde v France (5608/05) (2009) 48 E.H.R.R. 42; [2008] M.H.L.R. 331; [2008] Inquest L.R. 159; [2009] M.H.L.R. 25; [2010] 1 Prison L.R. 78 43–014

Richardson v Howie [2004] EWCA Civ 1127; [2005] P.I.Q.R. Q3; (2004) 101(37) L.S.G. 36; (2004) 154 N.L.J. 1361; (2004) 148 S.J.L.B. 1030 37–006

Roberts v Johnstone [1989] Q.B. 878; [1988] 3 W.L.R. 1247; (1989) 86(5) L.S.G. 44; (1989) 132 S.J. 1672 CA (Civ Div) 35–211

Robinson v Harman [1843–60] All E.R. Rep. 383; 154 E.R. 363; (1848) 1 Ex. 850 Ex Ct 2–041C

— v PE Jones (Contractors) Ltd [2011] EWCA Civ 9; [2011] 3 W.L.R. 815; [2011] B.L.R. 206; 134 Con. L.R. 26; [2011] 1 E.G.L.R. 111; (2011) 27 Const. L.J. 145; [2011] C.I.L.L. 2972; [2011] 4 E.G. 100 (C.S.) 4–004

Rowe v Dolman [2008] EWCA Civ 1040; (2008) 152(30) S.J.L.B. 31 .... 45–025A

Rozsa v Hungary (AG0003381) 43–045

Rubenstein v HSBC Bank Plc [2012] EWCA Civ 1184; [2012] P.N.L.R. 7 .....6–079, 6–154, 7–146A, 29–076

Rust-Andrews v First-tier Tribunal [2011] EWCA Civ 1548; [2012] P.I.Q.R. P7 8–078

Ruxley Electronics & Construction Ltd v Forsyth; Laddingford Enclosures Ltd v Forsyth [1996] A.C. 344; [1995] 3 W.L.R. 118; [1995] 3 All E.R. 268; [1995] C.L.C. 905; 73 B.L.R. 1; 45 Con. L.R. 61; (1995) 14 Tr. L.R. 541; (1995) 11 Const. L.J. 381; [1995] E.G. 11 (C.S.); (1995) 145 N.L.J. 996; (1995) 139 S.J.L.B. 163 HL 7–168, 23–056, 23–056A

S&D Property Investments Ltd v Nisbet [2009] EWHC 1726 (Ch) Ch D 3–011

Sadler v Filipiak Unreported October 10, 2011 35–281

Safeway Stores Ltd v Twigger [2010] EWCA Civ 1472; [2011] Bus. L.R. 1629; [2011] 2 All E.R. 841; [2011] 1 Lloyd's Rep. 462; [2011] 1 C.L.C. 80; [2011] U.K.C.L.R. 339 17–080

Saunders v Edwards [1987] 1 W.L.R. 1116; [1987] 2 All E.R. 651; [2008] B.T.C. 7119; (1987) 137 N.L.J. 389; (1987) 131 S.J. 1039 15–049

Savage v South Essex Partnership NHS Foundation Trust [2010] EWHC 865 (QB); [2010] H.R.L.R. 24; [2010] U.K.H.R.R. 838; [2010] P.I.Q.R. P14; [2010] Med. L.R. 292; [2010] M.H.L.R. 311 ....43–042, 43–050, 43–060

Sayce v TNT (UK) Ltd [2011] EWCA Civ 1583; [2012] 1 W.L.R. 1261; [2012] R.T.R. 22;
  [2012] Lloyd's Rep. I.R. 183; [2012] P.I.Q.R. P8 .... 7–68, 32–019
Scott v Kennedys Law LLP [2011] EWHC 3808 (Ch) 29–022A
Scullion v Bank of Scotland Plc (t/a Colleys) [2011] EWCA Civ 693; [2011] 1 W.L.R.
  3212; [2011] B.L.R. 449; [2011] H.L.R. 43; [2011] P.N.L.R. 27; [2011] 3 E.G.L.R.
  69; [2011] 37 E.G. 110; [2011] 25 E.G. 105 (C.S.); (2011) 155(25) S.J.L.B. 35;
  [2011] N.P.C. 6 ....5–007, 29–044, 29–052, 41–057A
Seager v Copydex Ltd (No.2) [1969] 1 W.L.R. 809; [1969] 2 All E.R. 718; [1969] F.S.R.
  261; [1969] R.P.C. 250; (1969) 113 S.J. 281 40–027
Seeff v Ho [2011] EWCA Civ 401; [2011] 4 Costs L.O. 443 34–044
Sempra Metals Ltd (formerly Metallgesellschaft Ltd) v Inland Revenue Commissioners
  [2007] UKHL 34; [2008] 1 A.C. 561; [2007] 3 W.L.R. 354; [2008] Bus. L.R. 49;
  [2007] 4 All E.R. 657; [2007] S.T.C. 1559; [2008] Eu. L.R. 1; [2007] B.T.C. 509;
  [2007] S.T.I. 1865; (2007) 104(31) L.S.G. 25; (2007) 157 N.L.J. 1082; (2007) 151
  S.J.L.B. 985 .... 15–003A, 15–060, 15–065
Shell UK Ltd v Total UK Ltd. See Colour Quest Ltd v Total Downstream UK Plc
Shi v Jiangsu Native Produce Import & Export Corp [2010] EWCA Civ 1582 .... 34–051B
Siemens Building Technologies FE Ltd v Supershield Ltd; sub nom. Supershield Ltd v
  Siemens Building Technologies FE Ltd [2010] EWCA Civ 7; [2010] 2 All E.R.
  (Comm) 1185; [2010] 1 Lloyd's Rep. 349; [2010] 1 C.L.C. 241; [2010] B.L.R. 145;
  129 Con. L.R. 52; [2010] N.P.C. 5 ....6–164A, 6–173E, 6–174, 17–062, 19–010, 20–094
Sienkiewicz v Greif (UK) Ltd; Knowsley MBC v Willmore; sub nom. Costello
  (Deceased), Re; Willmore v Knowsley MBC [2011] UKSC 10; [2011] 2 A.C. 229;
  [2011] 2 W.L.R. 523; [2011] 2 All E.R. 857; [2011] I.C.R. 391; [2011] P.I.Q.R. P11;
  (2011) 119 B.M.L.R. 54; (2011) 108(12) L.S.G. 21; (2011) 155(10) S.J.L.B. 30 ....8–020A,
                                                                                8–020B, 8–020C
Simmons v Castle [2012] EWCA Civ 1039 ....3–002, 3–013, 3–030, 34–019, 35–280, 35–287A,
                          36–019, 37–001, 37–012, 38–005, 39–028A, 40–003, 41–039, 41–059,
                                                                42–010, 42–022, 46–042
Simmons v Castle [2012] EWCA Civ 1288 ....3–002, 3–013, 3–030, 34–019, 35–287A, 37–001,
                          37–012, 38–005, 39–028A, 40–003, 41–039, 41–059, 42–010, 42–022,
                                                                               46–042
Simon v Helmot; sub nom. Helmot v Simon [2012] UKPC 5; [2012] Med. L.R. 394;
  (2012) 126 B.M.L.R. 73 ....35–132A, 35–132B
Skandia Property (UK) Ltd v Thames Water Utilities Ltd [1999] B.L.R. 338 CA (Civ Div) 26–011,
                                                                                34–006
Sklair v Haycock [2009] EWHC 3328 (QB) 35–185, 35–197
Smith v LC Window Fashions Ltd [2009] EWHC 1532 (QB) 35–223
Smith New Court Securities Ltd v Citibank NA; sub nom. Smith New Court Securities Ltd
  v Scrimgeour Vickers (Asset Management) Ltd [1997] A.C. 254; [1996] 3 W.L.R.
  1051; [1996] 4 All E.R. 769; [1997] 1 B.C.L.C. 350; [1996] C.L.C. 1958; (1996)
  93(46) L.S.G. 28; (1996) 146 N.L.J. 1722; (1997) 141 S.J.L.B. 5 HL 41–033A
Smithurst v Sealant Construction Services Ltd [2011] EWCA Civ 1277; [2012] Med. L.R.
  258 .... 8–043, 46–029
Sorguc v Turkey (AG0003400) 43–045, 43–092
South Australia Asset Management Corp v York Montague Ltd; United Bank of Kuwait
  Plc v Prudential Property Services Ltd; Nykredit Mortgage Bank Plc v Edward
  Erdman Group Ltd (SAAMCO) [1997] A.C. 191; [1996] 3 W.L.R. 87; [1996] 3 All
  E.R. 365; [1996] 5 Bank. L.R. 211; [1996] C.L.C. 1179; 80 B.L.R. 1; 50 Con. L.R.
  153; [1996] P.N.L.R. 455; [1996] 2 E.G.L.R. 93; [1996] 27 E.G. 125; [1996] E.G.
  107 (C.S.); (1996) 93(32) L.S.G. 33; (1996) 146 N.L.J. 956; (1996) 140 S.J.L.B. 156;
  [1996] N.P.C. 100 HL 6–132, 6–156, 6–164D, 29–052, 41–057C
Spelman v Express Newspapers [2012] EWHC 355 (QB) 42–007
Sprung v Royal Insurance (UK) Ltd [1997] C.L.C. 70; [1999] 1 Lloyd's Rep. I.R. 111 CA
  (Civ Div) 1–005
Stadium Capital Holdings v St Marylebone Properties Co Plc [2010] EWCA Civ 952 34–051
Stadium Capital Holdings (No.2) Ltd v St Marylebone Property Co Plc [2011] EWHC
  2856 (Ch); [2012] 1 P. & C.R. 7; [2012] 1 E.G.L.R. 103; [2012] 4 E.G. 108 34–051

Standard Chartered Bank v Pakistan National Shipping Corp (No.2) [2002] UKHL 43; [2003] 1 A.C. 959; [2002] 3 W.L.R. 1547; [2003] 1 All E.R. 173; [2002] 2 All E.R. (Comm) 931; [2003] 1 Lloyd's Rep. 227; [2002] B.C.C. 846; [2003] 1 B.C.L.C. 244; [2002] C.L.C. 1330; (2003) 100(1) L.S.G. 26; (2002) 146 S.J.L.B. 258 .... 5–005A
Stanton v Collinson [2010] EWCA Civ 81; [2010] C.P. Rep. 27; [2010] R.T.R. 26; (2010) 154(8) S.J.L.B. 29 5–006
Steel v United Kingdom (68416/01); Morris v United Kingdom (68416/01) [2005] E.M.L.R. 15; (2005) 41 E.H.R.R. 22; 18 B.H.R.C. 545 ECHR 43–092
Steele v Home Office [2010] EWCA Civ 724 (2010) 115 B.M.L.R. 218 .... 35–280, 46–041
Strand Electric and Engineering Co Ltd v Brisford Entertainments Ltd [1952] 2 Q.B. 246; [1952] 1 All E.R. 796; [1952] 1 T.L.R. 939; (1952) 96 S.J. 260 CA 33–067
Strange v Westbury Homes (Holdings) Ltd [2009] EWCA Civ 1247; 128 Con. L.R. 26 ..... 22–030A
Strategic Property Ltd v O'Se [2009] EWHC 3512 (Ch) 22–036
Strutt v Whitnell [1975] 1 W.L.R. 870; [1975] 2 All E.R. 510; (1975) 29 P. & C.R. 488; (1975) 119 S.J. 236 7–049
Suleman v Shahsavari [1988] 1 W.L.R. 1181; [1989] 2 All E.R. 460; (1989) 57 P. & C.R. 465; [1989] 09 E.G. 69; (1988) 85(32) L.S.G. 38; (1988) 138 N.L.J. Rep. 241; (1988) 132 S.J. 1243 Ch D 31–007
Sumpter v Hedges [1898] 1 Q.B. 673 CA 26–013
Supershield Ltd v Siemens Building Technologies FE Ltd. *See* Siemens Building Technologies FE Ltd v Supershield Ltd
Swain v Geoffrey Osborne Ltd [2010] EWHC 3118 (QB) 17–005
Sylvia Shipping Co Ltd v Progress Bulk Carriers Ltd [2010] EWHC 542 (Comm); [2010] 2 Lloyd's Rep. 81; [2010] 1 C.L.C. 470 ..... 6–173A, 6–173C, 6–173E, 6–173F, 6–173G, 27–032
TCP Europe Ltd v Parry Unreported July 23, 2012 QB 10–010
Takitota v Attorney General of the Bahamas [2009] UKPC 11; 26 B.H.R.C. 578 ....11–018, 37–012
Tanks & Vessels Industries Ltd v Devon Cider Co Ltd [2009] EWHC 1360 (Ch) 33–008, 33–067
Tate & Lyle Industries Ltd v Greater London Council; sub nom. Tate & Lyle Food & Distribution Ltd v Greater London Council [1983] 2 A.C. 509; [1983] 2 W.L.R. 649; [1983] 1 All E.R. 1159; [1983] 2 Lloyd's Rep. 117; 81 L.G.R. 4434; (1983) 46 P. & C.R. 243 HL 15–140
Tesla Motors Ltd v BBC [2011] EWHC 2760 (QB) 40–013
Texaco Melbourne, The. *See* Att Gen of Ghana v Texaco Overseas Tankships Ltd (The Texaco Melbourne)
Thornton v Telegraph Media Group Ltd [2011] EWHC 1884 (QB); [2012] E.M.L.R. 8 39–034
Tolstoy Miloslavsky v United Kingdom (A/323) [1996] E.M.L.R. 152; (1995) 20 E.H.R.R. 442 43–092
Tom Hoskins Plc v EMW Law (A Firm) [2010] EWHC 479 (Ch); [2010] E.C.C. 20; (2010) 160 N.L.J. 584 ....6–150, 8–055, 8–091, 29–027
Transfield Shipping Inc v Mercator Shipping Inc (The Achilleas) [2008] UKHL 48; [2009] 1 A.C. 61; [2008] 3 W.L.R. 345; [2008] Bus. L.R. 1395; [2008] 4 All E.R. 159; [2008] 2 All E.R. (Comm) 753; [2008] 2 Lloyd's Rep. 275; [2008] 2 C.L.C. 1; (2008) 105(28) L.S.G. 14; (2008) 158 N.L.J. 1040; (2008) 152(29) S.J.L.B. 30 ....6–156, 6–164D, 6–173A, 6–173B, 6–173C, 6–173E, 6–173F, 6–173G, 6–173I
UK Housing Alliance (North West) Ltd v Francis [2010] EWCA Civ 117; [2010] Bus. L.R. 1034; [2010] 3 All E.R. 519; [2010] H.L.R. 28; [2010] 18 E.G. 100; [2010] 9 E.G. 167 (C.S.); [2010] N.P.C. 23; [2010] 2 P. & C.R. DG9 13–009
UYB Ltd v British Railways Board (2000) 97(43) L.S.G. 37; (2000) 97(42) L.S.G. 45; (2001) 81 P. & C.R. DG19 CA (Civ Div) 2–026, 23–011
Van Colle v Chief Constable of Hertfordshire; Smith v Chief Constable of Sussex; sub nom. Chief Constable of Hertfordshire v Van Colle [2008] UKHL 50; [2009] 1 A.C. 225; [2008] 3 W.L.R. 593; [2008] 3 All E.R. 977; [2009] 1 Cr. App. R. 12; [2008] H.R.L.R. 44; [2008] U.K.H.R.R. 967; [2009] P.I.Q.R. P2; [2009] LS Law Medical 1; (2008) 152(32) S.J.L.B. 31 43–042
Van Dal Footwear Ltd v Ryman [2009] EWCA Civ 1478; [2010] 1 W.L.R. 2015; [2010] 1 All E.R. 883; [2010] 2 P. & C.R. 7; [2010] L. & T.R. 18 23–059
Van der Garde BV v Force India Formula One Team Ltd (formerly Spyker F1 Team Ltd (England)) [2010] EWHC 2373 (QB) 1–036A, 1–036C, 1–036D, 8–081, 12–035, 12–053, 26–006A, 29–005
Vasiliou v Hajigeorgiou [2010] EWCA Civ 1475 .... 8–029B, 8–038, 8–058

Ventouris v Mountain (The Italia Express) (No.3) [1992] 2 Lloyd's Rep. 281 QBD
(Comm) 1–005
Victoria Laundry (Windsor) v Newman Industries [1949] 2 K.B. 528; [1949] 1 All E.R.
997; 65 T.L.R. 274; (1949) 93 S.J. 371 .... 6–173H, 29–028
Virgo Fidelis Senior School v Boyle [2004] I.C.R. 1210; [2004] I.R.L.R. 268; *Times,*
February 26, 2004 EAT 3–011
Vitol SA v Conoil plc [2010] EWHC 1144 (Comm); [2009] 2 Lloyd's Rep. 466 ....13–028, 20–124
W v Veolia Environmental Services (UK) Plc [2011] EWHC 2020 (QB); [2011] EWHC
2020 (QB); [2012] 1 All E.R. (Comm) 667; [2012] Lloyd's Rep. I.R. 419 ......7–090A, 32–021A
Watford Electronics Ltd v Sanderson CFL Ltd [2001] EWCA Civ 317; [2001] 1 All E.R.
(Comm) 696; [2001] B.L.R. 143; (2001) 3 T.C.L.R. 14; [2002] F.S.R. 19; [2001]
Masons C.L.R. 57; (2001) 98(18) L.S.G. 44 1–037
Watson v Cakebread Robey Ltd [2009] EWHC 1695 (QB) 36–132
Webster v Attorney General of Trinidad & Tobago [2011] UKPC 22 11–018
Webster v Sandersons Solicitors [2009] EWCA Civ 830; [2009] 2 B.C.L.C. 542; [2009]
P.N.L.R. 37; [2010] Pens. L.R. 169; (2009) 106(32) L.S.G. 15 8–009
Wei v Cambridge Power and Light Ltd Unreported September 9, 2010 CC 32–021, 32–021A
Weir v Dobell. *See* Andrew Weir & Co v Dobell & Co
Wells v Wells; Page v Sheerness Steel Co Plc; Thomas v Brighton HA [1999] 1 A.C. 345;
[1998] 3 W.L.R. 329; [1998] 3 All E.R. 481; [1998] I.R.L.R. 536; [1998] 2 F.L.R.
507; [1998] P.I.Q.R. Q56; (1998) 43 B.M.L.R. 99; [1998] Fam. Law 593; (1998)
95(35) L.S.G. 35; (1998) 148 N.L.J. 1087; (1998) 142 S.J.L.B. 245 HL 35–132A
White & Carter (Councils) Ltd v McGregor [1962] A.C. 413; [1962] 2 W.L.R. 17; [1961]
3 All E.R. 1178; 1962 S.C. (H.L.) 1; 1962 S.L.T. 9; (1961) 105 S.J. 1104 HL 7–028A
White Arrow Express Ltd v Lamey's Distribution Ltd [1995] C.L.C. 1251; (1996) 15 Tr.
L.R. 69; (1995) 145 N.L.J. 1504 CA (Civ Div) 1–036C
Whiten v St George's Healthcare NHS Trust [2011] EWHC 2066 (QB); [2012] Med. L.R.
1; (2011) 108(33) L.S.G. 28 ....35–206, 35–221, 35–223
Willmore v Knowsley MBC [2009] EWCA Civ 1211; [2010] E.L.R. 227 .... 8–020C
Woodward v Leeds Teaching Hospitals NHS Trust [2012] EWHC 2167 (QB) 35–006, 35–188,
35–280
Woodlands Oak Ltd v Conwell [2011] EWCA Civ 254; [2011] B.L.R. 365 .... 7–076, 15–081
Wright (A Child) v Cambridge Medical Group (A Partnership) [2011] EWCA Civ 669;
[2011] Med. L.R. 496 ....6–024, 6–130, 8–044
Wrotham Park Estate Co Ltd v Parkside Homes Ltd [1974] 1 W.L.R. 798; [1974] 2 All
E.R. 321; (1974) 27 P. & C.R. 296; (1973) 118 S.J. 420 Ch D 12–010, 12–023, 12–035
XYZ v Portsmouth Hospital NHS Trust [2011] EWHC 243 (QB); (2011) 121 B.M.L.R.
13 .... 8–077A, 35–065, 35–078, 35–139, 35–188
Yasa v Turkey (1999) 28 E.H.R.R. 408; [1998] H.R.C.D. 828 43–014
Yearworth v North Bristol NHS Trust [2009] EWCA Civ 37; [2010] Q.B. 1; [2009] 3
W.L.R. 118; [2009] 2 All E.R. 986; [2009] LS Law Medical 126; (2009) 107
B.M.L.R. 47; (2009) 153(5) S.J.L.B. 27 3–025
Youlton v Charles Russell (A Firm) [2010] EWHC 1032; [2010] Lloyd's Rep. P.N. 227 ...15–073,
17–005, 29–038
Youlton v Charles Russell (A Firm) [2010] EWHC 1918 (Ch) 14–076
Zabihi v Janzemini [2009] EWCA Civ 851 ....8–002A, 8–002D, 8–008, 33–006, 33–049A
Zim Properties Ltd v Procter (Inspector of Taxes); sub nom. Procter (Inspector of Taxes)
v Zim Properties [1985] S.T.C. 90; 58 T.C. 371; (1985) 82 L.S.G. 124; (1985) 129
S.J. 323; (1985) 129 S.J. 68 Ch D 14–076
Zodiac Maritime Agencies Ltd v Fortescue Metals Group Ltd [2010] EWHC 903
(Comm); [2011] 2 Lloyd's Rep. 360 ....7–118, 7–125B, 20–115, 27–067A

TABLE OF STATUTES

1927 Landlord and Tenant Act (17
      & 18 Geo.5 c.36)
      s.18(1) 23–069A
1934 Law Reform (Miscellaneous
      Provisions) Act (24 & 25
      Geo.5 c.41)
      s.3 .... 15–031, 15–040
1945 Law Reform (Contributory
      Negligence) Act (8 & 9
      Geo.6 c.28) 5–005A
1951 Reserve and Auxiliary Forces
      (Protection of Civil Inter-
      ests) Act (14 & 15 Geo.6
      c.23)
      s.13(2) 11–031
1972 Defective   Premises   Act
      (c.35) 34–005, 34–006
1976 Fatal Accidents Act (c.30) 36–113,
                                      43–059A
      s.3(4) 36–028, 36–068A
1977 Patents Act (c.37) 40–047
      Sch.A1 40–036
1979 Sale of Goods Act (c.54) 20–001
1980 Limitation Act (c.58)
      s.33 43–019
      (2) 43–019
1981 Senior Courts Act (c.54) 1–009,
              1–015, 9–029, 10–010,
              15–031, 15–034, 15–036,
              15–056, 15–073, 15–131,
              25–022, 33–011

      s.35 15–038
      (3) 15–040
      (4) 15–003A
1984 County Courts Act (c.28)
      s.69 15–031
1988 Copyright, Designs and Pat-
      ents Act (c.48) 40–044
      s.191J(3) 40–047
      s.229(3) 40–047
1994 Trade Marks Act (c.26) 40–034
1997 Protection from Harassment
      Act (c.40) 1–010, 3–011
      s.3(2) 3–011
1998 Late Payment of Commercial
      Debts   (Interest)   Act
      (c.20) 15–038
1998 Human Rights Act (c.42) 43–019,
              43–027B, 43–059A,
              43–059B
      s.7 ....43–027C
      (5)(b) 43–019
      s.8 .... 43–024A, 43–027A
      (3) 43–024A, 43–024B,
              43–027B
2000 Financial Services and Mar-
      kets Act (c.8) 45–035
2006 Compensation Act (c.29)
      s.3 ....8–020B, 8–020C
2011 Damages (Scotland) Act (asp
      7)
      s.7(1)(d) 36–056
2012 Legal Aid, Sentencing and
      Punishment of Offenders
      Act (c.10) 46–042

TABLE OF STATUTORY INSTRUMENTS

2006   Intellectual Property (Enforce-
      ment, etc) Regulations
      (SI 2006/1028) 40–032F,
                             40–044
     reg.3 ....40–032A
      (2)(a) 40–032D, 40–032E

2009   Constitutional Reform Act
      2005 (Commencement
      No.11) Order (SI
      2009/1604) 15–031

TABLE OF CIVIL PROCEDURE RULES

1998   Civil Procedure Rules (SI
      1998/3132)
     r.3.1(2) 45–039
     Pt 36 .... 45–036, 45–037
     r.36.14(1A) 45–036

BOOK ONE
GENERAL PRINCIPLES

CHAPTER 1

DEFINITION, SCOPE, OBJECT AND TERMINOLOGY

			PARA.
■	1.	Definition of the term damages	1–001
	2.	Scope of a textbook on damages	1–019
■	3.	Object of an award of damages	1–021
□	4.	Terminology	1–029

Add at the end of the paragraph: The Supreme Court in *R. (on the application* **1–002** *of Lumba (Congo)) v Secretary of State for the Home Department* [2012] 1 A.C. 245 by a majority of six to three has effectively, and wisely, outlawed vindicatory damages for the infringement of a right from awards of damages at common law. See further at paras 42–009A and B, below.

Insert a new note after "under insurance policies" on line 6 of the **1–005** paragraph:

NOTE 8a: Curiously, by resort to a fiction, English law does see an action claiming money under a contract of indemnity insurance as an action for damages, with all the unfortunate results to which this leads: see *The Fanti* [1991] 2 A.C. 1 at 35G, *per* Lord Goff, *The Italia Express* [1992] 2 Lloyd's Rep. 281 and, in particular, *Sprung v Royal Insurance (UK) Ltd* [1999] 1 Lloyd's Rep. I.R. 111, CA. Fortunately, the Law Commission and the Scottish Law Commission have now produced a Joint Paper for consultation—the title is *Insurance Contract Law: Damages for Late Payment and the Insurer's Duty of Good Faith*—in which the reversal of *Sprung* is put forward as a solution and the isolation in this matter of England from Scotland and the rest of the common law world is documented. Responses to the Joint Paper showed strong support for reform and a full Consultation Paper Covering more ground—the title is *Insurance Contract Law: Post Contract Duties and Other Issues*—followed in late December 2011 setting out proposals for reform and requesting responses by late March 2012. We await developments.

NOTE 14: Insert after "Supreme Court Act" (and before "1981") on line 2 of **1–009** the note:—now renamed the Senior Courts Act (see para.15–031, fn.111a, below)—

NOTE 18: Add at the end of the note: The somewhat peculiar case of **1–009** *Brightlingsea Haven Ltd v Morris* [2009] EWHC 3061, QB, where the damages were for denial of the right of daytime occupation of lodges on a caravan park, seems to come within this category: see *ibid.*, paras 1, 41 and 44.

1–010   NOTE 22: Add at the end of the note: Another statute allowing actions for damages is the Harassment Act 1997. The liability being for deliberate conduct, the Court of Appeal has held in *Jones v Ruth* [2012] 1 W.L.R. 1495, CA (facts at para.34–020B, below) that foreseeability of harm is not essential: *ibid.*, para.32.

1–015   NOTE 42: Insert after "Supreme Court Act" (and before "1981"):—now renamed the Senior Courts Act (see para.15–031, fn.111a, below)—

1–015   NOTE 43: Insert after "Supreme Court Act" (and before "1981"):—now renamed the Senior Courts Act (see para.15–031, fn.111a, below)—

1–023   Insert a new note at the end of the paragraph:

NOTE 80a: The judge at trial in *Howard-Jones v Tate* [2012] 2 All E.R. 369, CA awarded damages based on the pre-contractual position and had to be corrected by the Court of Appeal: see the case at para.22–030, below.

1–031   Insert after fn.121 in the text of the paragraph: or the defendant's libelling of the claimant: *Cambridge v Makin* [2011] EWHC 12, QB (at para.39–034, below).

1–036   Add at the end of the paragraph: The Court of Appeal in Victoria, as opposed to the Court of Appeal in England, was in full agreement in *Environmental Systems Pty Ltd v Peerless Holdings Pty Ltd* [2008] VSCA 26 with the analysis in this paragraph, a large part of which from the main work it cited: at *ibid.*, para.87. See the Australian case further at para.1–038, below.

Insert new paragraphs after para.1–036:

1–036A   The passage in para.1–036 of the main work describing what is meant by the normal loss in the field of contract, as being the market value of the performance that should have been received under the contract, was cited by the claimants in *Van der Garde v Force India Formula One Team Ltd* [2010] EWHC 2373, QB in their support (*ibid.*, para.414). Contracts between the claimants, a motor racing driver and his company, and the defendant, a company which owned and operated a Formula One motor racing team, provided for the defendant, in return for a payment of $3 million which the claimants made, to permit the claimant driver to drive a Formula One racing car in testing, practising and racing for a minimum of 6,000 kilometres. In breach of contract, the defendant permitted the claimant driver to drive for only 2,004 kilometres. The claimants' claim in restitution having failed for want of a total failure of consideration, they turned to damages which they claimed on three fronts, each in the alternative. The primary claim (for the other two see paras 8–081 and 12–035, below) is the most interesting as it is the most controversial.

The primary claim was for damages based upon the value of that part of the **1–036B** defendant company's promised performance which, although paid for, had been denied to the claimant racing driver. It was argued for the claimant that this represented the normal measure of damages in contracts of services as well as in contracts for the sale of goods. There is no question that this is true in sale of goods as the normal measure for a short delivery is framed in terms of market value, less contract price where the contract price has not yet been paid. Stadlen J., after a careful, if too elaborate a, judgment, held that the same rule should apply to contracts for services, and upheld the claim.

This is a very important decision not only because the damages award was **1–036C** high, at just over $2 million (contrast the alternative award of $100,000 for the driver's loss of opportunity to advance his career, at para.8-081, below) but, more importantly, because the decision marks an interesting development in the common law. Little up to now has been thought of this issue and only strands of authority were available to Stadlen J. in coming to his decision. There were a few employment cases, of which *National Coal Board v Galley* [1958] 1 W.L.R. 16, CA, is perhaps the most important, in which it was accepted that, where an employee fails to carry out his duties, the employer is entitled to damages based on the value to him of the services which have not been provided: see the discussion in *Van der Garde* at para.420 *et seq*. Reliance was also placed (*ibid.*, para.419) on important dicta of Sir Thomas Bingham in *White Arrow Express Ltd v Lamey's Distribution Ltd* (1995) 15 T.L.R 69, CA. He there pointed out that, in his own words, it is obvious that in the ordinary way a party who has contracted for a superior service and received an inferior one has suffered a loss. He illustrated this by positing the case of the person who hires a luxury car and receives a small car, the person who orders an excellent meal and receives a run-of-the-mill meal, the person who contracts for violin lessons from a renowned violinist and receives violin lessons from a nonentity. In all these cases the one who has been short-changed should be entitled to more than nominal damages; the damages should be based not on the contract price but on the value of the services that he has not received. In other words it is the market value of what is not received that is relevant and not a slice of the contract price, a point emphasised by Stadlen J. (*ibid.*, para.487). While the contract price is relevant for restitutionary recovery, it is the market value that applies for damages. *Van der Garde* of course is not of the rendering of inferior services but simply of a short delivery of services, but the same principles must apply. In the event, Stadlen J. came to a valuation of the missing services at a figure of $1,865,000, which he awarded.

While *Van der Garde* is a first instance decision, the fact that the defendant **1–036D** sought to appeal only to be refused leave not only by Stadlen J. but also by the Court of Appeal may be some indication that the Court of Appeal would be in agreement with Stadlen J.'s holding unless it was simply focusing on the merits which clearly lay with the claimants. I suspect, however, that some further consideration will be given to the issue in the future.

1–037   Insert a new note at the end of the paragraph:

NOTE 156a: *Watford Electronics* is cited by Christopher Clarke J. in *Choil Trading SA v Sahara Energy Resources Ltd* [2010] EWHC 374 (Comm), para.164, in support of his holding that the loss there was not consequential because not within the second rule in *Hadley v Baxendale*. And at Court of Appeal level we have another such holding in Longmore L.J.'s judgment in *GB Gas Holdings Ltd v Accenture (UK) Ltd* [2010] EWCA Civ 912, para.66. In *Exportadora Valle de Collina SA v AP Moller-Maersk A/S* [2010] EWHC 3224 (Comm) Flaux J. had no difficulty in declaring summarily, without a mention of any of the authorities, that the clause excluding liability for consequential loss in the contract before him precluded recovery for losses which, while pleaded as consequential loss, did not appear to fall within the second rule in *Hadley v Baxendale*. It may be of course that he so held because of the claimant's manner of pleading.

1–038   Add at the end of the paragraph: Australia however has, as so often, seen the light. The opportunity came with *Environmental Systems Pty Ltd v Peerless Holdings Pty Ltd* [2008] VSCA 26, a decision of the Court of Appeal of the State of Victoria. Citing the whole of this paragraph in the main work other than its first sentence (at *ibid.*, para.90), together with most of para.1–036 of the main work, Nettle J.A., with whose valuable judgment his brethren agreed, was persuaded that our analysis was right and that, as he put it, "in point of principle . . . the English authority appears to be flawed" (*ibid.*, para.87), here referring to the four Court of Appeal decisions set out both at *ibid.*, para.89 by him and in para.1–037 of the main work. In consequence the court, reversing on this the judge below, held that various expenses incurred by the claimant, which constituted losses which went beyond the normal measure but were still in the ordinary course of things within the first rule in *Hadley v Baxendale*, were caught by the clause in the contract excluding liability for consequential loss: see *ibid.*, para.94.

1–039   NOTE 163: Add at the end of the note: Yet, as comes out clearly in what is said by the Victoria Court of Appeal in *Environmental Systems Pty Ltd v Peerless Holdings Pty Ltd* [2008] VSCA 26 at paras 91 to 93 (see para.1–038, above for this case), even resort to the *contra proferentem* rule should not lead to the conclusion that the contracting parties intended to depart from the natural meaning of the term "consequential loss" in favour of the forced and unrealistic meaning attributed to it by the English authorities.

BOOK ONE

PART ONE

THE HEADS OF COMPENSATORY DAMAGES

CHAPTER 2

PECUNIARY LOSSES

			PARA.
I.	CONTRACT		2–002
□	1.	Basic pecuniary losses: the normal measure of damages	2–002
■	2.	Consequential pecuniary losses	2–026
II.	TORT		2–042
□	1.	Basic pecuniary losses: the normal measure of damages	2–043
□	2.	Consequential pecuniary losses	2–046

Insert a new note before the last sentence of the paragraph: **2–020**

NOTE 43a: Damages which put the contracting party into the position he would have been in had the contact never been made are available only for expenses and not for money paid under a contract which can only be recovered as far as the law of restitution allows: *Khan v Malik* [2011] EWHC 1319, Ch, paras 129 to 132.

Insert a new note before "Such loss" on line 9 of the paragraph: **2–026**

NOTE 65a: Where the business continues after the breach of contract, the claim must be for loss of profits and cannot be for the value of the business as diminished by the breach. Flaux J. so held in *MMP GmbH v Antal International Network Ltd* [2011] EWHC 1120 (Comm) where a franchise agreement had been wrongly terminated. Only where the business has entirely ceased or been abandoned as a result of the breach of contract, as in the two lease and tenancy cases, distinguished by Flaux J. (damages at *ibid.*, paras 81 to 92), of *Crehan v Inntrepreneur Pub Co CPC* [2004] EWCA Civ 637 and the first instance decision in *U.Y.B. v British Railways Board*, 1999, unreported, can a valuation of the business as the basis for the damages take the place of lost business profits; see *U.Y.B. v British Railways Board* further, and in the Court of Appeal, at para.23–011 of the main text and at para.23–011, fn.28, below. The claim in the *MMP* case had to fail as it was based on valuation of the business and Flaux J. refused amendment to plead loss of business profits: [2011] EWHC 1120 (Comm) paras 5 to 9.

NOTE 130: Add at the end of the note: But not moneys paid under the   **2–032** contract: see *Khan v Malik* [2011] EWHC 1319, Ch at para.2–020, above.

Insert new paragraphs after para.2–041:

2–041A   *Omak Maritime Ltd v Mamola Challenger Shipping Co* [2011] 1 Lloyd's Rep. 47 is a very important case as it introduces a further qualification upon a contracting party's right to claim his wasted expenditure. In *Omak* Teare J. considered at length in a penetrating judgment the true basis in law of the principle which permits a contracting party to claim wasted expenditure as damages for breach of contract. The question as to true basis arose in the context of a long-term time charterparty terminated as a result of the owners' acceptance of the charterers' repudiation in unusual circumstances. The charterers had repudiated because of their inability to enter into an intended sub-charter, and repudiation came at a time when the market rate of hire was higher than the charterparty rate of hire. The owners were therefore able to trade their ship at the higher market rate unrestricted by the lower contract rate. They nevertheless claimed as damages the expenses they had incurred in preparing to perform the charterparty, the charterparty requiring them to make substantial modifications to the ship prior to its delivery.

2–041B   Arbitrators decided in favour of the owners on the basis that they were entitled to claim for their wasted expenditure rather than base their claim on the difference between contract and market rates. In other words, the expectation measure could be ignored and the reliance rate insisted upon. Teare J. did not agree.

2–041C   The question, as Teare J. saw it, was as to the true basis of the reliance measure. While there was no dispute that damages may be claimed on the reliance basis (*ibid.*, para.20), what required to be addressed here was whether the reliance measure was a measure separate from, and independent of, the normal expectation measure or whether it was a measure governed by the principle upon which the expectation measure is based, the principle, as stated famously by Baron Parke in *Robinson v Harman* in 1848, that the claimant is entitled to be put in the same position as if the contract had been performed. After a thorough review of the authorities (which appear at paras 2–032 to 2–041 of the main work), Teare J. came to the sensible conclusion that both the expectation claim and the reliance claim are governed by Baron Parke's fundamental principle, which requires the court to make a comparison between the claimant's present position and what it would have been had the contract been performed: *ibid.*, para.65. Accordingly, since the owners, by trading their ship at the higher market rates had more than recuperated the wasted expenditure, they were not entitled to damages. The appeal was allowed and the arbitrators' award set aside.

2–041D   It may be noted that, given this convincing rationale, the earlier cases on wasted expenditure fall neatly into line. One can see why it was held in *C&P Haulage v Middleton* (at para.2–034 of the main work) that the contracting party who has made a bad bargain cannot sue for his wasted expenditure; the expenditure would have been wasted, or at least wasted in part, if the contract had been performed. One can also see why there was recovery of expenditure incurred before the contract was made, and therefore not classifiable as reliance expenditure, in *Anglia Television v Reed* (at para.2–033 of the main work), because it was no doubt expected that the expenditure would be more than covered by the profits or other advantages coming from performance of the contract. As for later cases on wasted expenditure, *Omak* has been followed in *Ampurius Nu Homes Holdings Ltd v Telford Homes (Creekside) Ltd* [2012] EWHC 1820, Ch. A claim for wasted expenditure which had been incurred in a property development contract failed not because the claimant was seeking to escape from a bad bargain as it genuinely believed the contract to be for its advantage but because the defendant had established that the claimant would not have made a profit from the contract such as would have absorbed the expenditure claimed (see *ibid.*, para.131 *et seq.* and para.149).

It may also be noted that the same result could have been achieved in *Omak* **2–041E** by the application of mitigation principles, in particular by resort to Viscount Haldane's famous exposition in *British Westinghouse Co v Underground Railway* in 1912 of the rule that, when a contracting party has taken action arising out of the transaction which has diminished his loss, the effect in diminution of the loss by that action is to be taken into account. Here there can be no doubt that the owners' trading of their ship at the higher rate was such an action. Indeed it appears as if Teare J. himself felt able to decide against the owners on this reasoning, for not only did he cite substantial passages from Viscount Haldane in *British Westinghouse* (*Omak*, para.18) but also in his conclusion he added in the mitigation point to his basic ground (*ibid.*, para.65). But there was no need to resort to the principles of mitigation, here in its aspect of avoided, as distinct from, avoidable, loss. The correct solution came without them.

NOTE 190: Add at the end of the note: For recovery of profits lost through **2–046** fraud see *Parabola Investments Ltd v Browallia Cal Ltd* [2011] Q.B. 477, CA.

NOTE 206: Add at the end of the note: With tort as with breach of contract the **2–048** claim will be for loss of future business profits only where the business continues after the tort. If the business ceases or is abandoned because of the tort, a claim for the value of the business at cessation or abandonment takes the place of a claim for future business profits. For the relevant authorities on contract see para.2–026, fn.65a, above.

NOTE 220: Add at the end of the note: ; *Nationwide Building Society v Dunlop* **2–051** *Haywards (DHL) Ltd* [2010] 1 W.L.R. 258; *Borealis AB v Geogas Trading SA* [2011] 1 Lloyd's Rep. 482.

CHAPTER 3

NON-PECUNIARY LOSSES

		PARA.
■ I.	TORT	3–002
■ II.	CONTRACT	3–013

3–002   Insert a new note at the end of the paragraph:

NOTE 0: In changing its initial ruling in *Simmons v Castle* EWCA Civ 1039 for a 10 per cent increase to damages in respect of specified types of non-pecuniary loss in tort so as to include types of non-pecuniary loss generally (for which see, *inter alia*, para.37–001, fn.1a, below), the Court of Appeal in *Simmons v Castle* [2012] EWCA Civ 1288 considered that the best guidance was to be found in this chapter of the main work and set out, word for word, the five heads of loss following in the chapter as the heads of loss to which the 10 per cent increase was to apply.

3–004   NOTE 3: Substitute for £257,750 on line 2 of the note: £265,000 [With a new edition eventually coming out in late September, the figure now to substitute is £288,500]

3–004   NOTE 3: Substitute for "9th edn (2008)" on line 3 of the note: 10th edn (2010) [With a new edition eventually coming out in late September, now substitute: 11th edn (2012)]

3–009   Add at the end of the paragraph: Also, the Court of Appeal has now accepted that a car owner, who does not hire a substitute car for the time it takes for his negligently damaged car to be repaired, is entitled to general damages for the inconvenience of being without his own car: see *Beechwood Birmingham Ltd v Hoyer Group UK Ltd* [2011] Q.B. 357, CA at para.32–051A, below.

3–011   Insert a new note after "economic loss" on the last line but 12 of the paragraph:

NOTE 42a: The damages recoverable for non-economic loss by a car owner deprived of his car through negligence would seem to be for inconvenience rather than distress: see *Beechwood Birmingham Ltd v Hoyer Group UK Ltd* at para.3–009, above.

Insert in the text before "With all" on the last line but 6 of the paragraph: The **3–011** statutory tort involving harassment, *viz.*, under the Protection from Harassment Act 1997, allows for damages "for any anxiety caused by the harassment" (s.3(2)), and awards were made in *S&D Property Investments Ltd v Nisbet* [2009] EWHC 1726, Ch where it was rightly said that anxiety need not amount to mental illness (see *ibid.*, para.72 *et seq.*), and in *Rayment v Ministry of Defence* [2010] I.R.L.R. 768.

NOTE 47: Add at the end of the note: In *Da'Bell v National Society for the* **3–011** *Prevention of Cruelty to Children* [2010] I.R.L.R. 19, which involved disability discrimination, the Employment Appeal Tribunal held that the range for injured feelings damages in discrimination cases from £5,000 through £15,000 to £25,000 laid down by the Court of Appeal in *Vento* (see above in this note in the main work) should be adjusted upwards for inflation to £6,000, £18,000 and £30,000 respectively; *Vento* was decided in December 2002. But, as was said in *Bullimore v Pothecary Witham Weld* [2011] I.R.L.R. 18, there is no need for the court, as long as it takes inflation into account, explicitly to perform an uprating exercise when referring to the decided cases or to the guidelines that have been laid down: *ibid.*, para.31. Just as damages for injury to feelings may be awarded for most forms of discrimination, so damages for anxiety may be awarded for harassment under the Protection from Harassment Act 1997. An award of £7,000 was made in *S&D Property Investments Ltd v Nisbet* [2009] EWHC 1726, Ch, where it was said that awards should probably be modest (*ibid.*, paras 75 and 76), and an award of £5,500 in *Rayment v Ministry of Defence* [2010] I.R.L.R. 768 (*ibid.*, para.88). In many of the above cases, aggravated damages feature alongside damages for injury to feelings, whether given in a single award or having separate awards made, and in *Ministry of Defence v Fletcher* [2010] I.R.L.R. 25 the need to avoid double counting was stressed. The case involved victimisation of an army recruit as well as sexual discrimination. The Employment Appeal Tribunal's award of £30,000 for injured feelings was not appealed, though it was thought in the circumstances to be high, but its award of a further £20,000 for aggravated damages was held to include a degree of double counting and was reduced by the court to £8,000. Aggravated damages may be increased on account of conduct after the discriminatory dismissal from employment: *Bungay v Saini* [2011] Eq. L.R. 1130, EAT. In the wake of all these cases Underhill J., sitting as the President of the Employment Appeal Tribunal in *Commissioner of Police of the Metropolis v Shaw* [2012] I.C.R. 464, [2012] I.R.L.R. 291, a case involving the victimisation of a statutorily protected whistleblower (and *Virgo Fidelis Senior School v Boyle* [2004] I.C.R. 1210, [2004] I.R.L.R. 268 has held that damages in claims based on victimisation should be assessed on the same basis as awards in discrimination claims), adverted in a full and valuable judgment to the dangers of having separate awards for injured feelings and aggravated damages. There was the danger of double counting and there was the danger of the aggravated damages being thought of as punitive. Aggravated damages, he rightly said, are an aspect of injury to feelings (*ibid.*, para.21) and the right question to ask is: what additional distress have the aggravating features caused (*ibid.*, para.24). Underhill J. would have liked to follow the Scots law in which aggravated damages are not awarded as such but, instead, the aggravating features are taken into account in arriving at a single award for injury to feelings. However, since the Court of Appeal has time and again approved separate awards of aggravated damages, adopting the Scots approach was not a course open to the Employment Appeal Tribunal (*ibid.*, para.27). As far as Underhill J. could go was to suggest that it would be a healthy reminder of the true situation if in future aggravated damages awards were formulated as a sub-heading of injury to feelings rather than as a wholly distinct head of damages (*ibid.*, para.28). Whatever the Court of Appeal may make for the general law of Underhill J.'s approach, the case of *Shaw* has already had its effect in discrimination, harassment and victimisation cases in the employment field. In the appeals from two decisions arrived at before *Shaw* had reached the Employment Appeal Tribunal, the Tribunal eliminated the aggravated damages award in one of them, *Newcastle upon Tyne Hospitals NHS Foundation Trust v Bagley* [2012] Eq. L.R. 634, and upheld the refusal to award aggravated damages in the other, *Niekrash v South London Healthcare NHS Trust* March 7, 2012, unreported.

3–011   NOTE 48: Add at the end of the note: Tugendhat J. in *Hays Plc v Hartley* [2010] EWHC 1068, QB, para.24 stated categorically that "a corporation is not entitled to damages for injury to feelings". He said much the same in *Metropolitan International Schools Ltd v Designtechnica Corp* [2010] EWHC 2411, QB, para.14 and in *Cooper v Turrell* [2011] EWHC 3269, QB, with the result that in the latter he awarded more to the individual claimant than to the corporate claimant (see the case at para.39–043, fn.218a, below). Moreover, the proposals in the Civil Law Reform Bill 2009 on damages have been abandoned as thought by the Government not to be vote-catching, and hence the unfortunate proposal to allow in copyright claims recovery of aggravated damages to what are referred to as "bodies" as well as to individuals has gone. The details are at this paragraph and footnote in the First Supplement to the 18th edition.

3–013   Insert a new note at the end of the paragraph:

NOTE 52a: When extending its initial ruling in *Simmons v Castle* EWCA Civ 1039 for a 10 per cent increase to damages in respect of non-pecuniary loss from tort to contract in *Simmons v Castle* [2012] EWCA Civ 1288 (for which see para.3–030, fn.172a, below), the Court of Appeal's declaration that its ruling covers the five heads of loss taken from this chapter in the main work (see para.3–002, fn.0, above) will apply to contract as much as to tort.

Insert a new paragraph after para.3–018:

3–018A   Damages for loss of amenities may appear where there is no physical injury to the person. Thus in *Newman v Framewood Manor Management Co Ltd* [2012] EWCA Civ 159 there was recovery by way of loss of amenity where the lessor of an apartment in a block of flats was in breach of covenant in the provision of leisure facilities by way of swimming pool, jacuzzi and gym. The Court of Appeal allowed the claimant damages, though of a modest amount, for her loss of amenity in the use of the premises (*ibid.*, para.42 *et seq.*).

NOTE 107: Add at the end of the note: Recovery for a spoilt holiday is again **3–021** addressed by the Court of Appeal in *Milner v Carnival Plc* [2010] 3 All E.R. 701, CA. A contract for air transport, en route for a holiday, is not within this category so as to allow recovery for distress: cf. *Cowden v British Airways Plc* [2009] 2 Lloyd's Rep. 653.

Add at the end of the paragraph: What was said in *Farley v Skinner* was **3–025** adopted by the Court of Appeal in *Yearworth v North Bristol NHS Trust* [2010] Q.B. 1, CA to hold that claimants might recover for mental distress suffered on learning that sperm of theirs which had been banked with a fertility unit for later use had been damaged and lost to them. Here was breach of a bailment rather than breach of a contract but the Court of Appeal amalgamated the two in its analysis of what damages should be available.

Add at the end of the paragraph: However, Lord Scott's dictum has been firmly **3–026** disapproved by Newey J. in *Herrmann v Withers LLP* [2012] EWHC 1492, Ch (facts at para.7–091A, below). Citing with approval what is said in this paragraph in the main work, he held the claimant purchasers of a residential property entitled to damages for the disappointment and the loss of amenity in being unable to use a communal garden in addition to the damages awarded representing the diminution in value of the property from the lack of garden use: see *ibid.*, paras 125 to 128 and the full facts at para.7–091A, below.

Add at the end of the paragraph: Nor does *Edwards v Chesterfield Royal* **3–029** *Hospital NHS Foundation Trust* [2012] 2 W.L.R. 55, SC, which is dealt with at para.28–023A, below, take the matter further as the Supreme Court was disallowing a claim for financial loss, but it would follow that there could *a fortiori* be no recovery for mental distress.

Insert a new note at the end of the paragraph: **3–030**

NOTE 172a: The Court of Appeal's ruling in *Simmons v Castle* [2012] EWCA Civ 1039 that the level of general damages in all torts causing suffering, inconvenience or distress is to be increased by 10 per cent (for which see at, *inter alia*, para.37–001, fn.1a, below) has, surprisingly, no application to contract damages. [There has been a further hearing of *Simmons v Castle* by the Court of Appeal, the reasons for which appear at para.46–042, below, and judgment has been handed down ([2012] EWCA Civ 1288) just at the moment when final proofs were being returned to the publishers. In confirming its ruling for a general damages increase by 10 per cent (except for CFA claimants still entitled to a success fee, as to which issue see again para.46–042, below), the Court of Appeal has wisely extended its ruling to cover contract as well as tort: see *ibid.*, para.46.]

[15]

BOOK ONE

PART TWO

THE LIMITS OF COMPENSATORY DAMAGES

CHAPTER 4

THE GENERAL PROBLEM OF LIMITS

		PARA.
■ 1.	Interrelation of existence and extent of liability	4–002
2.	Interrelation of various facets of the extent of liability	4–014

Insert a new note at the end of the paragraph: **4–002**

NOTE 1a: Sometimes of course it is quite clear that one is only in the realm of existence of liability with no doubts about extent of liability appearing. This was so in *Mitchell v Glasgow City Council* [2009] 1 A.C. 874 where the House of Lords held that no duty lay upon a local council to warn one of its tenants that lawful actions on its part in respect of another of its tenants might cause the latter to inflict harm on the former.

NOTE 15: Add at the end of the note: A builder's liability to a house owner **4–004** for defective building lies in contract only and not in tort: *Robinson v P E Jones (Contractors) Ltd* [2012] Q.B. 44, CA.

NOTE 16: Add at the end of the note: Another illustration of solicitor **4–004** negligence in drafting of a will causing loss to a beneficiary is *Martin v Triggs Turner Bartons* [2010] P.N.L.R. 3, p.29: facts at para.29–038, below.

Insert a new note after "controls here," on the last line but 3 of the **4–004** paragraph:

NOTE 20a: *Leigh & Sillivan* was explained and distinguished by the Court of Appeal in *Shell UK Ltd v Total UK Ltd* [2011] Q.B. 86, CA so as to hold that an oil company which was the beneficial owner of tanks and pipelines destroyed in an explosion at an oil storage terminal was not precluded from claiming damages for economic loss.

Insert a new note at the end of the paragraph: **4–010**

NOTE 45a: Where in *Conarken Group Ltd v Network Rail Infrastructure Ltd* [2011] EWCA Civ 644 road drivers had inflicted damage to railway tracks causing disruption of rail services, duty, scope of duty and remoteness, together with foreseeability, causation and reasonableness, were all under discussion in the claim by the railway authorities against the road drivers: *ibid.*, para.29. See the case at para.34–023A, below.

4–011   Insert a new note after the last sentence but two of the paragraph:

NOTE 47a: The defence did succeed for a fall from a horse in *Goldsmith v Patchcott* [2012] EWCA Civ 183 where under statute liability was strict.

CHAPTER 5

REDUCTION OF DAMAGES FOR CONTRIBUTORY NEGLIGENCE

		PARA.
■ 1.	Liability in tort	5–003
2.	Liability in contract	5–009
3.	Liability under the Misrepresentation Act	5–017

NOTE 14: Delete and substitute: [2009] A.C. 1339 (CA) **5–005**

NOTE 15: Substitute for "[2009] 3 W.L.R. 167 HL" on line 2 of the note: **5–005**
[2009] A.C. 1339

Insert a new paragraph after para.5–005:

The Court of Appeal has now confirmed, in *Co-operative Group (CWS) Ltd v* **5–005A**
Pritchard [2012] Q.B. 320, CA, that contributory negligence cannot be a defence
to an intentional tort, neither at common law nor under the 1945 Act. The case
was one of assault and battery. It is therefore important as it takes this rule to
intentional torts causing physical damage, the earlier authorities which have
applied or stated the rule (collected at para.5–004 of the main work) having been
concerned with torts leading to economic loss. To arrive at this result, which was
thought by the court to be by no means certain, Aikens L.J., who gave the leading
judgment, found it necessary to conduct a lengthy and very thorough survey of
the law, going through cases, both domestic and Commonwealth, statutes and
textbooks (*ibid.*, paras 28 to 60), before basing his eventual conclusion (*ibid.*,
paras 61 and 62) on the clear statements of principle in the House of Lords in
Standard Chartered Bank v Pakistan National Shipping Corp and *Reeves v
Commissioner of Police of the Metropolis*, cases dealt with at paras 5–004 and
5–005, respectively, of the main work. At the same time, Smith L.J. expressed
regret that the law as it stood required her to come to this conclusion but thought,
as did Aikens L.J., that change could only come through Parliament: *ibid.*, paras
85 and 76. See a further aspect of the case at para.37–009A, below, where the
possibility of reducing the damages on the ground not of contributory negligence
but of provocation is examined.

NOTE 17: Add at the end of the note: The appropriate percentage reduction is **5–006**
again considered, together with that for driving with a driver known to have been
drinking heavily, in *Best v Smyth* [2010] EWHC 1541, QB, paras 12 and 13. If
indeed in cases of very serious injury it can be shown, exceptionally, from
medical or other evidence that the wearing of a seat belt was likely to have made

no difference, the trial judge will be justified in making no reduction in the damages for contributory negligence. This was accepted by the Court of Appeal in an extended review in *Stanton v Collinson* [2010] R.T.R. 26, CA, a review of seat belt contributory negligence which deserves attention.

5–007   Insert a new note after the first sentence of the paragraph:

NOTE 18a: Fault not causally contributing to the damage and therefore not to be taken into account in the damages is illustrated by *Scullion v Bank of Scotland Plc* [2011] P.N.L.R.5, p.68 (facts at para.41–057B, below): see *ibid.*, paras 81 to 86. The Court of Appeal has reversed on liability ([2011] 1 W.L.R. 3212, CA) but does not touch on this point.

5–007   NOTE 20: Add at the end of the note: In *Rehill v Rider Holdings Ltd* [2012] EWCA Civ 628, a typical road accident personal injury claim, Richards L.J., delivering the only reasoned judgment, said that he found it difficult to draw a clear distinction between considerations of causation and of fault: *ibid.*, para.30.

CHAPTER 6

REMOTENESS OF DAMAGE

		PARA.
I.	TORT	6–004
	(A) CAUSATION	6–005
	1. Cause in fact and cause in law	6–005
	2. Cause in fact: the norm and the exceptions	6–015
□	3. Cause in law: direct consequences	6–029
■	4. Cause in law: consequences following upon a new intervening force	6–033
	(B) SCOPE OF PROTECTION: THE LIMITS OF POLICY	6–080
	1. Damage where no separate liability has been established	6–081
□	2. Foreseeable damage caused in an unforeseeable manner or to an unforeseeable degree where a breach of duty to the claimant to take care has been established	6–084
	3. Damage to a secondary interest where a separate liability in respect of a primary interest has been established	6–120
■	4. Damage outside the scope of the duty	6–130
II.	CONTRACT	6–136
	(A) CAUSATION	6–137
	1. Direct consequences	6–139
■	2. Consequences following upon a new intervening force	6–140
□	(B) SCOPE OF PROTECTION: CONTEMPLATION OF THE PARTIES	6–155
	1. The rule in *Hadley v Baxendale*	6–157
	2. The rule restated in *Victoria Laundry v Newman* in 1949	6–159
□	3. The restated rule as qualified in *The Heron II* in 1967	6–161
□	4. The decision in *The Achilleas* in 2008	6–165
□	5. The degree of likelihood required	6–174
	6. The degree of knowledge required	6–186
	7. The overall requirements of public policy	6–200
	8. Main types of contract in which the rule in *Hadley v Baxendale* has been developed	6–203

NOTE 77: Add at the end of the note: In *Wright v Cambridge Medical Group* **6–024** [2011] EWCA Civ 669 there were two consecutive wrongs which, similarly, were said to have had a synergistic interaction (*ibid.*, para.36), a doctor's delay in referring a patient to a hospital for treatment and the hospital's delay in carrying out the treatment, and the doctor was held liable notwithstanding the later default of the hospital. See the case further at para.6–130, below.

Add at the end of the paragraph: Where in *Bullimore v Pothecary Witham Weld* **6–056** [2011] I.R.L.R. 18 the former employer of the claimant solicitor gave to her prospective employer an adverse reference which was discriminatory and the prospective employer retracted, also in a discriminatory manner, its offer of employment, both employers being considered as thereby having committed the statutory tort of sexual discrimination, the Employment Appeal Tribunal held that the former employer was liable for the resultant loss of earnings of the claimant despite the tortious act of the prospective employer. As was said, at *ibid.*, para.20, withdrawal of the offer was, in the words of Lord Reid in *Dorset Yacht* (in this paragraph of the main work), the very kind of thing that was likely to happen on receipt of a damaging reference.

6–059   Add at the end of the paragraph: Boy vandals entered an open and unattended medieval church and set off the fire extinguishers in the church, thereby covering the fabric, fittings and organ with a fine dust which had to be expensively cleaned. The church's claim in *Chubb Fire Ltd v The Vicar of Spalding* [2010] EWCA Civ 981 for the cleaning costs from the fire extinguisher suppliers, on the basis that the church should have been warned that discharge of the type of extinguisher installed could cause damage, foundered in the Court of Appeal as it was held that any such warning would have not been acted upon by the church. In addition, Aikens L.J. in a useful and detailed analysis in his leading judgment (*ibid.*, paras 50 to 73) decided that the church's claim must fail also on the ground that the fire extinguisher suppliers could not be held liable for the vandalism which constituted a new intervening act and, it may be noted, had occurred seven years after the extinguishers had been installed. On this the other members of the court preferred not to express a view.

6–063   NOTES 287 to 289: Substitute for "[2009] 2 W.L.R. 351 CA" in each note: [2009] A.C. 1339, CA

6–063   NOTE 290: Substitute for "[2009] 3 W.L.R. 167, HL" on line 2 of the note: [2009] A.C. 1339

6–063   NOTE 290: Add at the end of the note: As for the limits of the *ex turpi causa* rule as expounded by the House of Lords in *Gray v Thames Trains Ltd* [2009] 1 A.C. 1339, see *Griffin v UHY Hacker Young & Partners* [2010] P.N.L.R. 20, p.379.

Insert a new paragraph after para.6–079:

6–079A   The decision that the defendant was not liable for the claimant's loss in *Rubenstein v HSBC Bank Plc* [2012] P.N.L.R. 7, p.151 was on the basis of tort, breach of statutory duty and contract. The case is here dealt with under contract, at para.6–154, below, primarily because the trial judge made an award in contract for nominal damages, not available under the other two causes of action. [Between completion of text and proof stage the Court of Appeal has held the claimant entitled to recover for his loss, disagreeing with the trial judge's approach, in the particular circumstances of the case, to cause, remoteness and foreseeability: [2012] EWCA Civ 1184. Thus in dealing with the claimant's loss, tort and breach of statutory duty come back into the picture and the valuable judgment of the court, given by Rix L.J., is full of leading authorities on both the tortious and the contractual sides.]

Add at the end of the paragraph: That there can be recovery for loss of profits **6–104** where this kind of loss is foreseeable but its substantial extent and the manner of its coming about are not is well supported, in the context of tortious damage to land, by the Court of Appeal's decision in *Conarken Group Ltd v Network Rail Infrastructure Ltd* [2011] EWCA Civ 644. See the analysis of the remoteness aspect of the case at para.34–023B, below.

Add at the end of the paragraph: Moreover, it is interesting to see that the **6–130** Master of the Rolls, Lord Neuberger, in *Wright v Cambridge Medical Group* [2011] EWCA Civ 669, where a general practitioner practice being sued was arguing that a hospital, and not one of its doctors, had caused the injury, said at para.30:

> "It seems to me that this argument raises two questions. The first is whether . . . the defendants' negligence was a cause of . . . the claimant's permanent injury. The second question is whether that injury was, to use the traditional expression, too remote, or, to put it in more modern terms, whether that injury fell outside the scope of the defendants' duty."

The permanent injury was to the hip of a very young child which, at the time that her mother consulted the doctor in the practice, was capable of being righted with proper diagnosis and treatment. The doctor negligently delayed referring the child to the hospital for just over two days and the hospital negligently delayed proper treatment for nearly a further three days, by the end of which time permanent damage was inevitable. Curiously, the hospital had not been brought into the litigation—which was commented upon adversely by the Court of Appeal as it seemed the obvious thing to have done—so that the only issue was whether the practice was to be held liable for the negligence of its doctor. On this, the trial judge who had decided against liability was reversed but only by a majority of the Court of Appeal. Of the two questions posed by the Master of the Rolls (above), the first was answered by him in the affirmative and the second in the negative (*ibid.*, paras 31 to 41), Dame Janet Smith was in agreement, although regarding the case as being "very close to the line" (*ibid.*, para.132) on remoteness and scope of duty, Elias L.J. disagreed on scope of duty (*ibid.*, para.111). The reasoning in the judgments is detailed, close and complex; it requires careful perusal.

Insert a new note after the penultimate sentence of the paragraph: **6–132**

NOTE 667a: *Aneco* was distinguished and *SAAMCO* applied in *Capita Alternative Fund Services (Guernsey) Ltd v Drivers Jonas* [2011] EWHC 2336 (Comm). Surveyors had negligently advised the purchasers of a shopping centre development as to its value and commercial prospects. The damages were limited to the difference between what the purchasers had paid and what they should have paid on the basis of correct advice. They did not extend to all the business losses that followed purchase: see *ibid.*, paras 298 to 309.

6–135   Insert a new note after the second sentence of the paragraph:

NOTE 675a: However, in the interesting scope of duty case of *Haugesund Kommune v Depfa ACS Bank* [2011] 3 All E.R. 655, CA, the obligation of care, being that of solicitors, arose only in contract as Norwegian law applied: see further at para.6–156, below and the facts at paras 29–008A and 29–008B, below.

Insert a new paragraph after para.6–147:

6–147A   Another case not concerning ships where the claimant's intervening acts and omissions were held not to break the chain of causation is *Borealis AB v Geogas Trading SA* [2011] 1 Lloyd's Rep. 482, a case both factually and legally complex. The defendant supplied goods to the claimant, being butane feedstock which was heavily contaminated with fluorides. This caused extensive physical damage to the claimant's plant and equipment, with consequent disruption of business and loss of profits. The defendant argued that the chain of causation had been broken by the claimant's failure to react appropriately to the triggering of an alarm, which had sounded soon after the discharge of the goods had commenced at the claimant's plant, by taking no action in response. The alarm was not intended to deal with matters other than contaminants, the claimant was wholly unaware that there had been a breach of contract by the supply of contaminated goods and therefore wholly unaware of any impending danger. The claimant's response to the alarm, although well short of best practice, was held not to be unreasonable and, even if unreasonable, certainly not reckless, so that the chain of causation was not broken. This approach mirrors *County Ltd v Girozentrale Securities* and what was said there by Hobhouse L.J., at para.6–147 of the main work.

6–150   Add at the end of the paragraph: In contrast to *Galoo* is the recovery for trading losses in *Tom Hoskins Plc v EMW Law* [2010] EWHC 479, Ch. The claimant company instructed the defendant solicitor to sell its business properties since it was suffering financial difficulties, which the solicitor knew, and was trading at a loss, which the solicitor did not know. The solicitor's negligent handling of the sale meant that the company was only able to complete the sale late and on relatively unfavourable terms, and this caused it to be unable to close down its operations and stem its trading losses: see *ibid.*, paras 142 to 157.

6–154   Add at the end of the paragraph: In *Rubenstein v HSBC Bank Plc* [2012] P.N.L.R. 7, p.151 the defendant bank was held to have given not only information about a particular investment but also advice by way of recommending it to the claimant as a suitable purchase for him. The advice was negligent because the investment, a form of bond, was not the most suitable one for the claimant. However, when some years after the advice was given there was a run on the fund bringing loss to the claimant, it was held that he was not entitled to recover damages for his loss as it was caused not by the negligent advice but by the general collapse of markets which collapse was wholly unforeseeable at the time of the advice. [Between completion of text and proof stage the Court of Appeal has held the claimant entitled to recover for his loss, disagreeing with the trial judge's approach, in the particular circumstances of the case, to cause, remoteness and foreseeability: [2012] EWCA Civ 1184. The judgment of the court, given by Rix L.J., merits the reading.]

Add at the end of the paragraph: In the interesting scope of duty case of **6–156** *Haugesund Kommune v Depfa ACS Bank* [2011] 3 All E.R. 655, CA, fully considered at paras 29–008A and 29–008B, below, where the duty of care of solicitors arose only in contract as Norwegian law applied, it was agreed, indeed was common ground, that, in the words of Rix L.J., it was "appropriate to consider the scope of that (contractual) duty in the terms laid down in *SAAMCO* and the cases which follow it": *ibid.*, para.73. However, this was not introducing *SAAMCO* and scope of duty in the same way at all as Lord Hoffmann, as mentioned in this paragraph of the main work, was attempting to do in *The Achilleas*.

Insert new paragraphs after para.6–164:

Siemens Building Technologies FE Ltd v Supershield Ltd [2010] 1 Lloyd's **6–164A** Rep. 349, CA is a particularly interesting decision of the Court of Appeal on remoteness of damage in contract. It is particularly interesting because it allows recovery where it could be said that the loss claimed was unlikely to result from the breach of contract.

A connection on a float valve in the water tank supplying a sprinkler system **6–164B** in a new office building failed and water from the tank overflowed, flooding and extensively damaging electrical equipment in the basement of the building. Proceedings were commenced by occupier, lessee and owner of the building against the main building contractor and, one by one, a whole series of sub-contractors, who had contracted to supply and install the sprinkler system, were brought in. In this series of sub-contractors Siemens was the last but one and Supershield, who had done the work, the last. Siemens settled the claims with the parties up the contractual chain but maintained its claim against Supershield, claiming as damages the amount it had paid in settlement.

The water had overflowed into an area of the tank which had a high wall, **6–164C** referred to as the tank room, and which was designed to retain any overflowing water. Water would not overflow from the tank room as there were drains in its floor which were capable of carrying away escaping water indefinitely. The drains however had become blocked by packaging, insulating or other material on the tank room floor so that water could not drain away. In these circumstances Supershield argued that the amount for which Siemens had agreed to settle the claims against it was unreasonable. For, it was said, there was available to Siemens the defence of remoteness of damage on the basis that a failure of the float valve was unlikely to result in a flood because the probability was that the water would escape through the drains. The distinctive feature of the case, as was pointed out by the court (at para.44), was that the float valve and the drains were both designed to control the flow of water involved in the operation of the sprinkler system. Yet no case was cited nor indeed known with this feature of simultaneous failure of separate protective measures. In the annals of remoteness in contract the situation was novel.

6–164D   Toulson L.J., who gave a useful judgment with which his brethren simply agreed, regarded *Hadley v Baxendale* as remaining the standard rule, a rule which has been rationalised on the basis that it reflects the expectation to be imputed to the parties in the ordinary case, imposing a liability in damages only if, at the time of contracting, a reasonable person would have had damages of the kind suffered in mind as not unlikely to result from a breach. Yet, Toulson L.J. continued, there may be cases where the court, on examining the contract and the commercial background, decides that the standard approach would not reflect the parties' reasonable expectation. He was assisted in arriving at this conclusion by invoking the authority of *SAAMCO* and *The Achilleas*, House of Lords' decisions in which Lord Hoffmann, and in the second case also Lord Hope, had departed from the standard approach (for these cases in this context see, respectively, para. 6–131 and paras 6–169 to 6–170 in the main work). Toulson L.J. accepted that in these two cases the effect of departure from the standard approach was exclusionary by relieving the contract breaker from liability for loss that was not unlikely to occur, but correctly concluded that logically the effect can be inclusionary. All this is at para.43 of his judgment.

6–164E   Therefore even if failure of the proper operation of the float valve was unlikely to result in a flood because the probability was that the water would escape through the drains, Toulson L.J. did not accept that this made the loss resulting from the flood too remote. Siemens, he said, was responsible for installing the sprinkler system in such a way that the water used for it was properly contained. It therefore assumed a contractual responsibility to prevent its escape and he concluded that the flood resulting from the water escape, even if it was unlikely, was within the scope of Siemens's contractual duty to prevent: para.45. It followed therefore that the settlement made by Siemens was entirely reasonable.

Insert new paragraphs after para.6–173:

6–173A   As predicted in para.6–171 of the main work, Lord Hoffmann's and Lord Hope's speeches in *The Achilleas* were bound to bring forward defendants, and particularly shipping defendants, who would argue that the law of remoteness had been radically changed by the decision so that they could not now be liable for foreseeable losses as they had not assumed responsibility for them in the sense of agreeing to pay for them should they happen. Two such cases involving shipping rapidly appeared, *ASM Shipping Ltd of India v TTMI Ltd of England, The Amer Energy* [2009] 1 Lloyd's Rep. 293 and *Sylvia Shipping Co Ltd v*

Progress Bulk Carriers Ltd [2010] 2 Lloyd's Rep. 81. Both were appeals from arbitration awards by defendants on the basis that because of *The Achilleas* the arbitrators' awards of damages against them were wrong in law. Both concerned charterparties, a voyage charterparty for a single voyage in *The Amer Energy* and a time charterparty in *Sylvia Shipping*. Both concerned breach of contract by the shipowner rather than by the charterer, breach by providing the charterer with the ship late in *The Amer Energy* and breach by failure to maintain the ship, leading to delay in readiness to load, in *Sylvia Shipping*. Both breaches resulted in a loss of profit, the subject of the claims, through the cancellation of charters. In both cases the arbitrators had not considered *The Achilleas* because it had not yet been decided, in the one case at the time of the award, in the other at the time of the conclusion of the arbitration hearing. In awarding damages for these profit losses the arbitrators were vindicated by Flaux J. in *The Amer Energy* and by Hamblen J. in *Sylvia Shipping*.

6–173B   In upholding the arbitrators, both judges said that they were satisfied that the House of Lords in *The Achilleas* had no intention of laying down a completely new test for the recoverability of damages for breach of contract. For Flaux J. the rule in *Hadley v Baxendale*, as refined in subsequent cases, still ruled the day: see his judgment at para.17. Hamblen J. agreed and went on to say that it was important to make it clear that there is no new generally applicable test, so as to allay the confusion and uncertainty caused by cases being argued on the basis of, and decisions challenged for failing to apply, the assumption of responsibility test in place of the orthodox test: see his judgment at para.49. Only in unusual cases could the orthodox test be ousted by the new thinking and neither case displayed to the judge deciding it any unusual or exceptional quality.

6–173C   It is interesting to examine how, in coming to this conclusion, Flaux J. and Hamblen J. dealt with *The Achilleas* and what they saw as its *ratio decidendi*. Flaux J. would appear to regard those favouring the orthodox approach as forming the majority, and thus providing the *ratio*, though he does not say this outright: see his judgment at paras 17 and 18. By contrast, Hamblen J. in *Sylvia Shipping* is explicit, and explicit in the other direction. Recognising that there is confusion about the *ratio* on account of Lord Walker having agreed with both sides, he comes to the conclusion, supported by *Chitty on Contracts* but not by *McGregor on Damages*, both of which he cites, that the rationale of assumption of responsibility has the support of the majority: see his judgment at paras 36 to 39. But if one says that there was a majority for the broader approach because Lord Walker agreed with Lords Hoffmann and Hope, it must equally be the case that there was a majority for the orthodox approach because Lord Walker also agreed with Lord Rodger; indeed Hamblen J. recognises this.

6–173D   Given such a duality, one is left with a variety of solutions. One may say, unattractively, that there is no *ratio decidendi*, or say, more sensibly, that to find the *ratio* a choice must be made between the two approaches and that, in choosing, the old must prevail over the new. Indeed, the rules of precedent may take one further. There is the rule adopted by the distinguished Lord Greene M.R. in *Gold v Essex County Council* [1942] 2 K.B. 293, CA, when the Court of Appeal was considering the binding force on it of *Hillyer v St Bartholomew's Hospital* [1909] 2 K.B. 820, CA. He said, at *ibid.*, 298:

> "In a case when two members of the court base their judgments, the one on a narrow ground confined to the necessities of the decision and the other on wide propositions which go far beyond those necessities, and the third member of the court expresses his concurrence in the reasoning of both, I think it right to treat the narrow ground as the real *ratio decidendi*."

There is also 19th and early 20th century support for the proposition that, where the House of Lords is equally divided, it is the decision appealed from that stands. (For these rules of precedent, see section 9 of Ch.II of the definitive work on the subject, Cross and Harris, *Precedent in English Law*, 4th edn (Oxford: Clarendon Press, 1991).) Whichever way one turns, therefore, there is no room for the assumption of responsibility test.

6–173E   Yet, be that as it may, the views of Lords Hoffmann and Hope appear to be here to stay with us, at least for the time being and despite the strict rules of precedent which even in this day and age should not be disregarded, because not only are their views examined and adhered to by both Flaux J. and Hamblen J. but also they are applied by the Court of Appeal in *Siemens Building Technologies FE Ltd v Supershield Ltd* [2010] 1 Lloyd's Rep. 349, CA so as, somewhat ironically, to extend rather than restrict liability: see *Supershield* at para.6–164D, above. This is of course subject to the Supreme Court at some future date declining to adopt the new thinking—it will be recalled that Lord Rodger in *The Achilleas* was not prepared to take a view on the propriety of an assumption of responsibility test while Baroness Hale was very much against it: see paras 6–169 and 6–170 of the main work. At the same time it is fair to say that the assumption of responsibility approach has already been sidelined, requiring consideration only in very special cases. Thus, Hamblen J. in *Sylvia Shipping* [2010] 2 Lloyd's Rep. 81 concluded, at para.82, that, as the case was an ordinary one with the claimed loss arising in the ordinary course of things, there was no need to address the issue of assumption of responsibility.

6–173F   What then is a very special case, an extraordinary case, an exceptional case, an unusual case—word it as you will—in which the damages fall to be reduced below the norm? Thus far we only have the two reasons, given by Lord Hoffmann in *The Achilleas*, for placing that case into the extraordinary category. Hamblen J. usefully sets out these reasons of Lord Hoffmann in *Sylvia Shipping* [2010] 2 Lloyd's Rep. 81 at para.33. The one is that the loss claimed would have been completely unquantifiable at the time of contracting, the other that the general understanding of the shipping market was that the claimed loss was not a recoverable loss. In adopting these reasons, Hamblen J. somewhat elaborated on the first of them, speaking of liability for loss that is "unquantifiable, unpredictable, uncontrollable or disproportionate": *ibid.*, para.40.

It will be seen that in both *The Achilleas* and *Sylvia Shipping*, delay in **6–173G** procuring the ship resulted in the cancellation of a fixture and the loss of profit from the fixture. Yet in the one the profit was allowed and in the other disallowed. Why? The difference appears to lie in the fact that in the one the fixture lost was that of the shipowner and in the other it was that of the charterer. Thus, while there was a general market understanding that damages for a charterer's delay in returning the ship to the shipowner are limited to the difference between charter rates and market rates, there was no similar market understanding where there is a shipowner's delay in making the ship available to the charterer. So too, while a follow-on fixture made by a shipowner at the end of a charter can be made for any period of time however long, so that there is an unpredictable and unquantifiable element making the liability disproportionate, a fixture by way of sub-charter during the currency of a charter cannot be for longer than the period of the charter, so that the potential loss falls within fixed confines. This is how Hamblen J. argues the distinction: see his judgment at para.73.

It would seem unlikely that the assumption of responsibility approach will **6–173H** have much to work upon. In the first place, that there is a general understanding in a particular market as to levels of damages must surely be very rare, and in any event even if a general understanding can be found, one might hazard the thought that that understanding could just be wrong. In the second place, should the claimed loss be, in Hamblen J.'s words, unquantifiable, unpredictable, uncontrollable or disproportionate, in all likelihood the damages would be held to be too remote simply by application of the rule in *Hadley v Baxendale*—the irrecoverability of the profits from the exceptionally lucrative dyeing contracts in the familiar *Victoria Laundry v Newman* (see para.6–175 of the main work) comes to mind and is indeed referred to in this connection in the judgment of Hamblen J. at para.81—so that, again, there would be no need to resort to the assumption of responsibility test to exclude liability.

Now Tomlinson J. in *Pindell Ltd v Airasia Berhad (Pindell)* [2010] EWHC **6–173I** 2516 (Comm) has said that he agreed with the view expressed by Flaux J. in *The Amer Energy* and by Hamblen J. in *Sylvia Shipping* (cases at para.6–173A, above) that *The Achilleas* has not "effected a major change to the approach to be adopted to the recoverability of damages for breach of contract": *Pindell*, para.84. While *Pindell* did not, like the others, concern ships and charterparties but aircraft and their leasing, it was still, like the others, a claim for loss of profits. The claimant had contracted to sell aircraft to a third party on their return by the defendant lessee at the end of the lease. On the defendant's failure to return the aircraft on time, the sale fell through. Tomlinson J. decided against awarding the loss of profit on the sale, but to do so he did not think it relevant or necessary to resort to the new assumption of responsibility test (*ibid.*, para.87), finding that the loss was one which was not likely to result (*ibid.*, para.86) in the same way as Lord Rodger, Lord Walker and Baroness Hale had found in *The Achilleas*, to whose speeches Tomlinson J. specifically referred on this: *Pindell*, para.88.

6–174   Add at the end of the paragraph: For an important decision where recovery was allowed in respect of a loss which was in fact unlikely to result see *Siemens Building Technologies FE Ltd v Supershield Ltd* [2010] 1 Lloyd's Rep. 349, CA, fully considered at paras 6–164A to 6–164E, above.

6–185   Insert a new note at the end of the paragraph:

NOTE 895a: Loss of profits occurring almost a year after the incidence of the breach of contract were awarded as not being too remote in *Borealis AB v Geogas Trading SA* [2011] 1 Lloyd's Rep. 482 (facts at para.6–147A, above); see *ibid.* paras 48 and 120 *et seq.*

CHAPTER 7

MITIGATION OF DAMAGE

			PARA.
I.	VARIOUS MEANINGS OF THE TERM "MITIGATION"		7–001
☐	1.	Principal meaning: the three rules as to the avoiding of the consequences of a wrong	7–002
	2.	The two subsidiary or residual meanings	7–008
II.	THE RULE AS TO AVOIDABLE LOSS: NO RECOVERY FOR LOSS WHICH THE CLAIMANT OUGHT TO HAVE AVOIDED		7–014
■	1.	Various aspects of the rule	7–015
	2.	The rule and its relationship to the normal measure of damages	7–033
■	3.	Illustrations of circumstances raising the issue of whether loss should have been avoided	7–041
■	4.	Standard of conduct which the claimant must attain when assessing what steps should have been taken by him	7–070
■ III.	THE COROLLARY: RECOVERY FOR LOSS INCURRED IN ATTEMPTS TO MITIGATE THE DAMAGE		7–091
IV.	THE RULE AS TO AVOIDED LOSS: NO RECOVERY FOR LOSS WHICH THE CLAIMANT HAS AVOIDED, UNLESS THE MATTER IS COLLATERAL		7–097
	1.	The three subdivisions of the rule	7–099
☐	2.	Various aspects of the rule	7–102
☐	3.	Actions taken after the wrong by the claimant	7–106
■	4.	Actions taken after the wrong by third parties	7–137
☐	5.	Actions taken before the wrong by the claimant	7–147

Insert a new note at the end of the paragraph: **7–004**

NOTE 0: It is the loss that has to be avoided and not the wrong itself. The curious suggestion of an avoidable wrong appeared in the patent case of *Alan Nuttall Ltd v Fri-Jado UK Ltd* [2010] EWHC 1966 (Pat) at para.37 *et seq.*

NOTE 49: Add at the end of the note: On the other hand, a claimant must **7–019** establish that, while his tortiously damaged car is being repaired, he has a need for a replacement car and cannot require the defendant to prove the contrary: see *Park Lane BMW v Whipp*, May 20, 2009, unreported, at paras 16 and 17, approved on this by the Court of Appeal in *Beechwood Birmingham Ltd v Hoyer Group UK Ltd* [2011] Q.B. 357, CA. These two cases are at paras 7–062A and 7–062B, below.

Insert a new paragraph after para.7–028:

Isabella Shipowner SA v Shagang Shipping Co Ltd [2012] 2 Lloyd's Rep. 61 **7–028A** is a further charterparty case in which Cooke J. in a valuable judgment examined all of the earlier authorities in some detail and, departing from the decision of the arbitrator of whose legal analysis he was rather critical, held that the shipowners' refusal to accept redelivery by the charterers under a long term time charter was in order, so as to entitle the owners to keep the contract on foot and claim the hire that would fall due. Cooke J. rightly considered a time charter to be subject to the rule in *White and Carter v McGregor* as its performance by the owners did not need the charterers' co-operation and assistance (on this see para.7–023 of the main work); if the charterer failed to give any orders, Cooke J. said, the vessel would simply stay where it was, awaiting orders but earning hire (*ibid.*, para.37). Then for a finding that the owners had no legitimate interest in continuing with the charter, it had to be shown, and by the charterers, that it was wholly unreasonable for the owners to continue: see the points made at *ibid.*, paras 42 to 44. The charterers wished to compel the shipowners in mitigation of loss to trade in a difficult spot market where substitute time charters were impossible—something which with their right to sub-let the charterers could take the risk of doing themselves—and to argue about the quantum of damages at a much later date. Far safer from the owners' point of view to be entitled to the payment of hire up front, semi-monthly in advance, and on any default to bring suit for it: see the points made at *ibid.*, paras 47 and 48. Damages would thus be an inadequate remedy and the owners could not be faulted for their maintaining of the charter.

7–043   Add at the end of the paragraph: Various failures of the claimant in the wake of the delivery of defective goods in *Borealis AB v Geogas Trading SA* [2011] 1 Lloyd's Rep. 482 (facts at para.6–147A, above) were argued by the defendant, unsuccessfully, to be failures to mitigate: see *ibid.*, para.127 *et seq.*

7–049   NOTE 192: Add at the end of the note: Similarly, *Strutt v Whitnell* was applied by the Court of Appeal in *Activa DPS Europe SARL v Pressure Seal Solutions Ltd* [2012] EWCA Civ 943 where the buyer of machines, in breach by not having paid the purchase price, unsuccessfully argued that the seller had failed to mitigate by refusing the offer to return the machines that the buyer had not resold. Patten L.J., giving the only reasoned judgment, considered *Strutt v Whitnell* to be in point and obviously to apply since, while the victim of a breach of contract has to take such steps as are available to reduce the loss, there is no call to act so as to reverse the transaction: see *ibid.*, paras 33 to 36.

Insert new paragraphs after para.7–062:

7–062A   The claimant in *Beechwood Birmingham Ltd v Hoyer UK Group Ltd* [2011] Q.B. 357, CA was a substantial company of motor dealers. Whenever one of its cars suffered an accident necessitating a period off the road for repairs, it was the claimant's practice to provide a replacement during the repair period from its available pool of cars which was large enough to avoid the necessity to hire in from outside. The tortiously damaged car, which was the subject of the claim, had been allocated to the claimant's service manager whose contract of employment entitled him to the use of a company car. He, rather than simply reallocating to himself a similar car from the claimant's stock, this being the claimant's usual practice, hired an equivalent substitute vehicle. The claimant claimed the hire charges as special damages but in this was unsuccessful. The trial judge found the hiring to constitute a failure to mitigate and the Court of Appeal saw no reason to disturb this finding. The claimant had not acted reasonably in hiring a replacement vehicle when one was easily available from the claimant's stock, and the need for a replacement vehicle had not been shown: see *ibid.*, paras 25 to 32. The question as to what damages the claimant was entitled to recover in lieu is dealt with elsewhere: see paras 32–044A and 32–048A, below.

Also in *Park Lane BMW v Whipp*, May 20, 2009, unreported, hire charges for a substitute car were not allowed as special damages to the car dealership claimant as no need for a substitute car was shown. It is true that the car was an expensive sports touring car and not of the same type as the car damaged, but little was made of this; there was no need for a substitute car at all. This Oxford County Court decision was cited, clearly with approval, by the Court of Appeal in *Beechwood Birmingham* at para.28. **7–062B**

Add at the end of the paragraph (before the closing bracket): In another case of a "free" car being offered to and refused by the claimant while her own car was being repaired, *Sayce v TNT (UK) Ltd* [2012] 1 W.L.R. 1261, CA, the trial judge had refused to follow *Copley* and on account of this, and upon the ground of procedural irregularity, the Court of Appeal allowed the appeal that was brought. Moore-Bick L.J., who gave the leading judgment, was unhappy with, and rather critical of, the reasoning in *Copley* (*ibid.*, paras 27 to 29) while recognising that it had received support in this work; the other Lord Justices did not address the matter. In *Copley* leave to appeal was refused by the Supreme Court and, partly because of this, the Court of Appeal in *Sayce* refused leave to appeal, although Moore-Bick L.J. rightly said that it would be beneficial for the questions raised by these cases to be considered at the highest level as soon as a suitable opportunity arose: *ibid.*, para.30. **7–068**

NOTE 271: Add at the end of the note: For a whole series of ways in which the defendant argued unsuccessfully that the claimant should have acted to mitigate his loss see, at great length, *BSkyB Ltd v HP Enterprise Services UK Ltd* [2010] EWHC 86 (TCC), paras 1712 to 1800. **7–070**

Insert a new note at the end of the paragraph: **7–076**

NOTE 292a: House owners not giving their builders the opportunity to remedy defects, which the builders could have done with no cost to themselves or the house owners, was held to be a failure to mitigate in *Woodlands Oak Ltd v Conwell* [2011] EWCA Civ 254; see at *ibid.*, para.18 *et seq.*

Substitute for Nine as the first word of the paragraph: Ten **7–077**

7–082   Add at the end of the paragraph: Where in *Olafsson v Foreign & Commonwealth Office* [2009] EWHC 2608, QB a default judgment obtained in Iceland on a damages claim of the claimant had been set aside on account of defective service for which the defendant government department was responsible, the claimant sought to recover from the defendant the loss of the default judgment and attendant wasted costs. The defendant sought to argue that the claimant should have mitigated by seeking a second default judgment, but this argument failed as the outcome of a second claim was undoubtedly uncertain, the suit might well fail, the costs would be substantial and probably greater than on the first claim: see especially *ibid.*, para.33.

Insert a new paragraph after para.7–084:

7–084A   *Weir v Dobell* was given some consideration in the further charterparty case of *Glory Wealth Shipping PTE Ltd v North China Shipping Ltd* [2010] EWHC 1692 (Comm), the defendant there being said to have placed considerable emphasis on it when seeking leave to appeal against the arbitrators' award. The claimant had entered into a time charter with the shipowner and had sub-chartered the ship, again by way of time charter, to the defendant. The defendant sub-charterer repudiated, the claimant accepted the repudiation, and the ship was redelivered to the claimant just short of six months before the earliest date at which the sub-charter could have contractually been brought to an end by the defendant. For a time the claimant continued to sub-charter the ship on various charters but towards the end of the six months the claimant in its turn redelivered the ship to the owner without itself being, apparently, in breach of contract. The defendant argued that just as the claimant in *Weir v Dobell* should have cancelled the head charterparty in mitigation of damage, so the claimant's redelivery of the ship to the head charterer, the shipowner, relieving the claimant of the obligation to make hire payments, should be taken into account in mitigation of damage. David Steel J. however said that he found *Weir v Dobell* of no assistance and for two reasons: because the claimant had had a right to cancel the charterparty and because the length of the head charter did not run beyond the length of the sub-charter (*Glory Wealth*, para.13). There are indeed these two differences between the two cases but there is this far more important difference: the head charterer had in *Glory Wealth*, and had not in *Weir v Dobell*, returned the ship to the owner. *Glory Wealth* is therefore not about whether mitigation principles required the return of the ship in order to reduce loss but about whether the ship's actual return had in fact reduced loss. In other words, *Glory Wealth* is about whether loss has been avoided whereas *Weir v Dobell* is about whether loss should have been avoided. We have moved from questions of avoidable loss to questions of avoided loss, and *Glory Wealth* is considered in this connection at a later point: see para.7–125A, below.

7–085   NOTE 335: Substitute for [2009] L.S. Law Med. 229, CA on line 3 of the note: [2010] Q.B. 48, CA

NOTE 335: Add at the end of the note: That this principle that a claimant is **7–085** free to choose from whom to recover compensation has nothing to do with mitigation of loss was again emphasised and applied in *Haugesund Kommune v Depfa ACS Bank* [2010] 2 Lloyd's Rep. 323 where the claim being pursued was for damages, the claim for restitution having already been decided. The statements to this effect in *The Liverpool (No.2)* and in *Peters* were both prayed in aid as was this para.7–085 from the main work, which paragraph was cited in full and the formulation in which was preferred over the different formulation in *Halsbury's Laws*: all this at para.20 *et seq.* of *Haugesund*. The case has now gone to the Court of Appeal where it took a different direction. Nothing was said about mitigation and, while the principle in *The Liverpool (No.2)* was discussed and the conclusion reached that it was not in doubt (see [2011] 3 All E.R. 655, CA at paras 34 to 40), the principle was considered to be inapplicable to *Haugesund* because it was concerned with established loss and the real question in *Haugesund*, as the Court of Appeal saw it, was whether the loss had been properly established (see *ibid.*, paras 41, 84 and 85). This aspect of the case, which takes us far from mitigation and into scope of duty, is fully considered at paras 29–008A and 29–008B, below.

Insert a new note before the penultimate sentence of the paragraph as it **7–087** stands:

NOTE 342a: So too in *Deutsche Bank AG v Total Global Steel Ltd* [2012] EWHC 1201 (Comm), where the claimant had bought in a specialised market carbon emission units, the mitigating steps proposed by the defendant were not required as they would have prejudiced the claimant's reputation.

Add at the end of the paragraph: In *A Nelson & Co Ltd v Guna SpA* [2011] **7–087** EWHC 1202 (Comm), where there was breach of a distribution agreement, there was held to be no failure to mitigate. The claimant on the breach had found itself in an uncertain and complex situation where it was not called upon to take risks outside the normal course of business: see generally *ibid.*, paras 41 to 47.

Insert a new paragraph after para.7–090:

(x) A claimant need not be prejudiced by paying money in performance of a **7–090A** *contract which is unenforceable against him.* This rule is suggested by *W v Veolia Environmental Services* [2011] EWHC 2020, QB, another of the many credit car hire cases that are today appearing in the courts (facts at para.32–021A, below). The payment under a contract that was unenforceable against the hirer, so that there was no legal obligation for him to pay, of credit hire charges for a car needed by him while his car, damaged by the defendant, was being repaired did not constitute a failure to mitigate.

Insert new paragraphs after para.7–091:

7–091A   The peculiar feature in *Herrmann v Withers LLP* [2012] EWHC 1492, Ch was that the expense successfully claimed had not in fact been incurred by the claimants. The defendant solicitors, acting for the claimants in the purchase of a residential property in the Royal Borough of Kensington in London, advised them that the property enjoyed a statutory right of access to a communal garden when they should have advised that their construction of the relevant statute might not be right and have warned that there was scope for argument regarding entitlement to use the garden. After completion of the purchase had taken place, the claimants instructed fresh solicitors to advise them in relation to access to the garden. Correspondence over several months ensued between these new solicitors and the solicitors retained by the Borough to advise their garden committees, correspondence culminating in an offer made to the claimants by the Borough, through the relevant garden committee, of a licence to use the garden for a fee of £25,000. This offer the claimants did not accept and Newey J. held that this constituted a failure to mitigate as the grant of the licence offered would have alleviated to a great extent the disadvantage of not having the statutory right of access to the garden (his very detailed reasons for holding that the claimants ought reasonably to have pursued the offer of a licence appear at *ibid.*, para.82). Accordingly, the damages in respect of the diminution in the value of the residential property were limited to the difference between its value with the statutory right of access to the garden and its value with only a licence to use the garden. At the same time, however, Newey J. held that the claimants were entitled to damages represented by the costs that the claimants would have incurred in negotiating and agreeing a licence with the Borough's garden committee, such costs being the £25,000 for the licence itself and relevant legal costs.

7–091B   It will be seen that the claimants' recovery was not in respect of expenditure incurred in the taking of mitigating action but in respect of expenditure which was not incurred by reason of the failure to mitigate. It is thought that *Herrmann* is the first decision where damages have been claimed and allowed for expenditure which has not been incurred at all. One can see the logic and sense of this result. Had the claimants incurred the expenditure required by the mitigating action, they would have recovered for this expenditure in lieu of recovering for the greater loss that would have incurred had they not mitigated. If they fail to mitigate and so cannot recover for the loss that could and should have been avoided, they should still be entitled to recover for the loss that would have remained after they had mitigated, *viz.* for the expenditure not in fact incurred. In short, the claimants should be able to recover not only for the loss remaining after mitigation but also for what would have been the remaining loss had they mitigated: see Newey J. in *Herrmann* at paras 90 to 94.

Insert new paragraphs after para.7–096:

7–096A   A neat illustration of an action taken in mitigation which increases the loss is provided by a sale of goods case, *Choil Trading SA v Sahara Energy Resources*

Ltd [2010] EWHC 374 (Comm) (facts at para.20–059A, below). The claimant buyer's sub-buyer had, on account of defects, rejected the cargo of naphtha sold to it, thus leaving the claimant with the cargo on his hands. The claimant therefore decided to hedge against its open position, this being normal practice in a volatile market and constituting a reasonable attempt at mitigation. Because the market then rose the claimant was able to sell the cargo elsewhere for more than it had bought it, but the market rise meant that a loss was necessarily suffered on the hedge, which loss, as it turned out, was greater than the eventual profit made on the cargo sold to the claimant by the defendant. For this net loss the claimant was held entitled to recover: see Christopher Clarke J.'s complex computation at *ibid.*, paras 156 to 161.

It should be noted that Christopher Clarke J., in his discussion of the process **7–096B** of hedging, pointed out that the defendant was well aware of the likelihood that the claimant would hedge: *ibid.*, para.156. This may suggest that, in the absence of such knowledge he would have considered that, or would have had to consider whether, the damage was too remote. But remoteness does not come into the picture and has no application where acts taken in mitigation are concerned. The claimant has suffered damage, damage which is in no way too remote, and he is simply seeking by action to mitigate that damage. All that matters, to allow recovery, is that the action taken by the claimant is reasonable.

Add at the end of the paragraph: Another illustration of no loss is afforded by **7–105** *Murfin v Campbell* [2011] EWHC 1475, Ch. In reliance on what he maintained was the defendant's negligent advice the claimant gave a warranty which obliged him to pay over the amount by which the losses of a certain company exceeded a specified sum but the obligation to pay would only arise when a series of loan notes became redeemable. As things turned out the loan notes never did become redeemable so that no payment had to be made by the claimant. Nevertheless, he sought to recover the amount of the payment as damages on the basis that it represented his loss at the time of the wrong, whether regarded as breach of contract or negligence. He rightly failed because in the event he had suffered no loss. Many of the cases scattered throughout the main work were cited in support of his claim but none was really in point. The only case clearly in point, which the judge cited, was *Kennedy v Van Emden* (in this paragraph of the main work) and it was against him.

Insert a new note at the end of the paragraph as it stands: **7–110**

NOTE 432a: It is thought that this principle should have been applied in the sale of goods case of *M&J Marine Engineering Services Co Ltd v Shipshore Ltd* [2009] EWHC 2031 (Comm), dealt with at para.20–029A, below.

Add at the end of the paragraph (after fn.432a): A somewhat different case of **7–110** a buyer's loss reduced by action taken in mitigation occurred in *Glencore Energy UK Ltd v Transworld Oil Ltd* [2010] EWHC 141 (Comm). On the seller's repudiation of its sale of oil, the buyer, having accepted the repudiation, proceeded to reduce its loss by closing out its hedges, as to allow them to run on would have been to speculate in the movement of the price of oil, it being accepted that hedging was an integral part of the seller's business: see Blair J.'s analysis at *ibid.*, para.78 which somewhat confuses avoided loss and avoidable loss.

7–116 Substitute for *Lavarack v Colchester* on line 5 of the paragraph:

Lavarack v Woods of Colchester

7–116 Insert a new note at the end of the paragraph:

NOTE 448a: Where in *Red River UK Ltd v Sheikh* [2010] EWHC 1100, Ch the defendants in breach of contract had sabotaged certain refinancing so that the claimants had to abandon their planned development of a property site and merely sold the property, Henderson J., while holding that the claimants, for reasons not here relevant, were not entitled to the profit that would have been made on the development, said that he saw considerable force in the argument that, had he held the claimants so entitled, any profit on the sale of the property would have had to be taken into account against the development profit because the sale represented an alternative way of realising the development potential of the property and therefore formed part of a single commercial enterprise by the claimants: see *ibid.*, paras 165 and 168.

7–118 NOTE 454: Add at the end of the note: And in the context of charterparties and benefits to be taken into account, see the interesting and important *Omak Maritime Ltd v Mamola Challenger Shipping Co* [2011] 1 Lloyd's Rep. 47 at para.2–041A, above.

7–118 Add at the end of the paragraph: So too where in *Zodiac Maritime Agencies Ltd v Fortescue Metals Group Ltd* [2011] 2 Lloyd's Rep. 360 the claim was by the shipowner against the charterer for repudiation of the charterparty during its course (see para.27–067A, below) and the shipowner succeeded in nominating the ship for an earlier charter by negotiating for its substitution, it was held by David Steel J. that the earnings from that charter were to be taken into account in assessing the shipowner's loss since employing the ship under the earlier charter was part of a continuous dealing with the situation, the cause of the renegotiation of the one charter being the termination of the other: see *ibid.*, at paras 68 to 72. Again in *Dalwood Marine Co v Nordana Line SA* [2010] 2 Lloyd's Rep. 315 there was a wrongful repudiation of a charterparty by the charterer which prima facie entitled the shipowner to the contractual rate of hire up until the contractual date of redelivery less the hire that could be earned from alternative employment during that period. See the case further at para.27–067A, below. In *Linklaters Business Services v Sir Robert McAlpine Ltd* [2010] EWHC 2931 (TCC) tenants who had successfully claimed against contractors for the cost of replacing defective pipework (facts at para.26–011, below), and who had entered into an agreement with their landlords that for future rent reviews the defects would be regarded as remedied provided the landlords contributed £200,000 towards the replacement cost, were required to give credit for this sum in their damages claim: see *ibid.*, paras 156 to 163. Although nothing was said in this sensible decision of Viscount Haldane's test that for a subsequent transaction to be taken into account in mitigation it must arise out of the consequences of the breach (see para.7–007 *et seq.* of the main work), clearly this test was abundantly satisfied.

Insert new paragraphs after para.7–125:

The principle cogently stated by Lord Goff in *The Elena d'Amico*, a statement often turned to in the cases, was applied to a different charterparty situation in *Glory Wealth Shipping PTE Ltd v North China Shipping Ltd* [2010] EWHC 1692 (Comm). The claimant had entered into a time charter with the shipowner and had sub-chartered the ship, again by way of time charter, to the defendant. The defendant sub-charterer repudiated, the claimant accepted the repudiation, and the ship was redelivered to the claimant just short of six months before the earliest date at which the sub-charter could have contractually been brought to an end by the defendant sub-charterer. For a time the claimant continued to sub-charter the ship on various charters but towards the end of the six months the claimant in its turn redelivered the ship to the owner without itself being, apparently, in breach of contract. The defendant sub-charterer argued unsuccessfully that what the claimant had saved in having no further hire payments to make up the line under the head charter should be brought into account in the computation of the damages. David Steel J. was satisfied that the normal measure of the difference between the sub-charter rate and the market rate throughout the whole of the six-month period should apply, and had been applied by the arbitrators (see especially *ibid.*, paras 16 to 18). Therefore the redelivery by the claimant to the head owner did not reduce the claimant's loss and the reasons for making it were of no significance in the computation of the damages. As David Steel J. said at *ibid.*, para.15: "The early redelivery . . . should be treated as an independent speculation not caused by the repudiation of the sub-charter". The position had in effect crystallised at the time of the acceptance of the repudiation. This result follows precisely the reasoning in *The Elena d'Amico*. **7–125A**

Not only *The Elena d'Amico* but also *Norden v Andre* (for which see para.7–126 in the main work) was cited and relied upon by David Steel J. in *Zodiac Maritime Agencies Ltd v Fortescue Metals Group Ltd* [2011] 2 Lloyd's Rep. 360, another charterparty case but with the shipowner rather than the charterer as claimant (facts at para.27–067A, below). It was first held that there was no available market at the time of the charterer's breach so that the normal measure of the difference between market rate and charter rate could not be applied, and further held that the later appearance of an available market before **7–125B** the charter period would have expired was of no significance. A line had been drawn under the transaction after the occurrence of the breach, thereby removing subsequent market movements from the equation: see *ibid.*, paras 62 to 66. A somewhat unusual feature of the case is that it was the claimant and not the defendant who was contending for the application of the normal measure of the difference between market rate and charter rate.

7–125C   It is interesting that Briggs J., in *Anthracite Rated Investments (Jersey) Ltd v Lehman Brothers Finance SA* [2011] 2 Lloyd's Rep. 538 should have considered *Glory Wealth* as supporting the principle that the determination of loss should be at the breach date: *Anthracite*, paras 117 and 118.

7–145   Add at the end of the paragraph: *Linklaters Business Services v Sir Robert McAlpine Ltd* [2010] EWHC 2931 (TCC) is also a case which could be regarded as not falling within the conventional category of loss avoided by act of the claimant himself but as loss avoided by a third party's act but, whichever way one goes, the result, allowing deduction, is right: see the case at para.7–118, above.

Insert a new paragraph after para.7–146:

7–146A   By fortunate contrast, deduction of a benefit coming from a third party was held to be allowable in *Rubenstein v HSBC Bank Plc* [2012] P.N.L.R. 7, p.151 and *Needler* (at para.7–146 of the main work) was distinguished. While holding that there could be no recovery for the loss in respect of a bond on causation and remoteness grounds (see the case on this at para.6–154, above), the trial judge said that, if he should prove to be wrong on liability, he would have deducted from the damages the amount of an *ex gratia* payment made by the issuers of the bond to bondholders on account of a monetary recovery they had made on certain bond connected assets. This payment, to which the claimant had no contractual entitlement, arose directly in consequence of investment in the bond: *ibid.*, paras 129 and 130. [Between completion of text and proof stage the Court of Appeal, while holding the trial judge to be wrong on liability, upheld his decision that the *ex gratia* payment must be taken into account in reduction of damages: [2012] EWCA Civ 1184, paras 133 to 136.]

7–168   Add at the end of the paragraph: Indeed it has now been suggested that *Joyner* cannot stand after the decision of the House of Lords in a different context in *Ruxley Electronics & Construction Ltd v Forsyth* [1996] A.C. 344 (at para. 26–013 of the main work) with its accent on damages being confined to compensation for loss, and this suggestion has been accepted in *Pgf II SA v Royal & Sun Alliance Insurance Plc* [2010] EWHC 1459 (TCC) (facts at para.23–055, below) by H.H. Judge Toulmin: see his discussion at *ibid.*, para.23 *et seq.*

CHAPTER 8

CERTAINTY OF DAMAGE

			PARA.
■	I.	THE PROBLEM OF CERTAINTY	8–001
	II.	CIRCUMSTANCES IN WHICH DAMAGES MAY BE AWARDED ALTHOUGH THE NATURE OF THE DAMAGE PREVENTS ABSOLUTE CERTAINTY OF PROOF	8–004
	1.	Where damage is presumed	8–004
	2.	Where the loss is non-pecuniary	8–007
□	3.	Where it is uncertain how a pecuniary loss is to be measured	8–008
□	4.	Where it is uncertain how much of the loss, pecuniary or non-pecuniary, is attributable to the defendant's breach of duty	8–010
■	5.	Where it is uncertain whether a particular pecuniary loss will be or would have been incurred	8–021

Insert new paragraphs after para.8–002:

In *Zabihi v Janzemini* [2009] EWCA Civ 851, where the valuation of missing converted jewellery was in issue (facts at para.33–049A, below), the essence of the opening two paragraphs of this chapter, as set out by the Court of Appeal (*ibid.*, para.27), were relied upon by Blackburne J. below and distilled by him in the statement, also set out by the Court of Appeal (*ibid.*, para.29), that **8–002A**

> "the court must do its best on such evidence as it feels able to accept to place some kind of value on [the] jewellery . . . even if its precise identity cannot be established and therefore its value must be in doubt".

The Court of Appeal agreed that Blackburne J. was right to do his best to come to a valuation figure provided that he was entitled to accept the evidence on which he relied as sufficient evidence of value. By a majority it was held that he had had, in the words of para.8–002 of the main work, adequate data to support the award which he had made.

The issue of valuation and proof of value arose in a different context in *Experience Hendrix LLC v Times Newspapers Ltd* [2010] EWHC 1986, Ch with Blackburne J., now Sir William Blackburne, again as trial judge. A newspaper publisher had infringed the claimant companies' rights in the performance and recording of a concert by issuing a free CD of the concert to purchasers of its newspaper. The claimant companies claimed damages to compensate them for their resultant loss, the infringement having delayed the launch of their own project which related to a film of the concert. The judge found it impossible to forecast, so as to provide a reliable basis for computing losses, what the box office takings were likely to be for a film which had yet to be released, which at **8–002B** the time of the trial had not even been completed and which none of the independent experts had seen in any shape or form and, if they had, would not have had the relevant expertise to comment on. This great uncertainty, however, did not mean that the judge should award no damages on the basis that the claimant companies had not proved their loss; since they clearly had suffered loss, to award no damages would have been a most unsatisfactory outcome (*ibid.*, para.204). Fortunately, two figures emerged to which it was possible, as Sir William Blackburne put it, to anchor an assessment of the claimant companies' losses from the delay (*ibid.*, para.205). The first came from a distribution agreement with another company and the second from a rival offer made for some of the performance rights. See the case further at para.40–044, below.

8–002C   In *IRT Oil and Gas Ltd v Fiber Optic Systems Technology (Canada) Inc* [2009] EWHC 3041, QB the claimant company was the exclusive sales agent for Africa under a five-year contract with the defendant which entitled the claimant to a percentage of the purchase price of all sales in Africa that it negotiated. Some time into the contract the defendant wrongfully terminated the contract. In the claim for damages Tugendhat J. recognised that there was no way that he could make reliable findings as to what the prospective sales would have been over the remaining years of the contract but he did have evidence that sales had been made in other parts of the world and he was satisfied that the agency had some value. He agreed with the claimant's counsel that he must do the best that he could and arrived at an amount of damages by, as he put it, putting a figure on the chance that the claimant would have made a profit. On all this see para.94 *et seq.*

8–002D   Further cases presenting this difficulty of showing the amount of profitable sales that would have been made by the claimant had there been no tort or breach of contract by the defendant have indicated that the claimant is assisted by the principle in the very old case of *Armory v Delamirie* (at para.33–049 of the main work), which has today received a new lease of life, the principle being that the court is required to resolve uncertainties by making assumptions generous to the claimant where it is the defendant's wrongdoing which has created those uncertainties: see *Fearns v Anglo-Dutch Paint & Chemical Co Ltd* [2010] EWHC 1708, Ch at para.70 and *Double Communications Ltd v News Corp International Ltd* [2011] EWHC 961, QB at paras 4 and 5. What the courts in *Fearns* and *Double Communications* fail to notice is that the authorities bringing *Armory v Delamirie* into the modern world are concerned with proof of the loss of a chance in the strict sense, that is to say with situations where the chance is seen as an identifiable loss in itself, in particular where the chance relates to success in a damages action eliminated by a solicitor's negligence: see para.8–083, and the discussion at para.8–038, of the main work. The authorities do not go beyond this situation. In this connection the sensible comments of Moore-Bick L.J. in *Zabihi v Janzemoni* [2009] EWCA Civ 851 at para.33–049A, below are worth noting, while the subsequent refusal of Hamblen J. to apply the *Armory v Delamirie* principle to the facts in *Porton Capital Technology Funds v 3M UK Holdings Ltd* [2011] EWHC 2895 (Comm) is to be commended. In 2007 the defendants agreed to buy the entire shareholding of a company from the shareholder claimants. The consideration for the purchase was a cash sum together with what was referred to as an earn out payment based on net sales for the year 2009, the defendants being required to continue the business. The earn out payment was the principal return to be made by the claimants from the sale. The defendants in breach of contract closed down the business so that there were no sales in 2009. The claimants, relying on *Armory v Delamirie*, argued that, since the very actions of the defendants in breaching the contract had made the quantification of damages more difficult, the court should resolve any uncertainties in the claimants' favour. Hamblen J. did not accept the argument. The claim was for lost profits for breach of contract where there were evidence and documentation relating to the claim; the evidential playing field was a level one. The *Armory v Delamirie* principle should not be extended further than necessary: *ibid.*, paras 237 to 244.

NOTE 25: Add at the end of the note: For an interesting case where there was **8–008** uncertainty about how a pecuniary loss was to be measured see *Zabihi v Janzemini* [2009] EWCA Civ 851 at para.8–002A, above. Difficulty in valuing a pecuniary loss was also faced in *Experience Hendrix LLC v Times Newspapers Ltd* [2010] EWHC 1986, Ch, and in *IRT Oil and Gas Ltd v Fiber Optic Systems Technology (Canada) Inc* [2009] EWHC 3041, QB, considered at paras 8–002B and 8–002C, above.

NOTE 28: Add at the end of the note: *Webster v Sandersons Solicitors* [2009] **8–009** P.N.L.R. 37, p.773, CA is another case involving, *inter alia*, shareholders' reflective losses.

Insert new paragraphs after para.8–020:

In all the cases before *Sienkiewicz v Greif (UK) Ltd* [2011] 2 A.C. 229 the **8–020A** application of the *Fairchild* rule—or the *Fairchild* exception as it is referred to by the Supreme Court in *Sienkiewicz*—has been to situations where the exposure to asbestos resulting in mesothelioma has been by two or more defendants, generally employers of the victim. *Sienkiewicz* raised the question of whether the *Fairchild* exception applied where there is only one defendant responsible for exposure to asbestos, with the victim having been also at risk of developing mesothelioma from low level exposure to asbestos in the general atmosphere, referred to as environmental exposure. The Supreme Court sitting as a court of seven unanimously answered the question in the affirmative. As Lord Dyson put it at *ibid.*, para.212:

> "In view of the present state of medical knowledge, a single exposure claim would founder on the same rock of uncertainty [a term taken from Lord Bingham in *Fairchild* and adopted throughout the speeches in *Sienkiewicz*] as a multiple exposure claim. The [*Fairchild*] exception was devised as a matter of policy to overcome the

injustice that claimants would suffer if they were prevented by the rock of uncertainty from establishing causation in mesothelioma cases . . . . There is no reason in policy or principle why the exception should not apply to a single exposure claim just as it does to a multiple exposure claim."

And Lord Brown said, at *ibid.*, para.184, that in his opinion there was simply no logical stopping place between the case of successive negligent employers and the case before the court.

8–020B   The Court of Appeal had arrived at the same result in a curious way by construing s.3 of the Compensation Act 2006 (at para.8–019 of the main work) as laying down that a person is liable in tort in all cases where he has materially increased the risk of contracting mesothelioma. This was rightly regarded as a wrong interpretation by the Supreme Court. As Lord Phillips in the leading speech said at *ibid.*, para.70:

> "Section 3(1) does not state that the responsible person *will be* liable in tort if he has materially increased the risk of a victim of mesothelioma. It states that the section applies *where* the responsible person is liable in tort for materially increasing that risk. Whether and in what circumstances liability in tort attaches to one who has materially increased the risk of a victim contracting mesothelioma remains a question of common law." (italics his)

Lord Rodger explained the true position similarly: *ibid.*, paras 130 to 132.

8–020C   The Court of Appeal took the view that, aside from this faulty interpretation of s.3, the test of causation that it would have applied was not whether the defendant's participation had materially increased the risk of contracting meso-thelioma but whether the defendant's participation had at least doubled that risk. It is thought that the Court of Appeal in *Sienkiewicz* [2010] Q.B. 370 will have been drawn into this approach by making a comparison between the environ-mental exposure to asbestos which is at a low level and the exposure by the single defendant of the office worker victim at its factory, an exposure which was also light (even lighter in *Willmore v Knowsley Metropolitan Borough Council*, the co-joined appeal, where the victim had been exposed to asbestos as a girl in the single defendant's school) and concluding it to be somewhat unfair to expose to liability a defendant whose contribution to the contracting of the disease could have been less than that of the environment to which the whole world is exposed (also, views were very much in evidence on the propriety of the use of epidemio-logical evidence in this context). It was seen as particularly unfair in this type of case where there is no one from whom the single defendant can claim contribu-tion. Yet the Supreme Court would have none of this. Lord Rodger said:

> "There is no reason why a claimant needs to prove anything more than that the defendant's breach of duty materially increased the risk that he would develop the disease. So . . . the doubling of the risk approach is irrelevant": *ibid.*, para.161.

He added that the purported guidance to the courts from the Court of Appeal should not be followed: *ibid.*, para.162.

At the same time it was recognised by Lord Phillips that:

"The 2006 Act, coupled with *Fairchild's* case, has draconian consequences for an employer who has been responsible for only a small proportion of the overall exposure of a claimant to asbestos dust, or his insurers": *ibid.*, para.58.

Lord Brown went further. Citing Lord Phillips on draconian consequences, he doubted whether the special treatment given to mesothelioma cases was justified when it necessarily went so far as to apply, logically, to one negligent employer or negligent occupier unable to get any contribution from fellow tortfeasors: *ibid.*, para.184. He concluded his speech by saying that he had difficulty in accepting that the courts should now

"be thinking of creating any other special rules regarding the principles governing compensation for personal injury".

NOTE 107: Add at the end of the note: On the other hand, in *Cook v Cook* **8–025** [2011] EWHC 1638, QB, the same judge as in *Adan*, because the long-term outcome for the child claimant, injured from birth, was so uncertain and speculative, postponed the adjudication of future loss until she reached the age of 16 when the court would be in a far better position to assess her needs in adult life. For criticism of the result in *Cook v Cook*, see para.45–039, below.

Insert new paragraphs after para.8–029:

A very different result to that in *Bailey v Balholm* was arrived at in *Parabola* **8–029A** *Investments Ltd v Browallia Cal Ltd* [2011] Q.B. 477, CA. An individual trader through a company, the claimant, which had been set up by him for trading in stocks, shares and derivatives had for more than 10 years consistently made profits from his trading, profits sometimes of a spectacular nature, until for a period of about seven months he was defrauded by a broker employed by the defendant financial institution. The fraud took the form of misrepresenting that the trader was trading profitably and misrepresenting the size of the trading fund. Over the seven months the fund was depleted by several million pounds. The claimant company maintained that it was entitled to the substantial profits that would have been made had the amount by which the fund had been depleted been available for trading, both during the months while the fraud continued and during the much longer period from discovery of the fraud to trial. The defendant maintained that it should not be liable for more than the restoration of the trading fund plus interest, on the ground that the profits claimed were speculative. Flaux J. had decided in the claimant's favour, pointing out that the defendant's submissions that the claimant needed to prove that a specific amount of profits would have been earned was flawed since precise calculation was impossible: *ibid.*, paras 20 to 22. Beyond this he took the entirely proper view that the trader's past success had been a matter not of luck but of astuteness and the Court of Appeal saw no reason to interfere with his quantification of the claimant's loss of profits: *ibid.*, para.25.

8–029B   Recovery for loss of business profits again successfully featured in *Vasiliou v Hajigeorgiou* [2010] EWCA Civ 1475. The claimant had leased premises from the defendant for use as a restaurant and breaches by the defendant of the covenant of quiet enjoyment had made it impossible for the claimant to trade for two periods of time. The trial judge found the claimant to be an accomplished restaurateur whose restaurant would be successful and assessed his loss of profits on that basis, arriving, with the assistance of expert evidence, at an assessment of expected turnover, gross and net profit, and rate of growth. In upholding the award, the Court of Appeal confirmed that the judge had been right not to apply a discount, for which the defendant had contended, to recognise the chance that the restaurant might not have been successful. To do so would have been inconsistent with the judge's finding that the restaurant would be a success. See in particular Patten L.J.'s excellent analysis at para.15 *et seq.*

8–033   Insert a new note after "denied by the injury" on line 19 of the paragraph:

NOTE 138a: In *Clarke v Maltby* [2010] EWHC 1201, QB it was the loss of the chance of progressing up the solicitor ladder that was in issue.

8–038   Insert a new note at the end of the paragraph:

NOTE 151a: What Toulson L.J. convincingly says at para.23 of his judgment in the important case of *Parabola Investments Ltd v Browallia Cal Ltd* [2011] Q.B. 477, CA. (facts at para.8–029A, above) and what Patten L.J. equally convincingly says at para.25 of his judgment in the further important case of *Vasiliou v Hajigeorgiou* [2010] EWCA Civ 1475 (facts at para.8–029B, above), referring to Toulson L.J. in *Parabola*, fully support the analysis set out in this paragraph of the main work. The term "loss of a chance proper" is there used; Patten L.J. has "loss of chance as such". And see too, in *AerCap Partners Ltd v Avia Asset Management AB* [2010] EWHC 2431 (Comm), Gross L.J.'s exploration of the distinction between all or nothing causation and percentage loss of a chance in relation to an issue where there was no hope of loss of a chance applying: *ibid.*, paras 70 to 77, especially the detailed para.76.

8–040   Insert a new note after "professional boxer" on line 15 of the paragraph:

NOTE 163a: And see too *Clarke v Maltby* [2010] EWHC 1201, QB where a career in only one field had to be considered.

8–041   Insert a new note after the first sentence of the paragraph:

NOTE 164a: The damages in *IRT Oil and Gas Ltd v Fiber Optic Systems Technology (Canada) Inc* [2009] EWHC 3041, QB undoubtedly fell into the quantification category: see the case at para.8–002C, above. As for *Amalgamated Metal Corp Plc v Wragge & Co* [2011] EWHC 887 (Comm), where solicitors were sued for settling without authority at too low a figure their client's claim against the tax authorities in respect of advance corporation tax which should not have been paid to them, assessment of damages on a loss of a chance basis was out of the question: see *ibid.*, para.119 *et seq.*

Insert a new note at the end of the paragraph as it now stands in the main text: **8–041**

NOTE 170a: *Checkprice (UK) Ltd v Revenue and Customs Commissioners* [2010] EWHC 682 (Admin) is a further illustration of a lost chance that was so speculative that it had to be evaluated at nil, thereby allowing no compensatory damages: see the case at paras 33–009B and 33–009C, below.

Add at the end of the paragraph: *The Law Debenture Trust Corp Plc v Electrim*   **8–041**
SA [2010] EWCA Civ 1142 is a further quantification case. The amount of damages payable to bondholders for a breach of condition in the bonds issued to them turned upon the valuation of certain company assets which was to be carried out by investment bankers. It was held that, however difficult it might be to arrive at a value, the court must attempt an estimate and there was rejected the defendant's argument that, as the valuation depended upon the hypothetical actions of third party investment bankers, it was appropriate to assess the damages on the basis of the loss of the chance of the notional bankers arriving at a particular valuation: see *ibid.*, paras 40 to 49. The court did not consider the case to be a loss of a chance case at all and Arden L.J., delivering the judgment of the court, pointed to "the dangers of extending it [i.e. the loss of a chance doctrine] to commercial cases, especially valuation cases where permutations may be infinite": *ibid.*, para.48. See the case further at para.8–075, below.

Insert a new note at the end of the paragraph: **8–043**

NOTE 180a: The claimant employee in *Smithurst v Sealant Construction Services Ltd* [2011] EWCA Civ 1277 sustained a disc prolapse as a result of his employer's negligence and could no longer work. At the time he was at risk of suffering a similar disc prolapse which was likely to occur within the next two years. On the basis of causation of loss the trial judge considered that the claimant should have full damages for two years and none thereafter. The Court of Appeal disagreed with this reasoning, pointing out that the case was one of quantification of loss rather than of causation of loss, but regarded the result as acceptable. The result represented an adoption of the acceleration approach in place of the more usual assessment of risk approach: for all this see *ibid.*, paras 9, 16 and 22. In endorsing the acceleration approach the Court of Appeal followed its earlier decision in *Kenth v Heimdale Hotel Investments Ltd* [2001] EWCA Civ 1283.

Add at the end of the paragraph: The Court of Appeal agreed in *Wright v*   **8–044**
Cambridge Medical Group [2011] EWCA Civ 669 that the loss of a chance approach cannot be taken in claims for personal injury and particularly in claims

for clinical negligence. By the defendant doctor's negligent delay in referring the child claimant to a hospital for treatment, the claimant lost the chance of receiving prompt medical treatment which would have avoided permanent injury but which had not in fact been forthcoming. Though not strictly determinative of the case, the House of Lords' decision in *Gregg v Scott* (at this paragraph of the main work) was relied upon: *ibid.*, paras 82 to 84 and 93.

8–047   Insert in the text immediately before "no action of" in the last line but two of the paragraph: and also *Clarke v Maltby* [2010] EWHC 1201, QB.

8–055   NOTE 216: Add at the end of the note: Again in *Tom Hoskins Plc v EMW Law* [2010] EWHC 479, Ch the availability of evidence of how the third parties would have acted did not prevent the judge from taking the loss of a chance approach to the damages: *ibid.*, paras 125 to 128.

8–058   NOTE 230: Add at the end of the note: Two further cases allowing recovery for loss of business profits where loss of a chance proper had no part to play are *Parabola Investments Ltd v Browallia Cal Ltd* [2011] Q.B. 477, CA and *Vasiliou v Hajigeorgiou* [2010] EWCA Civ 1475. These cases are at paras 8–029A and 8–029B together with para.8–038, above.

8–063   Insert in the text before "Further successful" on the last line but 2 of the paragraph: In *Berry v Laytons* [2009] EWHC 1591, QB a solicitor had negligently advised his client as to his rights, so that he settled under his contract of employment and did not pursue his employer under the EU legislation which would have given him more. The trial judge took the view that the claimant would have settled with his employer and arrived at a settlement figure, which was awarded, calculated at 60 per cent of the amount that the claimant would have claimed against his employer.

8–063   NOTE 251: Add at the end of the note: Yet no question of loss of a chance arose in *Martin v Triggs Turner Bartons* [2010] P.N.L.R. 3, p.29, another case of solicitor's negligence in connection with a will affecting a beneficiary: facts at para.29–038, below.

8–066   Insert in the text before "are further" on the last line but 3 of the paragraph: and *Haithwaite v Thomson Snell & Passmore* [2010] Lloyd's Rep. P.N. 98.

8–066   Substitute in the text for "in both" on the penultimate line of the paragraph: in all three

8–066   NOTE 268: Substitute for "these two": these three

8–066   Add at the end of the paragraph: And in *Di Matteo v Marcus Lee & Co* [2010] EWHC 312, QB, where the statute-barred proceedings had themselves been against solicitors, there appears to have been even more losses of a chance: see this aspect of the case at para.8–091, below.

Insert in the text after "the lost chance." on the last line but 5 of the paragraph: **8–070**
Dennard v PricewaterhouseCoopers LLP [2010] EWHC 812, Ch on the other hand involved a sale to, rather than by, a bank. The defendant valuer had negligently undervalued certain private finance initiative projects, the interests of the claimants in which they were selling to a bank. The award of damages for the loss of the chance of increasing the purchase price was 75 per cent of the amount by which the trial judge estimated that the bank, on a proper valuation, would have been prepared to go higher: see *ibid.*, paras 200 to 207.

Insert a new paragraph after para.8–074:

Langford v Hebran again came under consideration in *Clarke v Maltby* [2010] **8–074A** EWHC 1201, QB where a career in only one field was under scrutiny. The career prospects of a badly injured solicitor were at the heart of her claim for loss of earnings. Three scenarios were advanced before the trial judge. Stated in summary, the claimant's progression was to be from a partnership in a regional law firm to one in a medium-sized city firm to one in a large city firm, and the chances of achieving this progression were held to be 100 per cent, 85 per cent and 30 percent respectively: see *ibid.*, paras 84 to 94 together with the elaborate calculations appearing in an appendix to the judgment. Thus the method adopted in *Langford v Hebran* was followed. Even more clearly the case is one of quantification and not of loss of a chance proper.

Add at the end of the paragraph: The Court of Appeal in *The Law Debenture* **8–075** *Trust Corp Plc v Electrim SA* [2010] EWCA Civ 1142 agreed, with reference to this paragraph in the main work, that in assessing loss of earnings in personal injury cases the loss of a chance approach ought not to replace the traditional approach of adjusting the multiplier and the multiplicand: *ibid.*, para.48.

NOTE 310: Add at the end of the note: In the appeal, *Collett v Smith* [2009] **8–077** EWCA Civ 583, the trial judge's award was analysed in detail by Smith L.J. in her leading judgment without resort to any authority and the trial judge was upheld, a principal issue being whether his discount of 15 per cent on the loss of future earnings had been too generous to the footballer claimant. While loss of a chance was naturally spoken of, the tenor of the judgment is in quantification terms.

Insert a new paragraph after para.8–077:

The uncertainties as to the future were even greater and more extensive than **8–077A** ever in *XYZ v Portsmouth Hospitals NHS Trust* [2011] EWHC 243, QB. The claimant had reached the top in the employed sector of the pharmaceutical industry and had already at the time of his severe injury resigned from his very senior post in order to set up his own pharmaceutical business where the rewards would be far greater. It thus fell to the court to consider whether the new business would have started at all, how quickly it would have succeeded, what level of turnover it would have reached and when, and finally the amount for which the business would have sold at the end of the day. In an elaborate, careful judgment Spencer J. arrived at a whole series of percentage chances: see his summary of each at *ibid.*, para.260. Once again, the case is one of quantification and not of loss of a chance proper.

8–078   NOTE 325: Add at the end of the note: In *Rust-Andrews v First-tier Tribunal* [2011] EWCA Civ 1548, a personal injury claim for compensation under the Criminal Injuries Compensation Scheme, deciding on the correctness of limiting the damages for loss of future earnings to a number of years brought in balance of probabilities and loss of a chance before the Court of Appeal.

8–081   Add at the end of the paragraph: The claimants in *Nicholas Prestige Homes v Neal* [2010] EWCA Civ 1552 were estate agents and the defendant was a house owner who sold her house through another estate agent in breach of her sole agency agreement with the claimants. The claimants were held entitled to damages for the loss of the chance of themselves selling the house and earning their commission. In *Van der Garde v Force India Formula One Team Ltd* [2010] EWHC 2373, QB (facts at para.1–036A, above) damages of $100,000 were held to be awardable for the claimant motor racing driver's loss of opportunity of enhancing his experience and reputation in the field of motor racing and thereby his ability to participate in remunerative Formula One testing and racing competitions: all at *ibid.*, paras 376 to 412. This was only the residual claim in *Van der Garde*, much larger sums, not far short of $2 million, being held to be awardable on either of two other grounds: see at para.1–036A, above and para.12–035, below.

8–082   NOTE 350: Add at the end of the note: and, at paras 33–009B and 33–009C, below, *Checkprice (UK) Ltd v Revenue and Customs Commissioners* [2010] EWHC 682 (Admin).

8–082   Add at the end of the paragraph: So too in *Nicholas Prestige Homes v Neal* [2010] EWCA Civ 1552 there was no chance that the estate agents would not have succeeded in selling the defendant's property (facts at para.8–081, above) so that, as Ward L.J. said, no discount had to be made for imponderables: *ibid.*, para.33.

8–091   Add at the end of the paragraph: Again in *Haithwaite v Thomson Snell & Passmore* [2010] Lloyd's Rep. P.N. 98, also a personal injury case, the 40 per cent chance of proving negligence was amalgamated with the 75 per cent chance of proving causation to give an award based on a 30 per cent loss of chance. In *Joyce v Bowman Law Ltd* [2010] P.N.L.R. 22, p.413, where the negligence of a firm of conveyancers had resulted in its client's failure to obtain a buyer's option over land he would have developed, the trial judge, while prepared to award the development profit, took four lost chances into account to pare down his award to the client to only 28.9 per cent of that profit—the chance of the client obtaining the buyer's option, the chance of his exercising it, the chance of his obtaining planning permission and the chance of his obtaining funding for the development—and this was the result even though one of the chances was assessed at 100 per cent. However, in *Tom Hoskins Plc v EMW Law* [2010] EWHC 479, Ch where the question as to whether a particular deal would have gone through involved multiple contingencies—agreement to the terms, attempts to renegotiate or extend completion and others—Floyd J. sensibly considered that it would be wrong for him to apply percentage upon percentage, and thereby reduce the damages to be awarded dramatically, because the contingencies were not independent of each other: *ibid.*, para.133. And in *Di Matteo v Marcus Lee & Co* [2010] EWHC 312, QB Slade J. arrived at an overall percentage figure without allocating separate percentages to each of the lost chances that she had identified. These were whether the claimant husband, who was suing the defendant solicitors for not issuing a writ in time against his divorce solicitors whom he had been suing for their failure to inform him of an offer by his wife in settlement, would, if so informed, himself have made an offer in settlement of a specific, somewhat lower amount, whether the wife would have accepted that offer if made, whether he would have pursued his claim against his divorce solicitors and whether that claim would have succeeded. After a very full review of the evidence Slade J. simply put the overall value of the loss of chance at 25 per cent, apparently unconcerned by her earlier having put the particular value of one of these lost chances, *viz.*, whether the wife would have accepted the offer if made, at 20 per cent: see *ibid.*, paras 61 and 67.

Insert new paragraphs after para.8–095:

Durham Tees Valley Airport Ltd v bmibaby Ltd [2011] 1 Lloyd's Rep. 68, CA **8–095A** is a valuable Court of Appeal decision in this area because of the rigorous analysis of the earlier cases, and the conclusion arrived at, by both Patten L.J. and Toulson L.J., the third member of the court, Mummery L.J., simply expressing agreement with the other two. The defendant airline had contracted to base and fly two aircraft from the claimant's airport over a 10-year period but the contract failed to specify criteria as to the manner of performance in terms of flight or passenger numbers. In these circumstances the defendant airline argued that damages had to be based on the minimum number of flights that it was contractually bound to operate and, since that was impossible to elicit from the contract, the award must be nil. Unsurprisingly, this argument did not appeal to the court.

It will be seen that the case was one where there was a single obligation—here **8–095B** were no alternatives, for which the law is clear—but a single obligation with discretion as to the manner in which it could be performed. In the forefront of the authorities considered was *Abrahams v Reiach* because it, like *Paula Lee v Robert Zehil & Co*, which was also fully considered, was of a similar nature to the case before the court (*Abrahams* and *Paula Lee* are at para.8–095 of the main work), and also because *Abrahams v Reiach* was a decision of a very strong Court of Appeal in which somewhat different views had been expressed. Atkin L.J. in that case effectively held that the court must attempt to make an estimate of how the contract would have worked out in practice, how it would have been performed by the defendant, Toulson L.J. saw Bankes L.J.'s judgment as saying much the same while Patten L.J. spoke of Atkin L.J. and Bankes L.J. as forming a majority. Therefore, Scrutton L.J.'s rather narrow view, as it was called, need not be gone into, as Patten and Toulson L.JJ. preferred Atkin L.J.'s approach. They also did not agree with the solution of Mustill J. put forward and applied by him in the *Paula Lee* case. Thought by them to be based on his misinterpretation of Atkin L.J.'s reasoning, Mustill J. saw the task of the court as being to look at the range of reasonable methods of performing and to select the one that was the least unfavourable to the defendant. See Patten L.J. at paras 75 and 76 and Toulson L.J. at paras 135 and 136.

8–095C   Patten L.J. put their conclusion in this way (*ibid.*, para.79). The court must carry out a factual enquiry as to how the contract would have been performed had it not been repudiated. The court must look at the relevant economic and other surrounding circumstances to decide on the level of performance that the defendant would have adopted. It has to be assumed that the defendant would have performed the contract in his own interests having regard to the relevant factors at the time but not to assume that he would act uncommercially merely to spite the claimant. Toulson L.J. (*ibid.*, para.147) explicitly agreed with all of this, pointing out that here was a contract of unusual length—and so distinct from the single transaction of publishing a book in *Abrahams v Reiach*—and, given the uncertainty of any prediction about the long-term future of the economy in general and the aircraft industry in particular, caution would be needed, when it came to trial, in arriving at the assessment of the damages. The decision in *Durham Tees Valley Airport* has thus cast a new light on how to deal with cases where there is a discretion as to the manner in which the contractual obligations are to be performed.

8–095D   Toulson L.J. (at para.96) usefully enumerated four categories of case which allow a defendant a degree of choice. These were:

> "1. The contract requires the defendant to do X or Y.
> 2. The contract requires the defendant, if he has not done X, to do Y.
> 3. The contract requires D to do X and the claimant has a reasonable expectation that he will do Y.
> 4. The contract requires the defendant to do X and allows him a discretion how he performs the obligation."

Category (1) presents no difficulty; the defendant may choose the alternative less burdensome to him. Cases of this nature are collected at para.8–093 *et seq.* of the main work. Nor is there any difficulty with category (2); the defendant, if he has not done X, must do Y. This category, apart from being uncommonly found, clearly does not fall within this area and has nothing to do with a defendant's entitlement to take the least burdensome path for him. The illustration given by Toulson L.J. (at para.111) appears elsewhere in the main work at para.13–119 when dealing with penalties. Category (3) is concerned with what the defendant need not do because not falling within his contractual obligations. It is illustrated by cases also appearing at para.8–093 *et seq.* of the main work of which *Lavarack v Woods of Colchester* (at para.8–093, fn.401) is probably the best. Category (4) is *Durham Tees Airport* itself.

In *Jones v Ricoh UK Ltd* [2010] EWHC 1743, Ch, Roth J. fully considered **8–095E** *Durham Tees Valley Airport*, the judgments and reasoning of both Patten and Toulson L.JJ. being gone into in much detail. Also in *Ricoh* Roth J. considered the rather earlier Court of Appeal decision in *Mulvenna v Royal Bank of Scotland Plc* [2003] EWCA Civ 1112 which, like *Ricoh*, is unreported on any issue of damages, although many citations from this work appear in Waller L.J.'s leading judgment. However, neither *Ricoh* nor *Mulvenna* was a decision on the quantum of damages, both being defendants' applications for summary judgment. Also, neither was a potential category (4) case like *Durham Tees Airport*. The two cases could fall only within category (3).

The Court of Appeal in *Mulvenna* effectively held the case to fall within **8–095F** category (3). The claimant had somewhat complicated banking arrangements with the defendant bank which had loaned moneys to him and his companies over a period. At one point under a refinancing agreement the bank had agreed to refund to the claimant's current account various excess interest and other charges which had been raised. In breach of that agreement the correct amount was refunded three years late. The claimant argued that if the refund had been made on time, the bank would then have returned him to normal mainstream banking arrangements and would, as the bank had agreed in principle, have extended to him an amount sufficient for him to embark on a specific property development which they had discussed. It was held that the claim for the profits lost on the development, lost because the claimant had to sell the undeveloped property for lack of funds, could not succeed as the bank was under no contractual obligation to advance the claimant the moneys needed for the development. Accordingly the bank was entitled to summary judgment.

In *Ricoh* the claimant was the principal shareholder and managing director of **8–095G** CMP Group Ltd, a company in voluntary liquidation which had assigned the causes of action vested in it to the claimant. The defendant company was a manufacturer of photocopying equipment and so-called office automation devices. CMG had provided assistance to other companies in the acquisition and management of such equipment and devices and had used the defendant company as its preferred manufacturer for these purposes. CMG entered into a confidentiality agreement with the defendant whereby the defendant could not use confidential information given to it by CMG for its own benefit but only for evaluating the purchasing terms available to CMG with a view to entering into agreements jointly with CMG with potential purchasers. The defendant was in breach of the confidentiality agreement by using confidential information in order to make a bid to a particular company, a bid which was successful. The claimant sought damages on the basis that if the defendant had not bid on its own, it would have successfully bid, as it had done before, together with CMG. The defendant, seeking summary judgment, contended that damages would be nominal as it was under no obligation to make a bid jointly with CMG. It was therefore a case of not doing what there was no obligation to do.

8–095H   In an interesting judgment, Roth J. disagreed with the defendant on this. What one was concerned with here was not the defendant's failure to bid jointly with CMG which it had no obligation to do but the defendant's decision to do something that it was contractually obliged not to do, which was to use confidential information to bid alone. Put another way, what mattered was not whether the defendant should have bid jointly but whether it should not have bid alone. The former did not constitute a breach of a contractual obligation, the latter did. Whether the defendant would have been prepared to bid jointly with CMG had it not made its bid alone in breach of contract was a matter that would have to be addressed when it came to the assessment of damages at trial. In any event the case was not suitable for summary judgment in relation to this particular breach of contract—there were other breaches not relevant here for which summary judgment was being sought—so this application of the defendant failed.

8–095I   In Roth J.'s careful analysis (at para.74 *et seq.*) he reached this correct result by drawing a distinction, in relation to breach of contract, between positive obligations and negative obligations. The only aspect of the reasoning that might be questioned is whether it is necessarily dependent on this distinction. This is because the positive scenario is about failure to do something which the defendant was *not obliged* to do whereas the negative scenario is about doing something which the defendant was *obliged* not to do. There surely could be situations where a contracting party has indicated that he would not act in a particular way without having so promised, and this would provide one with a category (3) case.

8–102   NOTE 433: Insert before "This is no doubt" on the last line but 4 of the note: (The appeal, on various grounds, does not touch on this point: *Cleveland Bridge UK Ltd v Multiplex Constructions (UK) Ltd* [2010] EWCA Civ 139.)

Insert new paragraphs after para.8–102:

8–103   In the course of a prolonged dispute giving rise to much litigation, applications for summary judgment came before Roth J. in *Leofelis SA v Lonsdale Sports Ltd* [2012] EWHC 485, Ch in respect of two actions which, though commenced in 2005 and 2009, were still to be heard by the courts. The licensee of a series of trade marks for sports clothing and leisure goods was the claimant in the 2005 action and the counterclaimant in the 2009 action, seeking damages against the licensor proprietor of the trade marks for breach of an exclusive licence agreement. The consideration for the licence was an obligation to pay royalties to the licensor, and the benefit to the licensee derived from royalties obtained by sub-licensing others to manufacture, distribute or sell goods bearing the trade marks. The licence agreement was for a period of six years from the beginning of 2003 renewable for a further six years, taking it to the end of 2014. The licensee's claim for damages in the 2005 action was for loss of royalty income to 2014 caused by the licensor's breach of the exclusivity of the agreement by sales of goods from Belgium. Then in late 2007 both licensor and licensee sought to terminate the agreement on account of the other's repudiatory breach, each claiming damages in the 2009 action which in the licensee's case were for its lost royalty income to 2014. The ground on which the licensee relied to repudiate the agreement was found, by an earlier court, not to be a repudiatory breach but the licensee subsequently discovered other breaches which would have allowed repudiation, and it has been long accepted, ever since *Boston Deep Sea Fishing and Ice Co v Ansell* (1888) 36 Ch.D. 339, CA, that a party can retrospectively justify termination of a contract by reference to a repudiatory breach of which the party was unaware at the time of termination.

One might expect that these breaches by the licensor would together lead in the normal way to recovery of lost royalty income to the end of the licence in 2014. Roth J. however held in both actions, but for different reasons as between the two, that the licensee could only claim lost royalty income to the time of the licensee's termination of the agreement in late 2007, which was a much smaller amount. Why should this be?   **8–104**

As far as the 2005 action was concerned, limiting recovery to late 2007 was on the basis that, while at the time of the breach and even at the time when the 2005 action was commenced the likely duration of the agreement was to 2014, it was now known that it came to an end in late 2007, knowledge which in the light of the House of Lords decision in *The Golden Victory* (at para.8–099 of the main work) had to be taken into account. Thus there remained in existence no licence on which to base damages. Reaching this result may seem rather strange when the cause of the agreement being terminated was a further, separate breach by the licensor. One would not expect that damages from a breach could be cut down simply by the appearance of another breach. It is suggested that the likely answer to this is that the breach that led to termination overtook the earlier breach which then became subsumed in the later breach, with the licensee able to include in the 2009 action the damages that would otherwise have been recoverable in the 2005 action in respect of the Belgian sales. Indeed that this was the position was specifically recognised by Roth J.: see his comments at *ibid.*, paras 50 and 60. This of course assumes that a claim for lost royalty income to 2014 was available in the 2009 action, to a consideration of which we now turn.   **8–105**

8–106   In the 2009 action Roth J. again held that there could be no claim for lost royalty income beyond late 2007. His reasoning was that entitlement to damages going to 2014 depended on the licence agreement's having been terminated by repudiation on account of a proper repudiatory breach. He argued that, because the licensee when terminating the agreement did not know of the breach entitling it to repudiate, the termination was not on account of a breach which allowed repudiation and therefore could not give an entitlement to claim damages based on loss of royalty income to the time that the licence would have ended: see his reasoning at *ibid.*, paras 65 and 66. This approach, while interestingly put forward by Roth J., is thought, with respect, to be too technical. The *Boston Deep Sea Fishing* principle (at para.8–103, above) allows a contracting party, in repudiating, to substitute a proper repudiatory breach for what turns out to be the non-breach relied upon in repudiating; it should allow the contracting party to do the same when it comes to considering the recoverable damages. Since a claimant is entitled to terminate for a breach not specified at the time of termination, he should be entitled to claim damages based on such a termination. Otherwise the advantages of the rule that a contracting party can adopt retrospectively a breach by the other party are likely to be lost. If the *Boston Deep Sea Fishing* principle does not take us as far as influencing the recovery of damages, it is in effect rendered valueless. It must surely be wrong to recognise the right to repudiate but not the remedy to which it gives rise.

CHAPTER 9

PAST AND PROSPECTIVE DAMAGE

		PARA.
I.	INTRODUCTORY: CIRCUMSTANCES IN WHICH THE SAME SET OF FACTS GIVES RISE TO MORE THAN ONE CAUSE OF ACTION	9–003
	1. Where there are two separate acts resulting in two separate wrongs	9–003
	2. Where a single act violates two separate interests protected by the law	9–004
	3. Where a single act constitutes a continuing wrong	9–010
	4. Where a single act not actionable *per se* causes separate damage on two separate occasions	9–014
II.	PAST LOSS: DAMAGE BEFORE ACCRUAL OF THE CAUSE OF ACTION	9–015
III.	PAST LOSS: DAMAGE BEFORE COMMENCEMENT OF THE ACTION	9–018
IV.	PROSPECTIVE LOSS: DAMAGE AFTER COMMENCEMENT OF THE ACTION	9–024
□	1. The rule	9–024
□	2. The corollary	9–030

NOTE 126: Insert after "Supreme Court Act" (and before "1981"):—now renamed the Senior Courts Act (see para.15–031, fn.111a, below)— **9–029**

NOTE 143: Insert after "these cases" in the last line of the note: and also *Cook v Cook* [2011] EWHC 1638, QB. **9–033**

BOOK ONE

PART THREE

DAMAGES NOT BASED STRICTLY ON COMPENSATION

CHAPTER 10

NOMINAL DAMAGES

PARA.

I. CIRCUMSTANCES GIVING RISE TO AN AWARD OF NOMINAL DAMAGES. 10–001
   1. Where there is *injuria sine damno* 10–001
   2. Where damage is shown but its amount is not sufficiently proved 10–004
II. AMOUNT AWARDED; NOMINAL AND SMALL DAMAGES DISTIN-
   GUISHED 10–006
III. PRACTICAL FUNCTIONS OF NOMINAL DAMAGES 10–007

10–002

NOTE 3: Insert after the second sentence of the note: The Supreme Court has now endorsed a nominal damages award in the false imprisonment case of *R. (on the application of Lumba (Congo)) v Secretary of State for the Home Department* [2012] 1 A.C. 245. Further awards of nominal damages in false imprisonment cases have followed in *R. (on the application of OM) v Secretary of State for the Home Department* [2011] EWCA Civ 909, *R. (on the application of Abdollahi) v Secretary of State for the Home Department* [2012] EWHC 878 (Admin) and *R. (on the application of Moussaoui) v Secretary of State for the Home Department* [2012] EWHC 126 (Admin). All four cases involved claimants, foreign nationals and asylum seekers, who, though unlawfully detained, could and would have been lawfully detained had the correct procedure for their detention been followed. And the Court of Appeal in *Hall v Harris* [2012] EWCA Civ 671 has endorsed a nominal damages award in trespass to land: *ibid.*, para.58.

10–006

NOTE 18: Add at the end of the note: and *Multi Veste 226 BV v NI Summer Row Unitholder BV* [2011] EWHC 2026, Ch for breach of a development contract with no established loss.

10–006

NOTE 22: Insert at the beginning of the note: Also in *R. (on the application of OM) v Secretary of State for the Home Department* [2011] EWCA Civ 909 £1 was awarded by the Court of Appeal (*ibid.*, para.57) and by Lindblom J. in *R. (on the application of Moussaoui) v Secretary of State for the Home Department* [2012] EWHC 126 (Admin) (*ibid.*, para.194), while in *Hodge Jones & Allen v McLaughlin* [2011] EWHC 2402, QB the nominal damages were provisionally assessed at £10 (*ibid.*, para.323).

10–006

NOTE 22: Add at the end of the note: And in *Checkprice (UK) Ltd v Revenue and Customs Commissioners* [2010] EWHC 682 (Admin) (facts at paras 33–009B and 33–009C, below) the surprising amount of £500 was awarded: *ibid.*, para.63. This must be wrong; even today £500 is for most people a considerable amount of money and far from being a nominal sum.

10–008   NOTE 26: Add at the end of the note: *R. (on the application of Lumba) v Secretary of State for the Home Department* [2012] 1 A.C. 245 is also illustrative.

10–010   NOTE 35: Insert after "Supreme Court Act" (and before "1981"):—now renamed the Senior Courts Act (see para.15–031, fn.111a, below)—

10–010   NOTE 40: Add at the end of the note: Thus in *TCP Europe Ltd v Parry*, QB, July 23, 2012, unreported, the claimant, who had been awarded nominal damages on establishing liability, was both deprived of his costs and ordered to pay the defendant his.

CHAPTER 11

EXEMPLARY DAMAGES

			PARA.
☐	I.	THE GENERAL BAN ON EXEMPLARY DAMAGES	11–001
☐	II.	CASES IN WHICH EXEMPLARY DAMAGES MAY BE AWARDED	11–009
■		1. Types of claim in which exemplary damages are possible	11–011
■		2. The three categories in which exemplary awards are possible	11–017
☐	III.	COMPUTATION OF THE EXEMPLARY AWARD	11–033
■		1. Various criteria applied by the courts	11–033
		2. The question of vicarious liability	11–047
☐		3. The irrelevance of the criteria in the second common law category	11–050

Insert in the text after "insolence or the like" on line 8 of the paragraph **11–001** (deleting the full stop after "the like"): , or as where, should the defendant be a government servant, it is oppressive, arbitrary or unconstitutional: see para. 11–017 of the main work and para.11–019, below.

Add at the end of the paragraph: However, the category of exemplary damages **11–009** authorised by statute is now expected to be removed by statute: see para.11–031, below.

Insert in the text after "and the like," on line 6 of the paragraph: behaviour **11–011** referred to, where it is the conduct of government servants that is in issue, as oppressive, arbitrary or unconstitutional (see para.11–017 of the main work and para.11–019, below),

NOTE 67: Add at the end of the note: Also in *Albion Water Ltd v Dwr Cymru* **11–014** *Cyfyngedig* [2010] C.A.T. 30.

Add at the end of the paragraph: By contrast, the Competition Appeal Tribunal **11–014** did award exemplary damages in a further case of breach of competition law, *2 Travel Group Plc v Cardiff City Transport Services Ltd* [2012] C.A.T. 19. For the reason for the difference between the two cases see para.11–043, fn.237, below.

NOTE 86: Insert before the last sentence of the note: In *Takitota v Attorney* **11–018** *General of The Bahamas* [2009] UKPC 11, where there was false imprisonment of the claimant in inhumane conditions over many years as well as breach of his constitutional rights and the Court of Appeal of The Bahamas had made an exemplary award, the Privy Council was unprepared to make a vindicatory award in addition, as counsel had argued for, regarding the award for breach of constitutional rights as having much the same object as the common law award of exemplary damages: *ibid.*, para.13. In the result the Privy Council upheld the exemplary award of the Court of Appeal as a vindicatory award. Where in *James v Attorney General of Trinidad and Tobago* [2010] UKPC 23 there had been discrimination arising out of breach of the claimant's constitutional rights, the Privy Council in an extensive judgment awarded neither compensatory damages, because no loss, material or immaterial, from the discrimination had been shown, nor vindicatory damages, because declaratory relief, which the claimant had obtained, was considered in the circumstances to be sufficient vindication. Subsequently, the Privy Council has held in *Webster v Attorney General of Trinidad and Tobago* [2011] UKPC 22 that, where the claimant has a claim in tort for assault and false imprisonment, it is wrong, as redundant, to add claims for constitutional relief, and has held in the circumstances of *Graham v Police Service Commission and Attorney General of Trinidad and Tobago* [2011] UKPC 46 that there was no call for an additional award of vindicatory damages (*ibid.*, paras 15 to 17). So we are seeing less and less of vindicatory damages in these Caribbean cases.

11–018   NOTE 86: Substitute for the last line of the note: 42–008 to 42–009A in the main work and below where it is shown that they have now taken a downturn.

11–018   Add at the end of the paragraph: Prison officers and immigration officials featured in *Muuse v Secretary of State for the Home Department* [2010] EWCA Civ 453 where substantial exemplary damages for false imprisonment were awarded to a Dutch national born in Somalia who was unlawfully kept in custody for over four months pending deportation to Somalia when it could very easily have been ascertained that there was no right to deport him. The conduct of the prison officers and immigration officials was categorised as an outrageous abuse of executive power.

11–019   NOTE 96: Add at the end of the note: The Employment Appeal Tribunal's award to a victimised army recruit was set aside as the conduct of the army officers involved, though deplorable, was held not to cross the high threshold set for a finding of oppressive or arbitrary behaviour: *Ministry of Defence v Fletcher* [2010] I.R.L.R. 25.

11–019   Add at the end of the paragraph: Where in *R. (on the application of Lumba (Congo)) v Secretary of State for the Home Department* [2012] 1 A.C. 245 the Secretary of State for the Home Department was held liable for the false imprisonment of foreign national prisoners pending their deportation, the Supreme Court was not prepared to award exemplary damages to the claimants since there had not been conduct so outrageous and so unconstitutional, oppressive or arbitrary as to justify such an award: see the careful analysis by Lord Dyson, with whom, on exemplary damages, the other eight Justices agreed, of the conduct of the senior Home Office personnel, at *ibid.*, paras 151 to 166. This unanimous view contrasts with the Justices being divided both on the issue of liability and on other aspects of the damages: see paras 37–013A and 42–009A, below.

Insert a new paragraph after para.11–019:

11–019A From his single reasoned judgment in *Muuse v Secretary of State for the Home Department* [2010] EWCA Civ 453 (facts at para.11–018, above) it appears that Thomas L.J.—and, it would seem, the defendant's counsel as well—failed to understand what is said in this paragraph of the main work. Thomas L.J. understands the paragraph to be advancing a proposition for which there is no authority by saying that the claimant must show not only that the government servant has acted oppressively, arbitrarily or unconstitutionally but also that his action has been motivated by malice, fraud, insolence, cruelty and the like: *ibid.*, paras 68 to 71. This is not at all what the paragraph is saying. It starts by stating that the first condition that must be satisfied in this category of case concerns the conduct of the defendant which must be shown to be oppressive, arbitrary or unconstitutional and, having so stated, it is concerned to make the point that, the central requirement for the imposition of exemplary damages being, and always having been, the existence of outrageous conduct on the defendant's part, should a claimant be relying on unconstitutional, as distinct from oppressive or arbitrary, action he must show the conduct to be outrageous, for an action which is simply unconstitutional may not constitute a misuse or abuse of constitutional or executive power. The reference to conduct disclosing malice, fraud, insolence, cruelty and the like is made only to emphasise the need for outrageousness in conduct, being the terminology appearing in the heyday of exemplary damages when they were widely available. The oppressive, arbitrary and unconstitutional trilogy simply introduces more suitable terms to indicate outrageousness in the misuse and abuse of power with which actions against government servants are concerned. It is clear that the trilogy takes the place of malice, fraud, insolence, cruelty and the like; it in no way adds to them.

Add a new note at the end of the third sentence of the paragraph: **11–020**

NOTE 100a: A bus undertaking owned by, but operated independently of, a local authority could not possibly fall within this category: *2 Travel Group Plc v Cardiff City Transport Services Ltd* [2012] C.A.T. 19.

NOTE 158: Add at the end of the note: In *AT, NT, ML, AK v Dulghieru* [2009] **11–028** EWHC 225, QB (facts at para.37–001, fn.4, below) Treacy J. said directly, at *ibid.*, para.68, that "the rationale behind the second category is not the punishment of the defendant but the prevention of his unjust enrichment", citing for this *Borders* and Sedley L.J. therein.

Insert a new paragraph after para.11–033:

[67]

11–033A The decision on exemplary damages of the Court of Appeal in *Ramzan v Brookwide Ltd* [2012] 1 All E.R. 903, CA, the facts of which are set out at paras 34–058B and 34–058C, below, causes some concern. For criteria relevant to computation, Arden L.J., who alone dealt with exemplary damages, the others simply agreeing with her, concentrated on the defendant's conduct in its expropriation of the property having taken place before it had been acquired by the claimant from his father (*ibid.*, para.78) and on the expropriation having had a deleterious effect on the health both of the claimant and of his father (*ibid.*, paras 78 to 80). These surely are matters that go to compensation by way of aggravated damages, which were here not allowed, and not to punishment by way of exemplary damages. Nor are convincing, or it may be said, with respect, even right, the statements that there is no scope for exemplary damages where an account of profits is claimed (*ibid.*, para.81), that the fact of making a compensatory award should largely be sufficient in itself (*ibid.*, para.82) and that there is little guidance on the quantification of exemplary damages (*ibid.*, para.82). On the basis of these various considerations, and primarily on account of the claimant not being the owner of the property at the time of the tort (see *ibid.*, para.83 *in init.*), Arden L.J. decided to reduce from £60,000 to £20,000 (*ibid.*, para.83 *in med.*) Geraldine Alexander QC's careful award in a case which she had described as one of the worst of its kind ([2011] 2 All E.R. 38, para.69).

11–037 Insert a new note at the end of the paragraph:

NOTE 193a: See the false imprisonment award of £27,500, upheld by the Court of Appeal, in *Muuse v Secretary of State for the Home Department* [2010] EWCA Civ 453 where there had been outrageous abuse of executive power: facts at para.11–018, above.

11–038 Add at the end of the paragraph: The trial judge's £60,000 in *Ramzan v Brookwide Ltd* [2011] 2 All E.R. 38, while at £60,000 higher than the general run of awards, was considered by her to fall within the criterion of moderation in the light of the seriousness of the wrong, the defendant's means and the need to provide a sufficient deterrent: see *ibid.*, paras 70 to 73. However, the Court of Appeal [2012] 1 All E.R. 903, CA has now reduced the award to £20,000, a move somewhat difficult to justify as suggested at para.11–033A, above. For the facts of this curious case see paras 34–058B and 34–058C, below.

11–039 Insert in the text before "On the other hand" on line 9 of the paragraph: That, together with its associated companies, the defendant in *Ramzan v Brookwide Ltd* [2011] 2 All E.R. 38 paid every year to their parent company some £18 million was a large factor in the trial judge's decision to award £60,000: see *ibid.*, para.70. However, the Court of Appeal, [2012] 1 All E.R. 903, CA, has now reduced the award to £20,000, a move somewhat difficult to justify as suggested at para.11–033A, above. For the facts of this curious case see paras 34–058B and 34–058C, below.

Insert in the text before "Similarly" on line 10 of the paragraph: An important **11–040** factor in the trial judge's decision to award £60,000 in *Ramzan v Brookwide Ltd* [2011] 2 All E.R. 38 was the defendant's conduct in deliberately expropriating the claimant's property, a most serious type of trespass, followed by no contrition, no apology and attempted cover-up by lying in evidence: see *ibid.*, paras 71 and 74. However, the Court of Appeal, [2012] 1 All E.R. 903, CA, has now reduced the award to £20,000, a move somewhat difficult to justify as suggested at para.11–033A, above. For the facts of this curious case see paras 34–058B and 34–058C, below.

Insert a new note at the end of the paragraph: **11–041**

NOTE 218a: Thus the Employment Appeal Tribunal's award of £50,000 exemplary damages to a victimised army recruit in order to match its award of £50,000 compensatory damages for aggravated injury to feelings was inappropriate: *Ministry of Defence v Fletcher* [2010] I.R.L.R. 25. In fact the exemplary award was set aside *in toto*: see para.11–019, fn.96, above.

Insert a new paragraph after para.11–042:

In the rather exceptional case of *Ramzan v Brookwide Ltd* [2011] 2 All E.R. 38   **11–042A** the total compensatory damages arrived at by the trial judge were in excess of half a million pounds but she nevertheless considered it appropriate to make an award of £60,000 in exemplary damages. She considered that this was called for because she foresaw the financially powerful defendant repeating its expropriatory actions elsewhere should it find an opportunity to do so: *ibid.*, para.73. However, the Court of Appeal, [2012] 1 All E.R. 903, CA, has now reduced the award to £20,000, a move somewhat difficult to justify as suggested at para. 11–033A, above. For the facts of this curious case see paras 34–058B and 34–058C, below.

NOTE 236: Distinguished in *Albion Water Ltd v Dwr Cymru Cyfyngedig*   **11–043** [2010] C.A.T. 30 where no penalty had been exacted and the exemplary damages claim was not struck out.

NOTE 237: Add at the end of the note: By contrast, exemplary damages were   **11–043** awarded in another case of breach of competition law, *2 Travel Group Plc v Cardiff City Transport Services Ltd* [2012] C.A.T. 19, by reason of the defendant company being by statute immune from a fine.

NOTE 239: Add at the end of the note: Similarly in *AT, NT, ML, AK v*   **11–043** *Dulghieru* [2009] EWHC 225, QB (facts at para.37–001, fn.4, below) an award of exemplary damages was held not to be precluded by the making of confiscation orders in criminal proceedings against the defendants: *ibid.*, para.71.

Insert before the last sentence of the paragraph: So too in *R. (on the applica-*   **11–046** *tion of Lumba (Congo)) v Secretary of State for the Home Department* [2012] 1

A.C. 245, another reason for holding it to be inappropriate to award exemplary damages (the main reason, and the basic facts, are at para.11–019, above) was the existence of potentially a large number of claimants and claimants who were not all before the court. For, as Lord Dyson asked (*ibid.*, para.167):

> "Unless all the claims are quantified by the court at the same time, how is the court to fix and apportion that punitive element of the damages? If the assessments are made separately at different times for different claimants, how is the court to know that the overall punishment is appropriate?"

Insert a new paragraph after para.11–050:

11–051   In *Ramzan v Brookwide Ltd* [2011] 2 All E.R. 38 Geraldine Andrews QC, sitting as a Deputy High Court Judge, expressed disagreement with the contents of para.11–050 of the main work and said that she was unpersuaded in a case such as the one before her that

> "the award of exemplary damages is simply designed to operate as an indirect method for extracting profits tortiously obtained by the defendant and thus to prevent his unjust enrichment . . . . In a case like this, which is one of the worst examples of its kind, forcing the wrongdoer to disgorge what turned out to be a modest profit is unlikely to provide a sufficient deterrent in itself": *ibid.*, para.69.

There is certainly something to be said for this if punishment is the real aim. However, the Court of Appeal, [2012] 1 All E.R. 903, CA, has now reduced the award to £20,000, a move somewhat difficult to justify as suggested at para. 11–033A, above. For the facts of this curious case see paras 34–058B and 34–058C, below.

CHAPTER 12

RESTITUTIONARY DAMAGES

		PARA.
I.	CONCEPT AND MEANING OF RESTITUTIONARY DAMAGES	12–001
II.	CIRCUMSTANCES GIVING RISE TO RESTITUTIONARY DAMAGES	12–007
■	1. Liability in tort	12–007
■	2. Liability in contract	12–023
□ III.	PARTICULAR ASPECTS OF THE CLAIM	12–045

Insert a new note at the end of the paragraph: **12–010**

NOTE 47a: Two recent cases at the highest level involving intentional torts, *Bocardo SA v Star Energy UK Onshore Ltd* [2011] 1 A.C. 380 in the Supreme Court and *Pell Frischmann Engineering Ltd v Bow Valley Iran Ltd* [2011] 1 W.L.R. 2370 in the Privy Council, do not advance the position. *Star Energy* concerned a highly unusual trespass to land (facts at para.34–051A, below). As to damages, there was no argument on the proper measure at common law as the parties were agreed as to what it was, and, while Lord Clarke sets out his view of how the law has developed (*ibid.*, paras 118 to 124), he does not say anything new, with no reference made to the damages being restitutionary (on all this see the case further at para.34–051A, below). *Pell Frischmann* concerned claims in conspiracy, deceit, inducing breach of contract and breach of confidence, although only the breach of confidence claim had succeeded below. Lord Walker, who gave the speech for the Board, embarked on an extended discussion of what he referred to as *Wrotham Park* damages (*ibid.*, paras 46 to 54)—that case is at para.12–024 of the main work—but again nothing new is said, and it is unfortunate that he speaks of damages which exceed the claimant's financial loss as compensatory (*ibid.*, para.46(1)). Moreover, it is not at all clear how the breach of confidence resulted in benefit to the defendant in excess of loss to the claimant, which after all is what this area of damages, whether called by the name of *Wrotham Park* or not, is about. In contrast to these two cases, the awarding to a claimant of a hypothetical licence fee is now seen by the Court of Appeal as extracting the benefit from the defendant: see the trespass to land cases of *Stadler* and *Enfield* at para.34–051, below.

NOTE 68: Add at the end of the note: Infringement of an easement of light   **12–013**
again featured in *HKRUK II (CHC) Ltd v Heaney* [2010] EWHC 2245, Ch where a mandatory injunction was awarded but an assessment of damages by the hypothetical licence route was made with no mention of the restitutionary route.

12–023   NOTE 108: Add at the end of the note: Lord Walker in *Pell Frischmann Engineering Ltd v Bow Valley Iran Ltd* [2011] 1 W.L.R. 2370, PC failed to understand why Lord Nicholls had referred to *Wrotham Park* as a "solitary beacon", which he said he found "a little surprising": *ibid.*, para.48(3).

12–033   Insert a new note at the end of the paragraph:

NOTE 138a: The possibilities may go somewhat beyond the three type situations specified as *Kettel v Bloomfold Ltd* [2012] EWHC 1422, Ch indicates. A lessor of flats that had granted to its lessees easements of designated parking spaces sought to develop the property by building further flats on the parking spaces. The trial judge held the lessees entitled to an injunction preventing the lessor from building but, in case the matter went further and he was held wrong to have granted an injunction, he indicated what damages he would have awarded in lieu. Relying principally on the recent trespass cases giving, in effect, restitutionary damages (cases at para.34–051, below), he would have awarded, in the absence of an injunction, damages on the hypothetical licence fee basis. These he would have assessed at half the value generated by the lessor's development after making an allowance for developer's profit. He was however wrong to describe such damages as compensatory (at *ibid.*, para.62) rather than restitutionary.

12–035   Add at the end of the paragraph: As for *Van der Garde v Force India Formula One Team Ltd* [2010] EWHC 2373, QB (facts at para.1–036A, above) Stadlen J. there made an award of what he called *Wrotham Park* damages based on the value of the kilometres of driving that the defendant had in breach of contract not allowed to the claimant racing driver, this breach being by way of a short delivery of services and so a form of skimped performance. Stadlen J. considered that there was nothing in the authorities to prevent such an award for this breach of contract (see the exhaustive, and exhausting, consideration of the authorities from *ibid.*, paras 509 to 539) but the case was one which was inappropriate for his *Wrotham Park* damages, which constituted the claimants' secondary claim for damages, as he had already acceded to their primary claim, awarding them the same amount of $1,865,000 by way of straightforward compensatory damages (see at paras 1–036B to 1–036D, above). Indeed, he upheld this secondary claim just in case he had gone wrong with the primary claim (*ibid.*, para.499), which it is believed he had not.

12–053   NOTE 226: Add at the end of the note: In *HKRUK II (CHC) Ltd v Heaney* [2010] EWHC 2245, Ch, a further case involving infringement of an easement of light, the trial judge took a variety of factors into account in arriving at the figure of £225,000 (*ibid.*, paras 81 to 89), which sum he would have awarded had he not been granting an injunction.

12–053   Add at the end of the paragraph: For an award of this nature *Van der Garde v Force India Formula One Team Ltd* [2010] EWHC 2373, QB was a very special case on damages (facts at para.1–036A, above), with 100 per cent of value being awarded (see Stadlen J.'s discussion of the appropriate amount to award at *ibid.*, paras 540 to 559), but there was no need to make such an award as the same amount had already been properly awarded on a purely compensatory basis in the same suit: see at para.12–035, above. The case was not one suitable for restitutionary damages at all.

CHAPTER 13

LIQUIDATED DAMAGES

		PARA.
1.	Historical development of liquidated damages and penalties	13–003
☐ 2.	Nature and effect of liquidated damages and penalties	13–009
☐ 3.	Rules for distinguishing liquidated damages from penalties	13–027
☐ 4.	Main types of contract in which the rules have been developed	13–051
☐ 5.	Related situations	13–089

13–009   NOTE 34: Add at the end of the note: A provision in a sale and leaseback contract that the lessor buyer need not pay the residue of the purchase price, amounting to 30 per cent of it, if it terminated the tenancy pursuant to a contractual right to do so, could not be construed as a penalty: *UK Housing Alliance (North West) Ltd v Francis* [2010] 3 All E.R. 519, CA.

13–014   Add at the end of the paragraph: Onus was again taken into account in the holding against penalty in *Azimut-Benetti SpA v Henley* [2011] 1 Lloyd's Rep. 473: see the case at para.13–020A, below.

13–018   NOTE 62: Add at the end of the note: The same is true of *Cantor Fitzgerald LP v Drummond*, August 4, 2009, unreported: see the case further at para. 13–123, below.

Insert a new paragraph after para.13–020:

13–020A   The new broad approach again appeared in *Azimut-Benetti SpA v Henley* [2011] 1 Lloyd's Rep. 473. The claimant yacht builder contracted to construct and sell to a company wholly owned by the defendant a luxury yacht for €38 million, the defendant giving his personal guarantee for payment of the purchase price, which was payable in instalments. The contract provided that the claimant could terminate the contract upon a failure to pay the instalments whereupon 20 per cent of the purchase price was to be due by way of liquidated damages. The defendant, when sued on the guarantee, argued that this was a penalty. Blair J., whose judgment merits the reading, was satisfied that the predominant function of this contractual provision was not to deter from breach but to compensate for breach. He did not agree with the defendant that he had to form a view as to the maximum possible loss that the parties would have expected to flow from any determination of the contract and the extent to which the stipulated sum exceeded that maximum possible loss (*ibid.*, para.29). He also referred to the accepted rule that upon the party claiming that a contractual provision was a penalty lay the onus of proving it (*ibid.*, para.14), pointed out that in commercial contracts what the parties have agreed should normally be upheld and stated that in his view the provision was not even arguably a penalty (*ibid.*, para.29). An important feature of the case was that the contract provided that instalments paid before the termination were to be returned to the extent that they exceeded the 20 per cent. The claimant was held entitled to summary judgment.

NOTE 118: Add at the end of the note: *Vitol SA v Conoil Plc* [2009] 2 Lloyd's **13–028** Rep. 466. This last case is considered at para.20–124, below.

Add at the end of the paragraph: Similarly, in *Hall v Van Der Heiden* [2010] **13–029** EWHC 586 (TCC) where in a contract for the refurbishment and remodelling of the claimants' flat the defendant builder was required to pay a specified sum for each day that completion was delayed, the main purpose of this provision was to allow for the cost of alternative accommodation while the work continued, but in the event, tired of their nomadic existence, the claimants had taken re-possession of their flat in advance of the delayed completion. This was not something that would have been anticipated at the time the contract was made and was therefore not capable of turning a perfectly good liquidated damages provision into a penalty: see *ibid.*, paras 70 to 75.

Add at the end of the paragraph: However, *Lansat Shipping Co Ltd v Glencore* **13–034** *Grain BV, The Paragon* [2009] 2 Lloyd's Rep. 688, CA may now be taken as an illustration of this situation. Breach of a time charter by the late redelivery of the ship would in the normal course allow damages to the shipowner at the difference between market and contract rates of hire for the overdue period, here six days, but the contract stipulated that such a breach would give rise to damages at that difference of rate for 30 days in addition to the six. For this see the case at paras 13–052 and 13–071, below.

Insert a new note before "Indeed the difficulty" on line 6 of the paragraph: **13–035**

NOTE 140a: The £2 million to which in *Keegan v Newcastle United Football Co Ltd* [2010] I.R.L.R. 94 the manager of a football club became entitled on his constructive dismissal was held not to be a penalty, the court saying that, in view of the near impossibility of estimating precisely what the manager's loss would be, it considered the amount agreed upon to represent a reasonable pre-estimate to the extent that it was possible to carry out such an exercise at all: *ibid.*, para.50.

Add at the end of the paragraph: So too, although not relating to general **13–052** provisions on either side of a charterparty, a clause in a time charter, which provided that, should the charterer be in breach of contract by late redelivery of the ship at a time when the market rate of hire exceeded the contractual rate of hire, the rate was to be adjusted to that market rate for the 30 days preceding the contractual redelivery date, was in *Lansat Shipping Co Ltd v Glencore Grain BV,*

The Paragon [2009] 2 Lloyd's Rep. 688, CA held to be a penalty. See analysis of the case further at para.13–034, above.

13–071   Add at the end of the paragraph: But a clause in a time charter, which provided that, should the charterer be in breach of contract by late redelivery of the ship at a time when the market rate of hire exceeded the contractual rate of hire, the rate was to be adjusted to that market rate for the 30 days preceding the contractual redelivery date, was in *Lansat Shipping Co Ltd v Glencore Grain BV, The Paragon* [2009] 2 Lloyd's Rep. 688, CA held to be a penalty. See analysis of the case further at para.13–034, above.

13–079   NOTE 339: Add at the end of the note: A sum to be paid for each day's delay in completion was without difficulty held to be liquidated damages and not a penalty in *Hall v Van Der Heiden* [2010] EWHC 586 (TCC). See the case at para.13–029, above.

13–123   Insert a new note before "Yet the reasoning" on line 15 of the paragraph:

NOTE 525a: In the factually complex case of *Cantor Fitzgerald LP v Drummond*, August 4, 2009, unreported, where a provision was introduced into a promissory note for the earlier repayment of funds should a certain consent not be forthcoming, it was said that the provision could constitute a penalty without there being any breach of contract; the question of penalty would go to trial. *Lordsdale Finance* was said to be applied.

BOOK ONE

PART FOUR

**VARIOUS GENERAL FACTORS IN THE ASSESSMENT
OF DAMAGES**

CHAPTER 14

THE INCIDENCE OF TAXATION

		PARA.
I.	INCOME TAX	14–002
	(A) THE RULE IN *GOURLEY'S* CASE	14–002
	(B) TYPE-SITUATIONS IN WHICH THE RULE IN *GOURLEY'S* CASE MAY APPLY	14–005
□	1. General considerations	14–005
	2. Tort	14–024
■	3. Contract	14–041
	(C) THE PRACTICAL APPLICATION OF THE RULE IN *GOURLEY'S* CASE	14–055
	1. Burden of proof	14–055
□	2. Calculation of the tax	14–059
II.	CAPITAL GAINS TAX	14–062
	1. General considerations	14–062
	2. Tort	14–066
□	3. Contract	14–071

Insert a new paragraph after para.14–021:

In *BSkyB Ltd v HP Enterprise Services UK Ltd* [2010] EWHC 862 (TCC), **14–021A**
after a very full review of the authorities (*ibid.*, paras 53 to 67) ending with a
reference to our strong approval of *Amstrad Plc v Seagate Technology Inc* (at
para.14–019 of the main work), Ramsey J. elected to follow *Amstrad* rather than
Deeny v Gooda Walker (at para.14–020 of the main work). All three cases were
concerned with profits which, had they been achieved rather than lost, would
have been taxable at a higher rate of tax than the rate at which the damages
representing them were to be taxable. Ramsey J. held that in awarding
damages

> "an allowance should be made for the difference between the corporation tax
> treatment which the lost benefit would have received and the corporation tax treat-
> ment which the sums awarded as damages are likely to receive": para.77 of *BSkyB
> Ltd.*

For his full discussion of the issue see *ibid.*, paras 68 to 77 together with
para.46.

NOTE 206: Add at the end of the note: The tax deduction issue which arose **14–049**
in the professional negligence case of *Capita Alternative Fund Services (Guernsey) Ltd v Drivers Jonas* [2011] EWHC 2336 (Comm) (see at para.29–052,
fn.265a, below) is entirely unrelated to the matters considered in this chapter.

NOTE 243: Add at the end of the note: Citing in *Johnson v Fourie* [2011] **14–060**
EWHC 1062, QB this ruling of Lord Goddard, Owen J. declined to take into

account statements of the Chancellor of the Exchequer of his intent to reduce rates of income tax and of corporation tax in the future: *ibid.*, paras 140 to 145.

14–076   NOTE 304: Add at the end of the note: What is said on the topic of tax on damages in *Youlton v Charles Russell* [2010] EWHC 1918, Ch, paras 2 to 9, where the assignment to the claimant of a cause of action featured, is probably of little or no general value. The reference to *Zim* (at *ibid.*, para.6) suggests that the court was concerned with capital gains tax rather than income tax.

Chapter 15

THE AWARDING OF INTEREST

		PARA.
☐	I. INTRODUCTORY	15–001
	II. THE POSITION BEFORE *SEMPRA METALS*	15–005
	A. Interest outside statute: interest as damages	15–005
☐	B. Interest conferred by statute: interest on damages	15–030
☐	1. Limits of the statutory provision	15–036
■	2. Categories to which statutory interest applies	15–043
☐	III. THE POSITION AFTER *SEMPRA METALS*	15–060
	1. The decision	15–061
	2. The analysis	15–065
	3. The results	15–069
	IV. CALCULATION OF THE AMOUNT OF INTEREST	15–073
☐	1. Period of time for which interest is awarded	15–073
■	2. Rate of interest awarded	15–104
☐	3. Amount on which interest is awarded: interest and taxation	15–135

Insert a new paragraph after para.15–003:

15–003A   The proposals in the Civil Law Reform Bill 2009 on interest damages have been abandoned as thought by the Government not to be vote-catching. The details are at this paragraph in the First Supplement to the 18th edition.

Insert a new note after "Supreme Court Act" (and before "1981") on line 4 of **15–031** the paragraph:

NOTE 111a: Renamed, from 2009, the Senior Courts Act: Constitutional Reform Act 2005 (Commencement No.11) Order 2009 (SI 2009/1604). It was apparently thought necessary to change the title to avoid confusion with our new Supreme Court.

Insert a new paragraph after para.15–031:

15–031A   The proposals in the Civil Law Reform Bill 2009 on interest damages have been abandoned as thought by the Government not to be vote-catching. Hence the proposal to replace the existing statutory provisions on interest, which are set out in various statutes and pieces of secondary legislation, with a single set of so-called modern provisions has gone. The details are at paras 15–031A and 15–031B in the First Supplement to the 18th edition.

Insert a new note after "Supreme Court Act" (and before "1981") on line 3 of **15–034** the paragraph:

NOTE 116a: Now renamed the Senior Courts Act: see para.15–031, fn.111a, above

15–036   Insert a new note after "Supreme Court Act" (and before "1981") on line 1 of the paragraph:

NOTE 118a: Now renamed the Senior Courts Act: see para.15–031, fn.111a, above.

15–038   NOTE 121: Add at the end of the note: Also, interest can be claimed on debts under the Late Payment of Commercial Debts (Interest) Act 1998 but not under s.35A where the debt is not included in a judgment. This is neatly illustrated by *Fitzroy Robinson Ltd v Mentmore Towers Ltd* [2009] B.L.R. 165: see *ibid.*, para.55 *et seq.* But it is not damages.

15–040   Insert a new note at the end of the paragraph:

NOTE 129a: The proposals in the Civil Law Reform Bill 2009 on interest damages have been abandoned as thought by the Government not to be vote-catching. Hence the unfortunate provision effectively reverting to the position under the earlier s.3 has gone. The details are at this paragraph in the First Supplement to the 18th edition.

15–043   Insert in the text before "The situation would" on line 12 of the paragraph: So too where in a contract for the sale of land the purchaser fails to pay the deposit, which is a regular feature of such contracts, it was held in *Ng v Ashley King (Developments) Ltd* [2011] Ch. 115 by Lewison J. that the seller, though not entitled to contractual interest, was entitled to statutory interest from the time that the deposit should have been paid: see *ibid.*, paras 53 to 60.

15–047   Add at the end of the paragraph: Similarly, no interest was awarded, either under contract, as damages or by virtue of the statute, in *Pattni v First Leicester Buses Ltd* [2011] EWCA Civ 1384 where interest on the credit car hire charges had not been paid by the claimant: for the case see para.32–021C, below.

15–048   Add at the end of the paragraph: However, where as in *Checkprice (UK) Ltd v Revenue and Customs Commissioners* [2010] EWHC 682 (Admin) (facts at paras 33–009B and 33–009C, below) the award was of market value at the time of conversion with no special damage or consequential loss, it was appropriate to allow interest on the market value: *ibid.*, para.55.

15–049   Add at the end of the paragraph: Also in *Dobson v Thames Water Utilities Ltd* [2012] EWHC 986 (TCC) interest was awarded by Ramsey J. on the damages for loss of amenity where the claimants' land was adversely affected by a serious nuisance, such damages being calculated by taking the notional rental value of the land year by year up to trial: see this aspect of the matter at paras 34–020A and 34–020B, below. This is correct if the courts are prepared to award interest on the non-pecuniary loss element in torts generally, but this has not yet been done in torts at common law outside the field of personal injury and wrongful death (which Ramsey J. rightly considered not to be a useful analogy: *ibid.*, para.10). Indeed the Court of Appeal has declined in a deceit action to award interest on non-pecuniary loss in *Saunders v Edwards* [1987] 1 W.L.R. 1116, CA and also in a claim for wrongful arrest and false imprisonment in *Holtham v Commissioner of Police for the Metropolis* [1987] C.L.Y. 1154, CA: see para.15–056 of the main work. The fact that the calculation was by way of the land's rental value makes no difference as this does not turn the loss into a pecuniary one. Ramsey J. said, at *ibid.*, para.17, that he considered the governing principle to be that set out by Lord Herschell L.C. in the early leading case of *London, Chatham & Dover Ry v S.E. Ry* [1893] A.C. 429, to the effect that an interest award to a claimant is to be regarded as compensation for being kept out of the money which should have been paid him. This however refers to a monetary loss, to a pecuniary benefit of which the claimant has been deprived by the defendant—indeed *London, Chatham & Dover* was a case of debt—and not to a non-monetary loss which is not truly calculable in money but where a monetary award is the best that the law can do by way of compensation. Neither *Saunders* nor *Holtham* appears to have been cited to Ramsey J.

Insert a new note after "Supreme Court Act" (and before "1981") on the last line but two of the paragraph: **15–056**

NOTE 197a: Now renamed the Senior Courts Act: see para.15–031, fn.111a, above.

Insert a new note at the end of the paragraph: **15–065**

NOTE 230a: While not dealing specifically with interest, *Parabola Investments Ltd v Browallia Cal Ltd* [2011] Q.B. 477, CA shows that recovery of damages for the loss of the use of money, in that case resulting from deceit, is now fully accepted: see this aspect of the case at para.41–033A, below. As Toulson L.J. put it (*ibid.*, paras 50 and 51), the hostile view of such claims has gone with *Sempra Metals* and the ghost of Lord Tenderden (who established the view in *Page v Newman* in 1829: see para.15–005 of the main work) has there been laid to rest.

Insert a new note at the end of the paragraph: **15–067**

NOTE 237a: "There is no necessary inconsistency between the existence of a substantive right to interest and the existence of a statutory discretion. Substantive rights to recover interest were already well known to the law when the 1934 Act was passed": *per* Moore-Bick L.J. delivering the judgment of the court in *Maher v Groupama Grand Est* [2010] 1 W.L.R. 1564, CA, a conflict of laws case, at *ibid.*, para.36.

15–073   Insert a new note after "Supreme Court Act" (and before "1981") on line 1 of the paragraph:

NOTE 256a: Now renamed the Senior Courts Act: see para.15–031, fn.111a, above.

15–073   Insert a new note at the end of the paragraph:

NOTE 257a: Where in *Youlton v Charles Russell* [2010] EWHC 1032, Ch damages had been awarded by Warren J. for loss of a chance (dealt with at para.29–038, below), he had then to consider the periods to which and from which interest should be awarded on the lost chance claim: see his later judgment on consequential matters at [2010] EWHC 1918, Ch, para.32 *et seq.*

15–081   NOTE 293: Add at the end of the note: The decision in *Aerospace Publishing* was in effect followed in *Woodlands Oak Ltd v Conwell* [2011] EWCA Civ 254 where interest was awarded on damages for defects in building works which had not been remedied by the time of judgment: see *ibid.*, paras 35 to 37.

Insert a new paragraph after para.15–087:

15–087A   Nevertheless in *Ramzan v Brookwide Ltd* [2012] 1 All E.R. 903, CA the Court of Appeal, on being offered by counsel, for the remedying of the trial judge's incorrect award of a constant rate of interest, the alternatives of calculating the interest on each element of the loss from the time at which it arose and of using the short-hand personal injury method of halving the interest (*ibid.*, para.87), chose the latter alternative, Arden L.J. in the leading judgment saying without more, at para.88: "There is no reason not to apply the practice in *Dexter v Courtaulds Ltd* to cases other than personal injury". It would seem that the commercial cases favouring, and using, the former alternative (set out at para. 15–087 of the main work) cannot have been brought to the court's attention. It may also be noted, though the point is here of no great importance, that this personal injury practice stems not from the *Dexter* case, which presented a rather special situation and is not now generally followed (see paras 15–093 and 15–094 of the main work), but from the earlier, more important, *Jefford v Gee* [1970] 2 Q.B. 130, CA (see paras 15–092 to 15–094 of the main work). The facts of this curious case of *Ramzan* are at para.34–058B and 34–058C, below. A rough and ready method was used in *Driver v Air India Ltd* [2011] EWCA Civ 986 by the Court of Appeal to deal with interest in an employee's claim for unpaid overtime over a number of years: *ibid.*, paras 7, 12 and 13.

15–094   Insert a new note before "Roch L.J." on line 9 of the paragraph:

NOTE 356a: So too in *Johnson v Fourie* [2011] EWHC 1062, QB; see at paras 138 and 139.

NOTE 360: Add at the end of the note: Some curious arguments for the **15–095** defendant appeared in *Manning v King's College Hospital NHS Trust* [2008] EWHC 3008, QB. It was argued that interest should run not from service of the writ but from the later service of the particulars of claim, argued that interest should run not to the date judgment was given but to the earlier date the trial commenced, and argued at one point, but later dropped, that interest should run not to the judgment on damages but to the much earlier judgment on liability. Naturally none of the arguments succeeded; they should have been given short shrift but were addressed at length by the trial judge: see *ibid.*, paras 71 to 81.

NOTE 372: Add at the end of the note: *Costain Ltd v Charles Haswell &* **15–098** *Partners Ltd* [2010] 128 Con. L.R. 154 (breach of building contract by defective design for foundation works); *Cooper v National Westminster Bank Plc* [2010] 1 Lloyd's Rep. 490 (breach of banking contract, where the reduction in interest for delay was tempered by the defendant bank's high-handed conduct towards the claimant customer: see *ibid.*, paras 91 to 95).

NOTE 414: Insert after "plus 3 per cent" on line 3 of the note: and in *Kinch* **15–106** *v Rosling* [2009] EWHC 286, QB it was 10 per cent

NOTE 421: Substitute for 2009 on line 3 of the note: 2010 **15–108**

Insert a new paragraph after para.15–109:

The proposals in the Civil Law Reform Bill 2009 on interest damages have **15–109A** been abandoned as thought by the Government not to be vote-catching. Hence the unfortunate proposal to turn the whole matter of rates of interest over to the Lord Chancellor has gone. The details are at paras 15–109A and 15–109B in the First Supplement to the 18th edition.

NOTE 452: Add at the end of the note: In *Fiona Trust & Holding Corp v* **15–112** *Privalov* [2011] EWHC 664 (Comm) (see the case at para.15–121, below) Andrew Smith J. recognised that the rate of interest achievable on investment was likely to fall below the rate exacted on borrowing but, citing cases, regarded the court's consistent practice to be to use the borrowing rate whatever the particular claimant's position—whether as a result of the wrong he had to borrow or had less to invest: *ibid.*, para.14.

Add at the end of the paragraph: In *Fiona Trust & Holding Corp v Privalov* **15–113** [2011] EWHC 664 (Comm) (see the case at para.15–121, below) where very substantial sums of interest were in issue, Andrew Smith J. was prepared to consider the personal circumstances of the claimants and examined at some length (*ibid.*, paras 23 to 31) the defendants' contention that the LIBOR plus 2.5 per cent rate that he had taken as a starting point (see para.15–121, below) was higher than the rate of interest that the claimants had in fact paid on their borrowings. Even so, he concluded that the defendants' contention was not made out (*ibid.*, para.32).

15–115   Add at the end of the paragraph: The trial judge in *Ramzan v Brookwide Ltd* [2011] 2 All E.R. 38 regarded as typical a rate of 2 per cent over base rate which she would have been prepared to award had not the defendant been prepared to accept an average rate of 6 per cent per annum over a nine-year period, a period which started with base rate, it was said, at 7.25 per cent and ended with it at 0.5 per cent: *ibid.*, para.79. The use of the rate of 6 per cent was not challenged in the Court of Appeal, [2012] 1 All E.R. 903, CA at para.85, though the trial judge's use of a constant rate of interest was: see para.15–087A, above. The facts of this curious case are at paras 34–058B and 34–058C, below. And in *Driver v Air India Ltd* [2011] EWCA Civ 986 the Court of Appeal awarded to an employee interest at 8 per cent for one period and at 5 per cent for another when overtime had not been paid him: see *ibid.*, paras 7, 12 and 13. Yet this was at least at 3 per cent higher than base rate had been during the two periods.

15–116   Add at the end of the paragraph: Certainly the award of LIBOR plus 3 per cent in *Pgf II SA v Royal & Sun Alliance Insurance Plc* [2010] EWHC 1459 (TCC) (facts at para.23–055, below) was on the assumption that this was the rate at which the claimant would have borrowed: see *ibid.*, paras 343 to 348.

15–117   Insert a new note at the end of the last sentence but 2 of the paragraph:

NOTE 489a: In *Attrill v Dresdner Kleinwort Ltd* [2012] EWHC 1468, QB, a claim for breach of employment contracts by two individual employees of an employer bank, Owen J. not only took borrowing rate but recognised that the rate at which commercial concerns could borrow was not available to private individuals; the result was awards of 5 per cent over the bank's base rate: *ibid.*, paras 2 to 5.

15–118   Insert a new note at the end of the paragraph:

NOTE 493a: So too the enhanced rate of 3 per cent over LIBOR in *Pgf II SA v Royal & Sun Alliance Insurance Plc* [2010] EWHC 1459 (TCC) (see para. 15–116, above) was not compounded. It should be noted that with awards of compound interest there is no settled rule as to how frequently the compounding is to be done, whether monthly, annually or for any other period of time. In *Fiona Trust & Holding Corp v Privalov* [2011] EWHC 664 (Comm) (see the case at para.15–121, below) Andrew Smith J. adopted three-monthly rests: *ibid.*, para.19.

15–119   NOTE 499: Insert before "But in" on line 1 of the note: Also in *Kinch v Rosling* [2009] EWHC 286, QB.

15–119   Insert in the text before the last sentence of the paragraph: By contrast, the trial judge in *Ramzan v Brookwide Ltd* [2011] 2 All E.R. 38 said rightly that judgment rate was inappropriate for pre-judgment interest: *ibid.*, para.78. For her award as to rate of interest, accepted by the Court of Appeal ([2012] 1 All E.R. 903, CA), see para.15–115, above.

Add at the end of the paragraph: By contrast, in *Fiona Trust & Holding Corp* **15–121**
v Privalov [2011] EWHC 664 (Comm), where the award to the claimants, who were very many Russian shipowning groups, was to be in US dollars, Andrew Smith J., while stating that it had become conventional in commercial cases to award US Prime Rate (*ibid.*, para.15), considered it more appropriate in the case before him to award US LIBOR plus 2.5 per cent rather than US Prime Rate. This was because those operating outside the United States were unaccustomed to Prime Rate and, more importantly, because borrowings by shipping companies were generally effected using LIBOR. The claim was for equitable compensation, there being breaches of fiduciary duty, but the same reasoning must be applicable to claims for common law damages.

NOTE 566: Insert after "Supreme Court Act" (and before "1981"):—now **15–131**
renamed the Senior Courts Act (see para.15–031, fn.111a, above)—

Insert a new heading and a new paragraph after para.15–134

(5) *The particular case of nuisance*

Interest having been awarded by Ramsey J. in *Dobson v Thames Water* **15–134A**
Utilities Ltd [2012] EWHC 986 (TCC) on the damages for non-pecuniary loss by way of loss of amenity in the enjoyment of land caused by a nuisance (see para.15–049, above), the question arose as to the appropriate rate of interest to apply. Ramsey J. awarded the special account rate sought by the claimants, which rate, though not generally used outside personal injury claims, he regarded as representing a suitable commercial rate: *ibid.*, para.19. At the same time he rejected the 2 per cent rate used for non-pecuniary loss in personal injury claims advocated by the defendant as he rightly regarded the analogy with general damages for personal injury an irrelevance—it should be noted that the claims for loss of amenity on account of the nuisance were only for the past years up to the trial and not, as with personal injury, also for future years which could be very many. It is thought, however, that the better solution may be to award no interest at all for the reasons set out at para.15–049, above.

Insert a new paragraph after para.15–139:

In *BSkyB Ltd v HP Enterprise Services UK Ltd* [2010] EWHC 862 (TCC) **15–140**
Ramsey J. adopted and applied the reasoning of Phillips J. in *Deeny v Gooda Walker (No.3)* (fully set out at para.15–138 of the main work) so as to base the award of interest on the net amount of damages after the deduction of tax. Ramsey J., unlike Phillips J., did not regard the *Tate & Lyle* case as standing alone with no progeny but took into account, with the assistance of this work, the

Court of Appeal's decision in *O'Sullivan v Management Agency and Music* (on all of which see paras 15–135 to 15–137 of the main work) together with *Amstrad Plc v Seagate Technology Inc* (dealt with on the related tax issue at para.14–019 of the main work). As in *Deeny* the damages were awarded for lost profits, referred to in *BSkyB* as lost benefits. See *BSkyB* on the related tax issue at para.14–021A, above.

CHAPTER 16

THE EFFECT OF CHANGES IN VALUE

		PARA.
1.	Changes in the value of property	16–002
2.	Changes in the value of services	16–006
3.	Changes in the value of money	16–008
	(1) General change in the internal value of sterling over the years	16–009
	(2) Particular changes in the internal value of sterling between the time of accrual of the cause of action and the time of judgment	16–013
	(3) Particular changes in the external value of sterling between the time of accrual of the cause of action and the time of judgment	16–018
	(a) The general rule before the *Miliangos* decision	16–019
	(i) Contract	16–021
	(ii) Tort	16–023
	(b) The *Miliangos* decision	16–024
	(c) The working out of the *Miliangos* decision	16–031
	(i) Contract debt and liquidated damages	16–032
	(ii) Contract: unliquidated damages	16–035
	(iii) Tort	16–046
	(d) The effect of the *Miliangos* decision	16–053

16–034

NOTE 143: Add at the end of the note: *Fearns v Anglo-Dutch Paint & Chemical Co Ltd* [2011] 1 W.L.R. 366 (in a judgment following on the judgment at [2010] EWHC 1708, Ch dealt with elsewhere in this Supplement) was primarily concerned with the operation of set-off, at law and in equity. A debt in euros fell to be set off against damages for trade mark infringement in pounds and an issue arose as to the proper date for conversion of the debt and the damages into a common currency (see at *ibid.*, paras 52 to 57), an issue of importance because of significant fluctuations at the time in the exchange rate between pounds and euros. While the decision of the judge, G. Leggatt QC, is not doubted, his view that damages can be recovered for a currency exchange loss caused by the late payment of a debt is inconsistent with the House of Lords decision in the *Lips* case (in this note in the main work), despite his citing it as illustrating the view put forward by him: see *ibid.*, para.53.

16–044

NOTE 193: Add at the end of the note: *The Texaco Melbourne* was distinguished by Gloster J. in *Milan Nigeria Ltd v Angeliki B Maritime Co* [2011] EWHC 892 (Comm) where the defendant shipowners were liable for damage to, rather than for the loss of, the claimants' cargo. Arbitrators had found no difficulty in holding that the loss was felt in US dollars and not in Nigerian naira, the currency where the cargo would, if not lost, have been discharged and sold, and where replacement goods might have been acquired. The arbitrators had so decided because they saw the cargo owners' claim as being related to international trade where the primary currency was US dollars, with the cost of the goods and the ocean freight being in that currency, and this conclusion was reached regardless of the fact that cargo, once discharged, would invariably be sold in the local currency. Gloster J. held that the arbitrators' decision must stand and that there could be no appeal against it: see generally *ibid.*, paras 46 to 68.

CHAPTER 17

THE RECOVERY OF COSTS, DAMAGES AND FINES INCURRED IN PREVIOUS PROCEEDINGS

			PARA.
■	I.	INTRODUCTORY: THE RECOVERY AS DAMAGES OF THE NOW CLAIM-ANT'S OWN COSTS IN THE PREVIOUS PROCEEDINGS	17–003
	II.	COSTS IN PREVIOUS PROCEEDINGS BETWEEN THE SAME PARTIES	17–020
		1. Further proceedings where no separate independent cause of action is available	17–021
□		2. Further proceedings where a separate independent cause of action is available...	17–023
	III.	COSTS, DAMAGES AND FINES IN PREVIOUS PROCEEDINGS BETWEEN THE NOW CLAIMANT AND THIRD PARTIES	17–039
		1. The rule as it has developed	17–039
□		2. Main type-situations in which costs, damages and fines have been claimed as damages	17–045
□		3. The various aspects of remoteness of damage involved	17–056
		4. Amount recoverable	17–085

NOTE 17: Add at the end of the note: Unfortunately, Warren J.'s decision on **17–005** this point did not feature in the appeal: see *Dadourian Group International Inc v Simms* [2009] 1 Lloyd's Rep. 601, CA, paras 128 and 129. Warren J. also in *Youlton v Charles Russell* [2010] EWHC 1032, Ch appears to assume that the *British Racing Drivers* case has, at least for the time being, changed the law (see *Youlton* at paras 529 and 539), but it is not at all clear where this gets him in his consideration of costs as damages, either in his judgment here (see *ibid.*, para.528 *et seq.*) or in his later judgment on consequential matters in the same case (see [2010] EWHC 1918, Ch at para.44 *et seq.*).

Add at the end of the paragraph: So too Foskett J. in *Swain v Osborne* [2010] **17–005** EWHC 3118, QB has felt obliged, though unenthusiastically, to follow Carnwarth J. on the grounds of judicial comity while expressing sympathy with the claimant's contention that Carnworth J.'s decision in *British Racing Drivers* is inconsistent with Sir Anthony Colman's decision in *National Westminster Bank Plc v Rabobank Nederland* (at paras 17–011 and 17–035 of the main work) and that the law has moved on: *Swain* paras 40 to 44.

NOTE 24: Add at the end of the note: It was however not given consideration **17–006** in *Dadourian* on appeal: see para.17–005, fn.17, above.

Insert a new note before "and it is thought" on line 6 of the paragraph: **17–013**

NOTE 33a: Nothing on this appears in the appeal: see para.17–005, fn.17, above.

17–017   NOTE 44: Add at the end of the note: but nothing on this appears in the appeal: see para.17–005, fn.17, above.

17–019   Add at the end of the paragraph: And now in *Herrmann v Withers LLP* [2012] EWHC 1492, Ch, Newey J., citing approvingly from this paragraph in the main work, has boldly decided in favour of awarding indemnity costs as damages to a claimant who had reasonably instructed solicitors to advise on a problem arising out of the negligence of the defendant solicitors (facts at para.7–091A, above). *British Racing Drivers' Club v Heskell Erskine & Co*, the decision of Carnwarth J. (at para.17–005 of the main work) which started the move to awarding costs as damages only on the standard basis, was doubted and not followed: see Newey J.'s extended discussion at *ibid.*, paras 105 to 116.

17–038   NOTE 109: Add at the end of the note: There was little hope of costs being allowed as damages in *Carroll v Kynaston* [2011] Q.B. 959, CA. Persistent litigants in what Ward L.J. described as the worst and most dreadful kind of litigation, the male party at one stage made an offer to settle all of their prior claims, an offer accepted by the female party. However, this did not end the matter, the male party now contending that the settlement was not contractually binding. To ascertain this he brought a further action which he lost. Undaunted, he then sued for breach of the settlement contract, claiming as damages the costs incurred in his preceding action. In this he clearly failed. He was not claiming for costs which he had been unable to recover in the earlier action, which is a feature of all the other cases in this field. He could and should have asked for costs in that action and if the judge had declined to make an order for costs he should have insisted and, were that of no avail, he should have appealed: see the analysis at *ibid.*, paras 20 to 22. Yet to reach this result, Ward L.J., who gave the only reasoned judgment, felt obliged to go through, in careful detail, most of the cases appearing in this section (paras 17–023 to 17–038) of the main work: *ibid.*, paras 23 to 31.

17–050   NOTE 159: Substitute for [2007] EWHC 454, Ch on line 1 of the note: [2009] 1 Lloyd's Rep. 601, CA

17–062   Add at the end of the paragraph: *Siemens Building Technologies FE Ltd v Supershield Ltd* [2010] 1 Lloyd's Rep. 349, CA (full facts at paras 6–164B and 6–164C, above) is a further case in which the amount paid in settlement was held to be reasonable and therefore recoverable. It is necessary, however, for recovery to show the causal link between the settlement by the claimant and the wrong of the defendant; on this the claimant failed in *Costain Ltd v Charles Haswell & Partners Ltd* [2010] 128 Con. L.R. 154.

17–080   Insert a new note at the end of the paragraph:

NOTE 268a: *Safeway Stores Ltd v Twigger* [2011] 2 All E.R. 841, CA is a rather special case considering whether a company could recover from its directors and employees a penalty, or fine, exacted from it by the Office of Fair Trading for anti-competition activities.

BOOK TWO
PARTICULAR CONTRACTS AND TORTS

CHAPTER 19

THE MEASURE OF DAMAGES IN CONTRACT AND TORT COMPARED

NOTE 48: Add at the end of the note: *Milner v Carnival Plc* [2010] 3 All E.R. **19–008**
701, CA is an up-to-date Court of Appeal decision, factually similar to *Jarvis* and
Jackson, allowing recovery for mental distress.

Insert a new note at the end of the paragraph: **19–010**

NOTE 94: An unusual illustration of contractual liability for a loss unlikely to
result, which might therefore not have founded recovery had the liability been in
tort, is provided by *Siemens Building Technologies FE Ltd v Supershield Ltd*
[2010] 1 Lloyd's Rep. 349, CA. The case is fully considered at paras 6–164A to
6–164E, above.

BOOK TWO

PART ONE

CONTRACT

CHAPTER 20

SALE OF GOODS

			PARA.
I.		BREACH BY SELLER	20–002
□	1.	Non-delivery	20–002
	2.	Delayed delivery	20–036
	3.	Breach of condition: goods properly rejected	20–056
■	4.	Breach of condition or warranty as to quality, fitness or description: goods accepted	20–057
	5.	Breach of condition as to title or of warranty of quiet possession	20–105
	6.	Breach of condition: loss of the right to reject the goods	20–107
II.		BREACH BY BUYER	20–109
□	1.	Non-acceptance	20–110
	2.	Failure to procure the opening of a letter of credit	20–127
	3.	Other breaches	20–129

Add a new note at the end of the paragraph: **20–001**

NOTE 1a: These damages provisions of the Sale of Goods Act can be applied to the sale of what are not, strictly speaking, goods, as in *Deutsche Bank AG v Total Global Steel Ltd* [2012] EWHC 1201 (Comm) where the sale was of carbon emission units: see the case at paras 20–059A and 20–062, fn.258a, below.

Insert a new note before "If he can" on the last line but 4 of the paragraph: **20–006**

NOTE 14a: No available market in *M&J Marine Engineering Services Co Ltd v Shipshore Ltd* [2009] EWHC 2031 (Comm) (facts at para.20–029A, below).

NOTE 21: Add at the end of the note: In *Luxe Holding Ltd v Midland*   **20–009**
Resources Holding Ltd [2010] EWHC 1908, Ch, which was a sale of shares rather than of goods and was not an action for damages but an application for a freezing order, the seller's resale price was taken, in that context, as evidence of market value. See the case at para.24–005A, below.

Insert a new paragraph after para.20–029:

(ia) Cost of acquiring substitute goods. The loss on a resale may not be caused   **20–029A**
by the resale itself being lost but be represented by the cost of acquiring at a price higher than the initial purchase price the nearest substitute goods should there be no market in which exactly equivalent goods can be bought, with which substitute goods the resale is then carried through. Here the buyer should recover as damages the price paid for the substitute goods less the contract price, in the

same manner as has been held where the substitute goods are required not for resale but for use: see the cases at para.20–024 of the main work. *M&J Marine Engineering Services Co Ltd v Shipshore Ltd* [2009] EWHC 2031 (Comm) was a case of this nature. A quantity of machined wheel rollers for which there was held to be no available market had been sold at a profit to a third party and the buyer had on the seller's non-delivery acquired substitute goods for its resale at a much higher price than that at which it had bought. It is however a curious case because the buyer had then succeeded in renegotiating with the third party an amount for it to pay which was even slightly above the price the buyer had paid for the substitute goods. In these circumstances the buyer was awarded as damages, apart from its costs in renegotiating the resale, the initial loss of profit on its resale—that is to say, the difference between the price the third party had initially agreed to pay and the contract price—less the small profit eventually made on the resale—that is to say, the difference between the price the third party had finally paid and the cost of the substitute goods: see the discussion at *ibid.*, paras 25 to 31 where the figures are a little difficult to work out. Yet it is thought that a better method of assessment would have been not to award the initial profit less the final profit but to have awarded the cost of the substitute goods less the initial contract price and then to deduct from this, as a form of mitigation (see the mitigation principles set out at para.7–106 *et seq.* of the main work), the difference between what the third party finally paid and what it had initially contracted to pay. The result mathematically is the same.

Insert a new paragraph after para.20–059:

20–059A   That the time, and place, taken for assessing the value of the goods is the time, and place, of delivery is only a prima facie rule. In *Choil Trading SA v Sahara Energy Resources Ltd* [2010] EWHC 374 (Comm) the rule was held displaced. Delivery to the buyer of a cargo of contaminated naphtha took place at the time of its shipment, on August 13, but it was not until tests carried out on board the ship had revealed the contamination that there was rejection, on August 28, of the cargo by the buyer's sub-buyer. It was held that the difference between the values of sound and contaminated naphtha fell to be assessed as at August 28: see para.115 *et seq.* together with para.131. So too in *Deutsche Bank AG v Total Global Steel Ltd* [2012] EWHC 1201 (Comm) a time later than that of delivery was taken as the buyer of the carbon emission units had delayed in order to give the seller a chance to put things right: see *ibid.*, para.166.

20–061   Add at the end of the paragraph: In *Choil Trading SA v Sahara Energy Resources Ltd* [2010] EWHC 374 (Comm) where the buyer on July 15 had sold the cargo of naphtha as sound to a third party (facts of the case at para.20–059A, above), there is a lengthy discussion by Christopher Clarke J. as to whether the price at which this sale was made could be taken as its sound value at August 28, the date on which sound value had to be assessed, leading to the conclusion that it could not: see *ibid.*, paras 132 to 150.

Insert a new note at the end of the second sentence of the paragraph: **20–062**

NOTE 258a: In the absence of an available market it was difficult to assess the value of the carbon emission units sold in *Deutsche Bank AG v Total Global Steel Ltd* [2012] EWHC 1201 (Comm): see *ibid.*, para.167 *et seq.*

Add at the end of the paragraph: In *Choil Trading SA v Sahara Energy* **20–062**
Resources Ltd [2010] EWHC 374 (Comm) where the buyer on September 12 had sold the cargo of naphtha in its contaminated condition to a third party (facts of the case at para.20–059A, above), Christopher Clarke J. held that the price at which this sale was made could be taken as the value of the naphtha in its contaminated condition on August 28, the date on which contaminated value had to be assessed: see *ibid.*, paras 132 and 151 to 155.

NOTE 312: Add at the end of the note: In *Borealis AB v Geogas Trading SA* **20–076**
[2011] 1 Lloyd's Rep. 482 (facts at para.6–147A, above) the claimant recovered for profits lost during repairs necessitated by the damage caused to the plant and equipment, without reduction, or even elimination, of the award on account of the claimant's having taken the opportunity to effect repairs to other equipment at the plant, the analogy of the shipping cases at para.32–037 of the main work being referred to: see *ibid.*, paras 156 to 160.

Insert a new paragraph before para.20–088, moving the heading to it so as to become the heading to para.20–087A:

That damages for loss on a resale are not recoverable merely because the seller **20–087A**
knows that the buyer is a merchant buying generally for resale, because what is contemplated is that the buyer on breach will go out into the market and buy substitute goods, is illustrated by *Choil Trading SA v Sahara Energy Resources Ltd* [2010] EWHC 374 (Comm), the facts of which are at para.20–059A, above. That this is the general rule was made clear in relation to breach by non-delivery by Devlin J. in *Kwei Tek Chao v British Traders* [1954] 2 Q.B. 459 (see para.20–026 of the main work) and *Kwei* was applied by Christopher Clarke J. to breach of warranty of quality in *Choil*: see *ibid.*, paras 128 to 130.

Add at the end of the paragraph: Though concerning building contracts rather **20–094**
than sales of goods *Siemens Building Technologies FE Ltd v Supershield Ltd* [2010] 1 Lloyd's Rep. 349, CA (dealt with at para.6–164A *et seq.*, above) has a useful passage by Toulson L.J., at para.28, on how the reasonableness of a settlement is to be assessed.

Insert a new paragraph after para.20–103:

(cc) Other losses. *Borealis AB v Geogas Trading SA* [2011] 1 Lloyd's Rep.482 **20–103A**
(facts at para.6–147A, above) is a sale of goods case in which the buyer was held entitled to recover for expenditure on managerial and staff time taken up in

dealing with remedial work: see *ibid.*, paras 144 to 149. This head of damages is already well established in relation to torts and other contracts: see the cases at para.2–051, fn.220 of the main work.

20–112   NOTE 482: Add at the end of the note: How far after a repudiation by a buyer of goods the seller's ability, or willingness, still to perform can affect the damages was much in issue in the complicated case of *Acre 1127 Ltd v De Montfort Fine Art* [2011] EWCA Civ 87 where the contract was for the supply of valuable items of contemporary art. The *Braithwaite* case (above in this note in the main work) was extensively referred to.

20–112   NOTE 483: Insert before "Provided always" on the first line of the note: and in *AerCap Partners Ltd v Avia Asset Management AB* [2010] EWHC 2431 (Comm).

20–115   NOTE 501: Add at the end of the note: This passage on the meaning of available market was cited and adopted by David Steel J. in *Zodiac Maritime Agencies Ltd v Fortescue Metals Group Ltd* [2011] 2 Lloyd's Rep. 360, para.56, which concerned breach of contract by a charterer of a ship rather than by a seller of goods: see the case at para.27–067A, below.

20–116   Insert in the text before "But apart" on line 9 of the paragraph: So too the seller of two Boeing aircraft was held entitled in *AerCap Partners Ltd v Avia Asset Management AB* [2010] EWHC 2431 (Comm) to the difference between the contract price and the substantially lower price at which it resold the aircraft a good many months after the buyer's repudiation of the contract, this apparently on the basis that the resale price was good evidence of the market value though possibly on the basis that no available market had appeared until the time of the resale. See the lengthy analysis of Gross L.J. at *ibid.*, para.90 *et seq.*

20–117   Insert in the text after the first sentence of the paragraph: It is however generally accepted today that the law gives the seller a reasonable period of time after breach in which to make the substitute sale. This was the case in *AerCap Partners Ltd v Avia Asset Management AB* [2010] EWHC 2431 (Comm): facts at para.20–116, above.

20–124   Insert in the text before "And an interesting" on line 9 of the paragraph: In *Vitol SA v Conoil Plc* [2009] 2 Lloyd's Rep. 466, where the seller sold large cargoes of gasoil under a number of contracts with delivery ex-ship and the buyer first delayed in taking them up and eventually did not take them up at all, a whole series of consequential losses was awarded. In addition to the normal measure of contract price less market price, the seller was awarded damages for financial losses caused by the delay—an item which was covered by what was construed as a liquidated damages clause though called a penalty—and damages in respect of various demurrage payments, together with recovery of storage charges for the gasoil until it could be resold.

CHAPTER 21

HIRE AND HIRE-PURCHASE OF GOODS

		PARA.
I.	BREACH BY LENDER	21–001
	1. Non-delivery	21–001
□	2. Breach of warranty	21–003
II.	BREACH BY HIRER	21–009
	1. Non-acceptance and related breaches	21–009
	2. Damage to the goods or their destruction	21–018
	3. Failure to surrender the goods	21–021

21–004 Add at the end of the paragraph: Where in *Lobster Group Ltd v Heidelberg Graphic Equipment Ltd* [2009] EWHC 1919 (TCC) a printing press which proved defective was hired, a claim for loss of profits was held to be available to the hirer. It however failed both on causation and on proof (*ibid.*, para.199 *et seq.*) and the hirer had to be content with the recovery of certain rectification costs (*ibid.*, para.234 *et seq.*).

21–007 NOTE 24: Add at the end of the note: Neither was there a reduction for the claimant's use of the car in *Brewer v Mann* [2010] EWHC 2444, QB (facts at para.21–007, below) but on the curious, and mistaken, ground that this would require a claim to be made in restitution: see *ibid.*, paras 226 to 230.

21–007 Add at the end of the paragraph: On the other hand, in *Brewer v Mann* [2010] EWHC 2444, QB the claimant, who had acquired a vintage car which turned out to be not quite vintage, successfully sued both the finance company and the dealer. The damages are worked out in a somewhat complicated and not too clear a fashion at *ibid.*, para.217 *et seq.* Among other things *Yeoman Credit Co v Odgers* (in this paragraph of the main work) is cited and relied on.

CHAPTER 22

SALE OF LAND

			PARA.
□	I.	BREACH BY SELLER	22–001
		(A) FAILURE TO COMPLETE	22–003
		(B) DELAY IN COMPLETION	22–010
		(C) BREACH OF COVENANTS	22–013
		1. The four usual covenants of title	22–014
		2. Covenant for quiet enjoyment	22–018
		3. Covenant for good right to convey	22–026
■		4. Covenants other than of title	22–030
□	II.	BREACH BY BUYER	22–031
□		(A) FAILURE TO ACCEPT	22–032
□		(B) BREACH OF COVENANTS	22–040
		1. Positive covenants	22–041
		2. Restrictive covenants	22–049

22–002 Insert a new note before the last sentence of the paragraph:

NOTE 3a: Should a seller of land be held in some way to have derogated from his grant, this can be regarded as another form of breach. This happened in a somewhat unusual way in *Carter v Cole* [2009] EWCA Civ 410 where it was sellers of land who turned out to be claimants. In their contract of sale to the defendants the claimants had stipulated for a right of way over the land sold in order to allow vehicular access to land retained by them, which they were letting out commercially. In short, interference with this access by the defendants, who were in effect sellers of the right of way granted by them, put paid for a time—there was a mandatory injunction to restore the position—to the claimants' commercial use. The damages, which were assessed by the Court of Appeal on very meagre evidence, were based on the value of the commercial use of which the claimants had been deprived: *ibid.*, para.19 *et seq.*

22–030 Add at the end of the paragraph: The work that the seller in *Howard-Jones v Tate* [2012] 2 All E.R. 369, CA contracted to carry out on the premises within six months of completion of the sale was the provision of electricity and mains water supplies. Unfortunately the judge at trial awarded damages on the wrong basis of restoring the pre-contractual position and the Court of Appeal, correcting him, directed that the damages be re-assessed. Kitchin L.J. in the leading judgment indicated that, as he saw it, the recoverable losses would comprise the cost to the claimant of having the services installed and any other losses suffered as a result of their not being installed in due time: *ibid.*, paras 31 to 36.

Insert a new paragraph after para.22–030:

The seller may also undertake to carry out, or to have carried out, work on the **22–030A**
premises before conveyance and it then turns out, after conveyance, that the work
is inadequate, indeed defective. This was the position in *Strange v Westbury
Homes (Holdings) Ltd* [2009] 128 Con. L.R. 26, CA where a developer sold a
number of plots to a number of buyers and it was a term of each contract that the
developer had completed, or soon would complete, the erection of the plots in a
thorough and workmanlike manner. This the developer failed to do. The Court of
Appeal upheld the trial judge's award of damages for the cost of remedial work
and in addition for the diminution in value of the properties following the
remedial work's completion. The trial judge had also made an award for distress
and inconvenience but there was no appeal against this.

NOTE 118: Add at the end of the note: Delay did feature in *Anglo Continental* **22–031**
Educational Group (GB) Ltd v ASN Capital Investments Ltd [2010] EWHC 2649
Ch where in issue was, *inter alia*, the compensation payable by the buyer for late
completion which was governed by the provisions of the Law Society's *General
Conditions of Sale*: see *ibid.*, para.53 *et seq.*

Insert a new note after the first sentence of the paragraph: **22–036**

NOTE 140a: In *Strategic Property Ltd v O'Se* [2009] EWHC 3512, Ch the
claimant had contracted to buy the property and had sold it on at a profit to the
defendant. On the defendant's failure to accept, the claimant did not complete the
head sale and so lost the profit on the sub-sale. This was not a consequential loss
for which there could be recovery. The claimant should have completed the head
sale and claimed the normal measure of damages. See the full discussion at *ibid.*,
para.33 *et seq.*

Insert in the text immediately before "Indeed" on the last line but three of the **22–039**
paragraph: In *Ng v Ashley King (Developments) Ltd* [2011] Ch. 115 Lewison J.
declined to follow *Essex v Daniell* (1875) L.R. 10 C.P. 538 and held that, where
the buyer is in repudiatory breach of a contract for the sale of land and the seller
forfeits the deposit, the buyer must give credit for the deposit in his claim for
damages even where no resale of the land has been made by him. Lewison J.
pointed out that since its Victorian genesis *Essex v Daniell* has not been referred
to in a single English judgment (*ibid.*, para.31) and stated that he agreed with the
statement in the text of this paragraph that it was difficult to see why there should
be a difference between the situation where, as in *Ockenden v Henly* (1858) E.
B. & E. 485, the seller has made a resale and where, as in *Essex v Daniell*, he has
not (*ibid.*, para.35). See his very full and helpful discussion from paras 16 to 52
in *Ng*.

CHAPTER 23

LEASE OF LAND

		PARA.
I.	BREACH BY LESSOR	23–001
	(A) FAILURE TO COMPLETE	23–003
	(B) DELAY IN COMPLETION	23–007
■	(C) BREACH OF COVENANTS	23–010
■	1. Covenant for quiet enjoyment and covenant against incumbrances	23–012
	2. Covenant to repair	23–023
	3. Covenant of fitness for habitation	23–033
	4. Covenant to renew and option to purchase	23–034
II.	BREACH BY LESSEE	23–037
	(A) FAILURE TO ACCEPT	23–038
	(B) BREACH OF COVENANTS	23–040
□	1. Covenant to repair	23–042
	2. Other covenants on the condition and use of the premises	23–081
	3. Covenant against assignment or underletting	23–091
	4. Covenant to deliver up possession	23–095

23–010 Insert a new note before "particularly those" on line 5 of the paragraph:

NOTE 18a: Recovery for breach of covenant as to the condition of the premises may be for non-pecuniary loss by way of loss of amenity, as in *Newman v Framewood Manor Management Co Ltd* [2012] EWCA Civ 159 where the lessor of an apartment in a block of flats was in breach of covenant in the provision of leisure facilities by way of swimming pool, jacuzzi and gym (*ibid.*, para.42 *et seq.*). The damages awarded to the claimant lessee by the Court of Appeal were modest.

23–011 NOTE 28: Add at the end of the note: It would seem that the Court of Appeal also endorsed the trial judge's award of the value of the business as at the time the carrying on of the business became impossible. Decided in a different field, *MMP GmbH v Antal International Network Ltd* [2011] EWHC 1120 (Comm), relying on the trial judge's award in *U.Y.B. v British Railways Board*, indicates that a claim for the value of a business runs only where the business has ceased or been abandoned. If it is continuing, the claim must be for lost future business profits. See para.2–026, fn.65a, above.

23–019 Insert a new note at the end of the paragraph:

NOTE 67a: The interference with an easement granted to lessees by their lessor took the trial judge to restitutionary damages in *Kettel v Bloomfold Ltd* [2012] EWHC 1422, Ch. See the case at para.12–033, fn.138a, above.

Add at the end of the paragraph: Both of these matters made an appearance in **23–055**
Pgf II SA v Royal & Sun Alliance Insurance Plc [2010] EWHC 1459 (TCC)
where the lessee and the sub-lessee of a prestigious six-storey office block in
London's financial centre built in the early 1970s were in breach of their
repairing covenants. It was undisputed that the lessor had carried out a scheme
of refurbishment which went well beyond that for which the lessees could have
been expected to pay to put the premises into repair (*ibid.*, para.54), which meant
that from the cost of the scheme as carried out fell to be deducted the cost of the
element of improvement. As for the loss of the use of the premises during repair,
it was accepted that loss of rent was in principle recoverable but the lessor must
prove that the carrying out of the repairs had prevented or would prevent the
letting of the premises for the whole of the claimable period of repair. This led
to a limited recovery for lost rent: see *ibid.*, paras 256 to 269.

NOTE 262: Add at the end of the note: , a view adopted in *Pgf II SA v Royal* **23–056**
& Sun Alliance Insurance Plc [2010] EWHC 1459 (TCC) (facts at para.23–055,
above) in the light of *Ruxley Electronics & Construction Ltd v Forsyth* [1996]
A.C. 344: see para.7–168, above.

Insert a new paragraph after para.23–056:

It would seem that these cases of common law damages are unlikely to be **23–056A**
followed today in the modern climate which views damages going beyond
compensation for loss as improper. In relation to the principal of these cases,
Joyner v Weeks [1891] 2 Q.B. 31, CA, H.H. Judge Toulmin in *Pgf II SA v Royal*
& Sun Alliance Insurance Plc [2010] EWHC 1459 (TCC) (facts at para.23–055,
above) was clear that continued reliance on it was precluded by the House of
Lords' decision in *Ruxley Electronics & Construction Ltd v Forsyth* [1996] A.C.
344 (at para.26–013 of the main work). Nevertheless this is a somewhat academic conclusion since *Joyner v Weeks* and the other cases have been overturned
by the statutory changes of 1927, to which we now turn.

Add at the end of the paragraph: In assessing the market value of the property **23–059**
in its unrepaired state it is the property as it reverts to the lessor that is to be
taken, so that the Court of Appeal in *Van Dal Footwear Ltd v Ryman Ltd* [2010]
1 W.L.R. 2015, CA held the trial judge to be wrong to have increased that value
because the former tenant might have taken a further lease of the property in its
unrepaired condition.

NOTE 299: Add at the end of the note: The trial judge in *Pgf II SA v Royal &* **23–062**
Sun Alliance Insurance Plc [2010] EWHC 1459 (TCC) (facts at para.23–055,
above) concerned himself very much with the question of the date at which a
lessor's intention about what to do with the property is to be considered,
concluding rightly that it had to be taken as the date of the termination of the
lease and no later: see *ibid.*, para.41 *et seq.*

23–067 NOTE 320: Add at the end of the note: and would not be followed today according to H.H. Judge Toulmin in *Pgf II SA v Royal & Sun Alliance Insurance Plc* [2010] EWHC 1459 (TCC) (facts at para.23–055, above): see para.7–168, above.

Insert a new paragraph after para.23–069:

23–069A (9) No account is to be taken of latent development value of the property so as to increase its market value in its unrepaired state. A lessor's damages are not to be reduced, or eliminated, because of a development value which at the date of the termination of the lease the lessor had no intention of realising. As was pointed out in *Pgf II SA v Royal & Sun Alliance Insurance Plc* [2010] EWHC 1459 (TCC) (facts at para.23–055, above) this had not been argued successfully since section 18(1) of the Landlord and Tenant Act 1927 had been passed, and it was not successfully argued there: see *ibid.*, paras 54 to 68.

23–070 Add at the end of the paragraph: Nevertheless such damages were allowed in *Pgf II SA v Royal & Sun Alliance Insurance Plc* [2010] EWHC 1459 (TCC) (facts at para.23–055, above) where it may be that they did not extend the award beyond the diminution in value ceiling: see *ibid.*, paras 328 to 342. While one is sympathetic to allowing such damages even should they exceed the diminution in value, it is thought that *Maud v Saunders* is right in disallowing the cost of the schedule of dilapidations. It may be that here section 18(1) has gone too far in its limiting of the damages recoverable.

CHAPTER 24

SALE OF SHARES AND LOAN OF STOCK

		PARA.
I.	BREACH BY SELLER	24–003
□	1. Non-delivery	24–003
	2. Other breaches	24–006
II.	BREACH BY BUYER	24–008
	1. Non-acceptance	24–008
	2. Other breaches	24–011
III.	BREACH BY LENDER	24–012

Insert a new paragraph after para.24–005:

Where the sale is of a shareholding in a company, whether the sale be of a **24–005A** tranche of the shares or be of all the shares and therefore effectively of the company itself, a different approach may be required as there may be no open market for the shareholding. Under a share option agreement with the defendant the claimant in *Plumbly v BeatthatQuote.com Ltd* [2009] EWHC 321, QB was entitled to buy a 10 per cent holding in the company but the defendant refused to allot the shares to him. In the claimant's action for damages for this breach of contract the value of the shares was arrived at by applying a multiplier of 1.2 to the figure for the company's annual revenue and then applying a 65 per cent discount to reflect the fact that the holding to which the claimant was entitled was a minority one: see *ibid.*, para.131 *et seq. Luxe Holding Ltd v Midland Resources Holding Ltd* [2010] EWHC 1908, Ch concerned a company which, having contracted to sell its shareholdings in 20 companies, largely incorporated in Russia or the Ukraine, to another company which broke the contract on finding another buyer, a company to which it resold the shareholdings at a higher price. *Luxe Holding* was not itself a claim for damages but an application by the initial buying company for a freezing of the selling company's assets in support of its damages claim—as well as in support of its proprietary and account of profits claims—and this effectively required the initial buying company to show that the proceeds of the resale would be likely to form the measure of damages. There being no open market for the shareholdings, Roth J. considered that at this very early stage of the proceedings it was entirely acceptable to take the resale price as evidence showing a good arguable case of the value of the shareholdings: see *ibid.*, para.57 *et seq.*, especially para.59. On this basis he was prepared to grant the requested freezing order.

CHAPTER 25

CONTRACTS TO PAY OR TO LEND MONEY

		PARA.
I.	BREACH BY PARTY PROMISING TO PAY	25–001
☐	1. Failure to pay money in general	25–002
☐	2. Dishonour of bills of exchange and promissory notes	25–011
II.	BREACH BY LENDER	25–028
III.	BREACH BY BORROWER	25–030

Insert a new paragraph after para.25–010:

25–010A *Cooper v National Westminster Bank Plc* [2010] 1 Lloyd's Rep. 490 is a case which may be introduced at this point as it involved a failure to pay over money in the form of a bank draft. A bank draft for an amount in euros which the claimant had requested his bank to issue in his favour was not delivered to him, but was cancelled, by the bank. The bank thereby made the foreign exchange profit which the claimant customer should have made, the rate of exchange between euro and sterling having moved in sterling's favour between the bank draft's issue and its cancellation. The damages were assessed by analogy to a claim for damages for non-delivery under a contract of sale of goods. This took the value at the time that the bank failed to deliver less the value at the time of issue, thereby giving the foreign exchange profit to the claimant: see *ibid.*, paras 82 to 89.

25–013 Insert a new note at the end of the paragraph:

NOTE 48a: One 21st century case has now appeared. However, not only, like all the 20th century cases, did it contain a foreign element but also the proper law was foreign. Accordingly in *Karafarin Bank v Mansoury-Dara* [2010] 1 Lloyd's Rep. 236 Iranian law had to be applied. For the dishonour of a number of very large cheques the claimant bank recovered the amount of the cheques together not with interest, prohibited under Iranian law, but with an amount calculated on an index reflecting the rate of inflation from cheque issue to judgment.

25–014 Insert a new note before "When some" on line 13 of the paragraph:

NOTE 52a: As was the case in *Karafarin Bank v Mansoury-Dara* [2010] 1 Lloyd's Rep. 236: facts at para.25–013, fn.48a, above.

25–022 NOTE 108: Insert after "Supreme Court Act" (and before "1981"):—now renamed the Senior Courts Act (see para.15–031, fn.111a, above)—

CHAPTER 26

BUILDING CONTRACTS

			PARA.
I.	BREACH BY BUILDER		26–004
	1.	Failure to build at all or in part	26–004
	2.	Delay in completing building	26–008
	3.	Defective building	26–011
II.	BREACH BY OWNER		26–022
	1.	Prevention resulting in non-completion	26–022
	2.	Prevention resulting in delay	26–025
	3.	Other breaches	26–026

Insert a new paragraph after para.26–006:

De Beers UK Ltd v Atos Origin IT Services UK Ltd [2010] EWHC 3276 **26–006A**
(TCC), [2011] B.L.R. 274 concerned a contract for information technology
suppliers to build and deliver a software system to a diamond trader where the
suppliers were in repudiatory breach of their contract so that no system was
provided by them to the trader. Edwards-Stuart J. held that the trader was entitled
to damages for the cost of upgrading its existing software system and the cost of
purchasing a new system elsewhere while at the same time being unprepared to
allow employee costs to the claimant trader. These software system costs were
allowed as it was accepted that the claimant had need for a new system but there
was no certainty that the claimant would acquire one see *ibid.*, para.342 *et seq.*
There is a hint here of the argument that had already succeeded in *Van der Garde
v Force India Formula One Team Ltd* [2010] EWHC 2373, QB: see paras
1–036A to 1–036D, above.

Insert in the text at the beginning of line 11 of the paragraph: What was termed **26–011**
the usual rule was applied in *Hall v Van Der Heiden* [2010] EWHC 586 (TCC)
so as to allow as damages the costs, which were not shown to be in any way
unreasonable, of putting right defective and incomplete performance by the
builder: see *ibid.*, paras 62 to 67.

Add at the end of the paragraph: In *Linklaters Business Services v Sir Robert* **26–011**
McAlpine Ltd [2010] EWHC 2931 (TCC) solicitors claimed for the faulty
installation by contractors of insulated air conditioning pipework in the solicitors' office premises, of which they were lessees, pipework which had become
extensively corroded on failure of the insulation. The solicitors had, on proper
expert advice, replaced the corroded pipework throughout the building, rather

than attempting a less costly remedial scheme for which the contractors contended, and were held by Akenhead J. to have acted wholly reasonably in so doing (his extended reasons are set out by him at *ibid.*, para.145), thereby entitling them to damages measured by the cost of replacement. *Skandia Property v Thames Water*, a tort case at para.34–006 of the main work, was distinguished: *Linklaters* para.146. In *Brit Inns Ltd v BDW Trading Ltd* [2012] EWHC 2143 (TCC) Coulson J. set out, with authorities, the proper approach to a claim for reinstatement costs (*ibid.*, paras 54 to 58), stating that, where the work was already done by trial, the actual costs were almost always the starting point in assessing what was reasonable and were particularly significant where carried out on professional advice, but holding that the claim before him had been grossly exaggerated.

26–013   NOTE 40: Add at the end of the note: It is true that the rule in *Sumpter v Hedges* has been widely, and rightly, criticised but the Court of Appeal in *Cleveland Bridge UK Ltd v Multiplex Constructions (UK) Ltd* [2010] EWCA Civ 139 considered that the case "remains intact and binding, at least for the moment": para.138. See the extended discussion around the case from *ibid.*, paras 82 to 140.

26–016   NOTE 62: Add at the end of the note: Where a fire was negligently caused by a sub-contractor, the question of how far damages were available to the developer owner if prevented by the fire from developing other properties was elaborately considered by Akenhead J., in the light of both the facts and very many legal authorities, in *Aldgate Construction Co Ltd v Unibar Plumbing & Heating Ltd* (2010) 130 Con. L.R. 190.

26–020   Add at the end of the paragraph: So we find that no damages were awarded at first instance in *Eribo v Odinaiya* [2010] EWHC 301 (TCC) for "the stress, inconvenience and overall unpleasantness" during the course of design and refurbishment works at the claimant's home which went badly wrong: see *ibid.*, paras 141 and 142. Yet, by contrast, recovery was allowed for distress as well as inconvenience, also as first instance, in *Hall v Van Der Heiden* [2010] EWHC 586 (TCC) (facts at para.13–029, above): see *ibid.*, paras 90 to 92.

CHAPTER 27

CONTRACTS OF CARRIAGE

		PARA.
I.	BREACH BY CARRIER	27–002
	(A) CARRIAGE OF GOODS	27–002
☐	1. Non-delivery including delivery in a damaged condition	27–002
☐	2. Delayed delivery	27–026
	3. Failure to carry or to carry to the right place	27–048
	(B) CARRIAGE OF PERSONS	27–055
	1. Injury and death in carriage	27–055
	2. Delay in carriage	27–056
	3. Failure to carry or to carry to the right place	27–058
II.	BREACH BY CARGO OWNER	27–060
☐	1. Failure to supply cargo	27–062
	2. Detention of the transport	27–075
	3. Damage to the transport	27–077

27–004 NOTE 21: Add at the end of the note: So too in *Exportadora Valle de Collina SA v AP Moller-Maersk A/S* [2010] EWHC 3224 (Comm) the difference between the sound arrived value of the goods and the actual arrived value was awarded: *ibid.*, para.188.

27–032 Add at the end of the paragraph: Where there is breach by shipowners resulting in delay in making the ship available to charterers for the loading of cargo (and with charterparties, whether of the voyage or time variety, it is the shipowner that is the carrier and the charterer that is the cargo owner: see para.27–001 of the main work), loss to the charterers from loss of a fixture, and the consequent loss of the profit from that fixture, have generally been held recoverable, and this result is not adversely affected by the House of Lords decision in *The Achilleas* [2009] 1 A.C. 61. This is made clear by the decisions in *ASM Shipping Ltd of India v TTMI Ltd of England, The Amer Energy* [2009] 1 Lloyd's Rep. 293 and *Sylvia Shipping Co Ltd v Progress Bulk Carriers Ltd* [2010] 2 Lloyd's Rep. 81: see the discussion on remoteness at paras 6–173A to 6–173G, above, especially at para.6–173F; contrast para.27–076 of the main work.

27–063 Insert a new note after "supply cargo." on line 7 of the paragraph:

NOTE 258a: For the position where, exceptionally in the context of breach of a contract to supply, the market rate is higher than the contract rate, see *Omak*

Maritime Ltd v Mamola Challenger Shipping Co [2011] 1 Lloyd's Rep. 47 at para.2–041A, above.

Insert a new paragraph after para.27–067:

27–067A   One of the issues which arose in *Zodiac Maritime Agencies Ltd v Fortescue Metals Group Ltd* [2011] 2 Lloyd's Rep. 360, where the charterer had repudiated a five-year voyage charter about a year after its commencement (and with charterparties, whether of the voyage or time variety, it is the shipowner that is the carrier and the charterer that is the cargo owner: see para.27–001 of the main work), was whether there was an available market so that, in the shipowner's claim for damages, the normal measure of contract rate less market rate, these rates here being expressed in terms of so many US dollars per day, could be applied. David Steel J. held on the facts that there was no available market: see *ibid.*, paras 56 to 61. Further issues concerning mitigation arising in consequence of this holding are dealt with at paras 7–118 and 7–125A, above, and for more on available market in the context of contracts of carriage see para.27–005 of the main work. In *Dalwood Marine Co v Nordana Line SA* [2010] 2 Lloyd's Rep. 315 there was again a premature wrongful termination of a charterparty by the charterers and, there being no available market in the relevant area, the shipowner sailed the ship to another location and delivered her pursuant to another charterparty which had a hire rate significantly higher than that under the breached charterparty. The importance of the case is that the arbitrators were held to have been right to take into account the earnings of the ship after the date on which she would have been notionally redelivered under the breach charterparty. On this basis the shipowner claimant had made a gain rather than a loss, entitling him to no damages. The case is seen from a mitigation angle at para.7–118, above. Also in *Glory Wealth Shipping PTE Ltd v Korea Line Corp* [2011] 2 Lloyd's Rep. 370, where a charterer's repudiation of a time charter took place when there was no market for the unexpired period of the charter but the market revived at a much later date, it was held that, mitigation apart (and mitigation was not an issue in the case: *ibid.*, para.28), the revived market rate was not to be taken in assessing the owners' damages, their actual loss forming the correct measure: *ibid.*, para.31.

CHAPTER 28

CONTRACTS OF EMPLOYMENT

		PARA.
I.	BREACH BY EMPLOYER	28–001
■	1. Wrongful dismissal	28–001
	2. Breach of obligation of trust and confidence	28–027
	3. Injury and death	28–029
□	4. Miscellaneous breaches	28–030
II.	BREACH BY EMPLOYEE	28–031
	1. Failure or refusal to work	28–032
	2. Careless or defective work	28–035
□	3. Miscellaneous breaches	28–036

Insert a new paragraph after para.28–023:

Johnson v Unisys was held to govern in *Edwards v Chesterfield Royal Hospital*   **28–023A**
NHS Foundation Trust [2012] 2 W.L.R. 55, SC. The claimant was appointed as consultant surgeon at a National Health Service hospital under a contract providing that either party could terminate it on three months' notice to the other, and providing expressly that the consultant was entitled to a formal disciplinary hearing where allegations of misconduct were made against him. He was wrongfully dismissed on the grounds of personal and professional misconduct and was on this account unable to obtain similar employment elsewhere. His claim was for damages for the defendant's failure to implement the contractual disciplinary procedure properly, arguing that but for this failure there would have been no finding of misconduct and therefore no dismissal. It was held by the Supreme Court that *Johnson* prevented the recovery of damages not only for loss arising from dismissal but also for loss arising from failures in the steps leading to dismissal even if these failures amounted to a breach of contract, unless the loss claimed could be regarded as occurring quite independently of the dismissal. This result was however a close thing, being arrived at by a bare majority of four Justices to three and by their reversing the Court of Appeal. *Botham v Ministry of Defence*, which was heard by the Supreme Court together with *Edwards*, was factually more in the employer's favour and the appeal in *Botham* was allowed by the court with only a single dissent.

NOTE 208: Add at the end of the note: Consequential losses by way of huge   **28–036**
losses on unauthorised speculative trading in aluminium futures were allowed in *Noble Resources SA v Gross* [2009] EWHC 1435 (Comm) for breach of employment contracts (there were also claims for conspiracy and in deceit which took more prominence): see *ibid.*, paras 222 to 227 and the case at para.40–024, below.

CHAPTER 29

CONTRACTS FOR PROFESSIONAL AND OTHER SERVICES

		PARA.
I.	BREACH BY THE PARTY ENGAGING THE SERVICES	29–002
II.	BREACH BY THE PARTY RENDERING THE SERVICES	29–003
☐	(A) IN GENERAL	29–003
	(B) PARTICULAR CATEGORIES	29–006
■	1. Solicitors	29–007
■	2. Surveyors and valuers	29–043
	3. Accountants	29–075
■	4. Bankers	29–076
	5. Stockbrokers	29–081
	6. Estate Agents	29–084
☐	7. Travel Agents	29–085

29–005   Add at the end of the paragraph: The claim in *Van der Garde v Force India Formula One Team Ltd* [2010] EWHC 2373, QB was against a company which owned and operated a Formula One motor racing team, the claim being for failure in breach of contract to provide services to a motor racing driver: facts at para.1–036A, above. The claim in *De Beers UK Ltd v Atos Origin IT Services UK Ltd* [2010] EWHC 3276 (TCC), [2011] B.L.R. 274 was in respect of a failure to construct and supply a computer software system which the trial judge categorised as a failure of services: facts at para.26–006A, above.

29–008   NOTE 38: Add at the end of the note: Solicitors' negligent advice was held by the Court of Appeal, reversing the judge below, to be causative of their client's pursuing of a claim against a third party in *Levicom International Holdings BV v Linklaters* [2010] P.N.L.R. 29, CA, p.566, but the question of loss was not addressed and the assessment of damages was remitted. The case therefore need not detain us.

29–008   Add at the end of the paragraph: In *Berry v Laytons* [2009] EWHC 1591, QB a solicitor failed to advise his client that his rights under EU legislation were far better than his rights under his employment contract. In the absence of this advice the employee came to an agreement with his employer, and in his ensuing claim for damages the solicitor was held liable for the employee's loss of the opportunity of doing a better deal than he had done.

Insert new paragraphs after para.29–008:

29–008A   Because the loss that occurred did not fall within the scope of the duty of solicitors in *Haugesund Kommune v Depfa ACS Bank* [2011] 3 All E.R. 655, CA, they were held not liable in damages for that loss. An Irish bank had entered into so-called swap contracts with two Norwegian municipalities, the practical effect of such contracts being to achieve a form of borrowing by the municipalities and of lending by the bank. The bank instructed solicitors to advise on whether the municipalities had the capacity to enter into swap contracts. The solicitors advised, wrongly and negligently, that there was capacity, also advising, correctly, that it was not possible for the bank to obtain execution in any form against the municipalities. The result of the contracts being ultra vires and void was that the apparent contractual obligation to repay the moneys advanced at various times in the future became a real restitutionary obligation to repay at once.

When some years after the conclusion of the contracts the truth became **29–008B** known, the municipalities, both of which had made disastrous investments with the moneys borrowed and were therefore very short of funds, declined to make any further payments under the contracts. The bank then claimed against its solicitors damages based on the moneys which it might no longer receive from the municipalities. The Court of Appeal, departing from the court below, held the solicitors not liable for the bank's loss as it fell outside the scope of their duty. The bank's claim against the municipalities would founder either on the municipalities' impecuniosity or on the municipalities' reliance on their immunity from execution risk, both of which risks—the credit risk and the no execution risk —lay squarely on the bank and not on the solicitors. As Rix L.J. put it, liability of the solicitors for the bank's loss could arise only if the municipalities were prevented from repaying the bank by something that arose from their legal incapacity and from the invalidity of the transactions, and there was nothing to indicate that this was so: see his whole discussion at *ibid.*, paras 73 to 87. Indeed the reality was that an equal, or even more than equal, claim had risen up in place of the claim in contract.

NOTE 52: Add at the end of the note: In *Joyce v Bowman Law* [2010] P.N.L.R. **29–012** 22, p.413 where, through the negligence of a licensed conveyancer advising the claimant, not a developer, on his purchase of a dilapidated cottage, the claimant failed to secure a buyer's option over adjacent land, the profit he would have made had he been able to develop the whole property to its fullest was allowed, although heavily discounted on loss of a chance principles (at para.8–091, above).

Insert a new paragraph after para.29–022:

In *Scott v Kennedys and Vertex Law* [2011] EWHC 3808, Ch a husband and **29–022A** wife bought a guest house and its associated business which they would not have bought but for their solicitor's negligent failure to inform them that the planning permission which had been given required the guest house and its adjoining, attached property to be in the same occupation. Vos J. in a full judgment considered many items of the claimed damages, this taking him to general principles involving remoteness, foreseeability and contemplation of the parties, and ended up awarding the claimants, who had eventually sold the property, their capital loss, thereby following and applying *Hayes v Dodd* (at para.29–012 of the main work).

29–027   Add at the end of the paragraph: A further case is *Tom Hoskins Plc v EMW Law* [2010] EWHC 479, Ch where damages were allowed for a company's trading losses which had not been avoided by reason of the negligent handling by its solicitor of the sale of its businesses.

29–028   Insert a new note after "that was lost;" on line 7 of the paragraph:

NOTE 106a: *Nahome v Last Cawthra Feather Solicitors* [2010] P.N.L.R. 19, p.352 is a further illustration of solicitors' negligent failure in breach of contract to renew a lease, here of protected business premises. The claimants maintained that the minimally profitable jewellery business which they ran from the premises would have developed into a highly successful largely internet-based business, and claimed the very large profits that it was alleged would have been made had the business not had to close down; the defendants argued for damages based on the value of the lease and retail business that had been lost, which came to a fairly small figure (*ibid.*, para.2). The trial judge embarked on a lengthy analysis of, among others, cases cited at this point in the main work (*ibid.*, paras 59 to 70) which took him to the somewhat uncertain conclusion that the appropriate way to compensate the claimants was by reference to the value of the business of which they had been deprived (*ibid.*, para.71). As for the internet business, since the defendants had not been made aware either of its existence or of its alleged dependence on the leasehold promises, profits which might have been made from it were held to be too remote, effectively applying the well-known *Victoria Laundry v Newman* [1949] 2 K.B. 528, CA (facts at paras 6–159 and 6–173 of the main work): see para.91 *et seq.* of *Nahome*.

29–038   Add at the end of the paragraph: Also, where in *Youlton v Charles Russell* [2010] EWHC 1032, Ch solicitors were negligent in failing to ensure that agreements between a company and the trustees of its pension scheme were not open to challenge on grounds of want of authority and conflict of interest, damages were to be assessed on the basis of the lost chance of the trustees enforcing their claims had the agreements been beyond challenge. However, no question of loss of a chance arose in *Martin v Triggs Turner Bartons* [2010] P.N.L.R. 3, p.29, where a power of advancement to a deceased's widow granted a life interest in residue was negligently drafted by the deceased's solicitors so as to apply only to £100,000 from the estate rather than to the whole of the estate except for £100,000. There was no loss of a chance because the widow suffered an immediate loss in that the value of the benefit she received was reduced: see *ibid.*, paras 73 and 74. The court's task was therefore the difficult one of valuing the widow's loss, a matter of quantification: see *ibid.*, paras 75 to 92.

NOTE 206: Add at the end of the note: See also the solicitor's negligence case **29–042** of *Herrmann v Withers LLP* [2012] EWHC 1492, Ch and the various issues arising therein, at paras 3–026, 7–091A and 17–019, above.

Insert a new note at the end of the italicised heading to paras 29–044 to **29–044** 29–055:

NOTE 207a: Occasionally there will be no contract between the purchaser and the valuer when the claim can only be in tort. *Scullion v Bank of Scotland Plc* [2011] P.N.L.R.5, p.68 was such a case but the Court of Appeal, reversing, has now held against tortious liability: [2011] 1 W.L.R. 3212, CA. The case is considered at paras 41–057A to 41–057D, below.

Insert a new note after the penultimate sentence of the paragraph: **29–052**

NOTE 265a: This was the result in *Scullion v Bank of Scotland Plc* [2011] P.N.L.R. 5, p.68 (facts at para.41–057B, below) where the claim was in tort only and there was an overvaluation of the property. *SAAMCO* was applied so as not to allow recovery for loss caused by a collapse in the market. (The Court of Appeal reversed on liability ([2011] 1 W.L.R. 3212, CA but does not touch on this point.) Similarly, in *Capita Alternative Fund Services (Guernsey) Ltd v Drivers Jonas* [2011] EWHC 2336 (Comm), where surveyors had negligently advised the purchasers of a shopping centre development as to its value and commercial prospects, *SAAMCO* was applied, limiting the damages to the difference between what the purchasers had paid and what they should have paid on the basis of correct advice and not extending the damages to all the business losses that followed purchase: see *ibid.*, paras 298 to 309. No deduction, however, fell to be made from these damages on account of the tax reliefs available on the purchase price to the investors in the trust which was the purchaser and claimant: *ibid.*, paras 310 to 313.

Insert in the text before the last sentence of the paragraph: In *Rubenstein v* **29–076** *HSBC Bank Plc* [2012] P.N.L.R. 7, p.151 the defendant was held to have given advice, negligently, to the claimant to invest in a form of bond which he would not have done but for the advice. Damages were however nominal as it was the general collapse of markets which caused the claimant's loss and which was unforeseeable at the time of the negligent advice. [Between completion of text and proof stage the Court of Appeal has reversed the trial judge on this, disagreeing with his approach, in the particular circumstances of the case, to cause, remoteness and foreseeability: [2012] EWCA Civ 1184.]

Insert a new paragraph after para.29–086:

In *Milner v Carnival Plc* [2010] 3 All E.R. 701, CA the Court of Appeal **29–086A** addressed the question of what is the correct measure of damages for a ruined holiday and the judgment of Ward L.J. on this—the only reasoned judgment given—deserves study. The ruined holiday was that of a husband and wife who had embarked on a cruise on a Cunard luxury liner. The host of county court decisions on ruined holidays appearing in *Current Law Yearbooks*, referred to in the main work's para.29–086, giving, as pointed out also in para.29–086, awards in the hundreds occasionally moving into the thousands and often in favour of a number of holiday makers, had been marshalled by counsel who were praised by Ward L.J. for their industry in producing up to 56 cases of this nature: *ibid.*, para.35. He said that "counsel's diligent analyses tend on the whole to show rather low awards": *ibid.*, para.37; see the various amounts of damages in the cases usefully set out by him there. In the result the Court of Appeal arrived at the much higher award of £12,000 (although this was a reduction of the trial judge's even higher £22,000), being £3,500 for the diminution in the value of the cruise, on the basis that there had been diminution by about a third of its value (*ibid.*, para.46), together with £4,000 to the husband and £4,500 to the wife for their inconvenience and distress (*ibid.*, para.60). This however must not be taken as a representative award for today. For Ward L.J. not only was careful to point out that each case presented different facts and different holiday features which would affect the damages awarded—see his useful analysis of types of holiday at *ibid.*, para.37—but also regarded *Milner* as an exceptional case (*ibid.*, para.52)—the cruise was billed in ecstatic terms as a legendary experience while for the claimants it was the unrepeatable holiday of a lifetime—calling for an exceptional award (*ibid.*, para.55). Nonetheless the impression gained from his judgment is that in the future awards are likely to be somewhat higher than in the few cases in the law reports and the many in the *Current Law Yearbooks*.

CHAPTER 30

CONTRACTS CONCERNING PRINCIPAL AND AGENT

		PARA.
☐	I. BREACH BY PRINCIPAL	30–002
	II. BREACH BY AGENT	30–005
	(A) Agents Employed to Enter into Contracts on behalf of the Principal	30–005
	1. Breach by failure to conclude the contract as instructed	30–006
	2. Breach other than by failure to conclude the contract as instructed	30–008
	(B) Agents Dealing with the Principal's Property	30–010

NOTE 8: Add at the end of the note: In *IRT Oil and Gas Ltd v Fiber Optic Systems Technology (Canada) Inc* [2009] EWHC 3041, QB a company that was the exclusive sales agent for another company recovered for its loss of profit on the principal's repudiation of the contract: facts at para.8–002C, above.   **30–003**

Add at the end of the paragraph: Where the estate agent claimants in *Nicholas Prestige Homes v Neal* [2010] EWCA Civ 1552 had a sole agency agreement with the defendant house owner who was in breach of the agreement by selling the house through another estate agent, the claimants were held entitled to their full commission as damages since the chance they had lost of selling the house was considered to be a certain one: *ibid.*, para.32.   **30–003**

Chapter 31

CONTRACTS OF WARRANTY OF AUTHORITY BY AGENT

		PARA.
1.	The contractual measure of damages	31–001
■ 2.	Warranty of authority to contract on the principal's behalf	31–003
3.	Other warranties of authority by an agent	31–017

31–007 Add at the end of the paragraph: The same result was arrived at in *Greenglade Estates Ltd v Chana* [2012] EWHC 1913, Ch where the defendant auctioneer sold without, as it turned out, authority long leasehold properties to the claimant consortium. The formula in *Suleman* was followed and applied by postponing the date of valuation of the properties for as long as the claimant was acting reasonably in trying to have the contract enforced. However, this was done only at the instance of counsel for both parties (*ibid.*, para.14), the trial judge expressing himself as finding serious difficulty in subscribing to the approach of the judge in *Suleman*, giving reasons for this which are not convincing and somewhat unclear (*ibid.*, para.12).

BOOK TWO

PART TWO

TORT

CHAPTER 32

TORTS AFFECTING GOODS: DAMAGE AND DESTRUCTION

			PARA.
I.	DAMAGE		32–003
■	1.	Normal measure	32–003
■	2.	Consequential losses	32–013
II.	DESTRUCTION		32–052
	1.	Normal measure	32–052
	2.	Consequential losses	32–058

NOTE 44: Add at the end of the note: In *Coles v Hetherton* [2012] EWHC **32–007**
1599 (Comm) (facts at para.32–021B, below) Cooke J. cited at length all of the
preceding cases in this paragraph of the main work to reach the conclusion that,
where a negligently damaged vehicle is repaired, the measure of the claimant's
loss is the reasonable cost of repair whether or not the repair has been effected,
since this measure is only a means of ascertaining the diminution in the value of
the vehicle: paras 15 to 42.

Insert a new note after the first sentence of the paragraph: **32–019**

NOTE 89a: The Court of Appeal in *Pattni v First Leicester Buses Ltd* [2011]
EWCA Civ 1384 has expressed a preference for the use of "basic hire rate" since
spot rate is a misnomer, being more appropriately applied to rates of freight or
charter hire or to the open market price of a commodity where the service or
commodity is for immediate rather than future delivery: *ibid.*, para.30(4).

NOTE 91: Add at the end of the note: In *McLaren v Hastings Direct*, **32–019**
unreported July 1, 2009, CC District Judge, the issue of no recovery for additional benefits and the issue of mitigation were sensibly kept separate so that, the
credit hire company hiring apart, the claimant was held to have hired at an
unreasonably expensive rate.

NOTE 94: Add at the end of the note (before the closing bracket): *Copley* was **32–019**
followed by the Court of Appeal, somewhat reluctantly, in *Sayce v TNT (UK) Ltd*
[2012] 1 W.L.R. 1261, CA: see para.7–068, above.

Add at the end of the paragraph: As to what constitutes impecuniosity H.H. **32–020**
Judge Mackie was prepared to hold impecunious for these purposes an actuary
living in a good part of London whose damaged car was an old Bentley but
whose finances were in a very poor state: see the judge's analysis of the

claimant's position at *ibid.*, paras 60 and 61. He was therefore held entitled to recover the credit hire charges in their entirety.

32–021 NOTE 105: Add at the end of the note: That *Bee* does not affect the House of Lords' holding in *Dimond* (for which see para.32–018 of the main work) is illustrated by *Wei v Cambridge Power and Light Ltd*, County Court unreported September 9, 2010 (see *ibid.*, paras 21 and 26) and to a degree by *W v Veolia Environmental Services* [2011] EWHC 2020, QB.

Insert new paragraphs after para.32–021:

32–021A The continuing saga in the contest between providers of credit hire cars and defendants in car accident claims has produced in *W v Veolia Environmental Services* [2011] EWHC 2020, QB yet another point requiring a solution. The claimant had entered into a credit hire agreement, with the hire charges being insured in the usual way, which agreement H.H. Judge Mackie held to be unenforceable against the claimant. This was not by reason of the provisions of the Consumer Credit Act, as in the controlling House of Lords' case of *Dimond* (see para.32–017 of the main work), but by reason of Regulations directed against agreements concluded at the hirer's home or place of work (held unenforceable following the somewhat earlier decision in *Wei v Cambridge Power and Light Ltd*, County Court unreported September 9, 2010). The crucial difference from *Dimond* (and indeed from *Wei*) was that here the credit hire charges had been actually paid to the credit hire company, not by the claimant himself but, as is usual in these cases, by his insurers. It was immaterial that it was the insurers that had paid over the money, and for tactical reasons, rather than the claimant himself. The essential point was that there would be no double recovery by the claimant since on receipt of the damages he would have to account to the insurers for them. However, because the insurers had, curiously, paid over the full hire charges despite their being a good deal higher than the insurance cover, the judge limited the recovery to the amount of that cover: see *ibid.*, para.40. The separate question of whether making the payment could be regarded as a failure to mitigate is considered at para.7–090A, above.

32–021B *Coles v Hetherton* [2012] EWHC 1599 (Comm) is a further case in this burgeoning corner of the law of damages. In *Coles* insurers indemnified the various owners of negligently damaged vehicles by having them repaired for them and then bringing subrogated claims in the names of the owners as the policyholders. The insurers were able to have the repairs done at a lower cost than the policyholders would have had to pay on the open market and the defendants, insurers for the tortfeasors, maintained that the lower cost to the claiming insurers should form the measure of damages. Cooke J. disagreed. He pointed out that it was the policyholder who had suffered the loss, that it was his asset that was diminished in value and that loss was suffered at the outset when the collision occurred and before any decision had been made about repair: *ibid.*, para.51.

On two new fronts in the long and continuing war between credit car hire **32–021C** companies and motor insurance companies were fought out two appeals, heard consecutively and leading to a single and very fully reasoned judgment of Aikens L.J. The first appeal, *Pattni v First Leicester Buses Ltd* [2011] EWCA Civ 1384, concerned interest. Under his contract with the credit car hire company the claimant was obliged to pay interest on the credit hire charges for the period between the end of the hire of the replacement car and the date when the claim against the defendant driver was finalised. The Court of Appeal decided that this contractual interest charge constituted the cost of an additional benefit to the claimant and was therefore not a recoverable loss on the reasoning of the majority of the House of Lords in *Dimond v Lovell* (for which see para.32–019 of the main work): *ibid.*, paras 50 to 63. Nor was interest recoverable as damages or under the statute, it having been a finding of fact that no interest had been paid: see *ibid.*, paras 64 to 70. This refusal to award interest on all three bases claimed was in affirmation of the two courts below.

The second appeal, *Bent v Highways and Utilities Construction* [2011] EWCA **32–021D** Civ 1384, concerned the method of determining the basic hire rate to which the claimant was entitled as damages, the Court of Appeal preferring the terminology of basic hire rate to that of spot rate (for the reason for this see para.32–019, fn.89a, above). Since it was accepted that it was reasonable for the claimant to have hired the particular make and model of the car that he did, the method to use was to find, on the evidence available, the basic hire rate for that car which had been hired on credit hire terms: see *ibid.*, paras 73 to 80. As the trial judge was considered not to have carried out this task properly (see *ibid.*, paras 80 to 85), the Court of Appeal decided for itself, coming up with a different figure (*ibid.*, para.86 *et seq.*)

Insert new paragraphs after para.32–044:

Beechwood Birmingham Ltd v Hoyer Group UK Ltd [2011] Q.B. 357, CA, the **32–044A** facts of which are set out at para.7–062A, above, is an important case in this area of damages. This is because it allows general damages to be awarded for loss of use not of a non-profit earning chattel but of a chattel which was profit-earning but which would not have been used for earning profits during the period of repair. The chattel was not one used for utility, like the harbour authority's dredger in *The Greta Holme*, the harbour authority's lightship in *The Mediana*, the town corporation's bus in *Birmingham Corp v Sowsbery*, but a motor car from the stock of a company of motor dealers. It is true that in *The Hebridean Coast*, where general damages for loss of use were again allowed to a non-profit earning claimant, there an electricity authority (all these cases are dealt with at length both in *Beechwood Birmingham* and in the main work at paras 32–038 to 32–051), Lord Reid said that he did "not proceed on any supposed distinction in principle between a profit-earning ship and a non-profit-earning ship", but the shipping cases, together with the corporation bus case, all had non-profit earning claimants. All this makes for *Beechwood Birmingham* being an important case. As for the computation of the damages which were allowed, this is dealt with at para.32–048A, below.

32–044B A distinction is however drawn in *Beechwood Birmingham* between claims by a company for loss of use of a car employed in the course of the company's business and claims by an individual owner of a car used solely for convenience and not for profit. It had already been said in *Alexander v Rolls Royce Motors*, as noted in the main work at para.32–044, that private cars were different from lightships, dredgers and corporation buses; the principles first developed in *The Greta Holme* and *The Mediana* (at para.32–038 *et seq.* of the main work) do not apply to private cars so that, where no substitute car is hired by the owner, there can be no recovery by him of general damages of a financial nature. This is now confirmed by the Court of Appeal, admittedly *obiter*, in *Beechwood Birmingham* on the basis that with the individual car owner there is no business loss that calls for compensation: see at *ibid.*, para.48. The distinction is therefore strictly not between the corporate claimant and the individual claimant but between the claimant with a business and the claimant without, so that the individual running a business using cars, either alone or in partnership, will be in the same position as to damages as is the equivalent company. The private car owner is, however, not denied all damages; his entitlement is dealt with at para.32–051A, below.

Insert a new paragraph after para.32–048:

32–048A *Beechwood Birmingham Ltd v Hoyer Group UK Ltd* [2011] Q.B. 357, CA (facts at para.7–062A, above) has extended the rule as to non-profit-earning ships, and buses, to cars which, though held for the generation of profit, are not in fact being used for profit at the time of the tortious damage (para.32–044A, above). Of the two methods for calculating the damages established for non-profit-earning ships, *viz.*, taking interest on capital and depreciation and taking the cost of maintenance and operation, the Court of Appeal preferred the former: *ibid.*, para.52. This is in marked contrast to Geoffrey Lane J.'s choice of the latter in *Birmingham Corp v Sowsbery* (at para.32–048 of the main work), a choice made for good reasons set out in a passage fully cited by the Court of Appeal in *Beechwood Birmingham*: *ibid.*, para.51.

Insert a new paragraph after para.32–051:

32–051A None of the above on the amount of general damages applies to private cars not used for profit, for the reason indicated in *Beechwood Birmingham Ltd v Hoyer Group UK Ltd* [2011] Q.B. 357, CA (see at para.32–044B, above). Instead, as is also indicated in *Beechwood Birmingham*, the private car owner should be entitled, by way of general damages for non-pecuniary loss, for, as it is put by the Court of Appeal, "the lack of advantage and inconvenience caused by not having the use of a car ready at hand and at all hours for personal and/or family use": *ibid.*, para.48.

Perusal of the *Current Law Yearbooks* had revealed to the Court of Appeal that county courts up and down the land have for some time been awarding modest sums along these lines, said to be £40 to £50 a week in 1995 rising to £100 per week in 2005: *ibid.*, para.49. While the Court of Appeal was not dealing with a private car owner in *Beechwood Birmingham*, it may be taken that it is confirming this approach of the county courts.

CHAPTER 33

TORTS AFFECTING GOODS: MISAPPROPRIATION

			PARA.
I.	INTRODUCTORY: AND IN PARTICULAR OF THE DEMISE OF DETINUE...		33–001
II.	CONVERSION		33–006
■	1.	Normal measure	33–006
☐	2.	Time at which value is to be taken: changes in the value of the goods	33–011
	3.	Place at which value is to be taken	33–042
☐	4.	Some special cases of value	33–043
☐	5.	Claimant with a limited interest in the goods	33–050
☐	6.	Consequential losses	33–066
☐	7.	Effect on damages of redelivery of the goods or their equivalent	33–074
☐	8.	Exemplary damages	33–081
III.	TRESPASS		33–083
IV.	WRONGFUL DISTRESS		33–088
	1.	Distress for rent	33–090
	2.	Other forms of distress	33–101
V.	REPLEVIN		33–102

33–006   NOTE 25: Add at the end of the note: In *Checkprice (UK) Ltd v Revenue and Customs Commissioners* [2010] EWHC 682 (Admin) the trial judge held the market value of the cider converted (facts at paras 33–009A and 33–009B, below) formed the proper measure of damages, and left the parties to try to agree it: *ibid.*, paras 51 to 53.

33–006   NOTE 29: Add at the end of the note: The fact that the parties in *Zabihi v Janzemini* [2009] EWCA Civ 851 may have envisaged a private sale of converted jewellery at a substantially higher price than the market value was neither here nor there: see *ibid.*, paras 42 to 44 and para.60 (facts at para.33–049A, below).

33–008   NOTE 38: Add at the end of the note: Conversion by seizure of two luxury cars led to an award of replacement cost in *Lightning Bolt Ltd v Elite Performance Cars Ltd*, November 2, 2011, unreported. This measure was described as the replacement cost of the value without warranty with a 12 per cent mark-up to reflect retail value.

33–008   Add at the end of the paragraph: In the absence of any other evidence of the market value of the two items of industrial plant and equipment converted in *Tanks and Vessels Industries Ltd v Devon Cider Co Ltd* [2009] EWHC 1360, Ch, it was ruled that the market value for which the company owning them could claim was to be taken as the value for which it could have disposed of them at

[130]

the time of their conversion (*ibid.*, para.58); the problem before the court lay in discovering what that value was (*ibid.*, paras 59 to 61).

Insert new paragraphs after para.33–009:

In *Jabir v HA Jordan & Co Ltd* [2011] EWCA Civ 816 the claimant, a dealer **33–009A** in pearls, had bought what was described as a remarkable pearl from another dealer for $500,000 and had sold it on to a third dealer for $650,000, agreeing with him to have it mounted in a ring. All three were experienced dealers in a trade where deals were done in confidence without documentation. To do the mounting the claimant took the pearl to the defendant specialists who proceeded to lose it. The Court of Appeal upheld the trial's judge's award of $650,000 in damages, preferring these practical views on market value of the three experienced traders who had all seen the very unusual pearl, and who were willing and informed buyers and sellers, over the substantially lower valuation views of the experts called in who had not seen the pearl.

Exceptionally, a claimant may find that the normal entitlement to damages **33–009B** based on market value falls away. This was so on the somewhat complex facts of *Checkprice (UK) Ltd v Revenue and Customs Commissioners* [2010] EWHC 682 (Admin). Revenue and Customs has power to detain goods for a reasonable period in order to investigate whether they are liable to forfeiture because customs duty has not been paid on them. If this is not established by the end of such reasonable period, Revenue and Customs has the option of returning the goods or exercising its power of seizure by commencing proceedings in the magistrates' court for an order that the goods should be forfeit. *Checkprice* involved quantities of alcoholic beverages held for sale by the claimant company which were taken by Revenue and Customs on suspicion that customs duty had not been paid on them. The beverages were detained for such a length of time that they passed their sell-by date or became infected so that they had to be destroyed. When the reasonable time for investigation was over, Revenue and Customs neither returned the beverages nor exercised its powers of seizure over them by starting the necessary court proceedings. At that point there was a conversion of the beverages.

Sales J. held that on a quantity of cider among the detained beverages the **33–009C** claimant was entitled to damages represented by the market value of the cider since it was established that duty had been paid, and paid at a time when the cider was still saleable, so that the powers both of detention and of seizure had come to an end. This aspect of the case is considered variously at paras 15–048 (interest) and 33–006, fn.25 (market value), above, and at para.33–066, fn.317 (consequential loss), below. As for the rest of the beverages there was no entitlement to market value as damages. This was because, it not having been established that customs duty had been paid on the beverages, the loss suffered by the claimant was the loss of the opportunity or chance to prove to the magistrates' court that duty had been paid, and since Sales J. took the view that the chance of doing so was speculative there was no loss for which compensatory damages could be awarded: *ibid.*, paras 56 to 62. The appropriate award was of nominal damages, conversion, though an action on the case, being nevertheless a tort actionable *per se*: *ibid.*, para.63.

33–011   NOTE 54: Insert after "Supreme Court Act" (and before "1981") on line 6 of the note:—now renamed the Senior Courts Act (see para.15–031, fn.111a, above)—

33–049   NOTE 247: Add at the end of the note: *Jabir v HA Jordan & Co Ltd* [2011] EWCA Civ 816 is another case where jewellery which could not be produced, here a very special pearl, had to be valued for damages, but the valuation issue was somewhat different: see the case at para.33–009A, above.

Insert a new paragraph after para.33–049:

33–049A   *Zabihi v Janzemini* [2009] EWCA Civ 851, where the need to ascertain the value of missing converted jewellery reappeared nearly three hundred years after *Armory v Delamirie*, has gone to the Court of Appeal. The claimant handed over to the defendant for the purposes of sale four sets of gold and diamond jewellery which the defendant converted by his failure to produce and account for them. The Court of Appeal considered that some limitations must be placed upon the principle in *Armory v Delamirie* and that for a variety of reasons it could not apply to the case before the court. Since both sides had given dishonest evidence as to the jewellery's value, any presumption against the defendant was, in the view of the Chancellor of the High Court, matched by an equal and opposite presumption against the claimant: *ibid.*, para.32; the claimant here was hardly in the same position as the boy chimney sweep in *Armory v Delamirie*. More importantly, the Chancellor thought that the principle could not be applied by reason of the factual difference between the two cases. He said:

> "In *Armory v Delamirie* the socket from which the stones had been removed was available to indicate the size of stone required to replace those taken. No doubt they testified to a range of values and the jury, as directed, took the top of the range. But . . . in this case there are no similar parameters, save that the jewelry [*sic*] comprised diamonds mounted in gold, by which the extent of the presumption may be restricted. Without such parameters an application of the principle would lead to little more than guesswork": *ibid.*, para.32.

Moore-Bick L.J. went further. He was rather unhappy with the decision in *Armory v Delamirie*, considering that the assuming of the existence of facts that are the most favourable to the claimant was difficult to reconcile with the indemnity principle and with the requirement that a claimant must prove his loss: *ibid.*, paras 50 and 51. He said:

> "It can, perhaps, be justified in a case where the defendant has wilfully suppressed evidence that would otherwise have been available to the claimant to enable him to prove his case, but I find it difficult to accept that that the ability to make the goods available for inspection is of itself sufficient for that purpose. In the absence of

evidence to the contrary, it would seem more logical to assume that the goods were of fair average quality rather than the best or worst of their kind": *ibid.*, para.51.

The third member of the court, Sullivan L.J., did not address the principle in *Armony v Delamirie*, merely saying that there was nothing that he could usefully add to the Chancellor's judgment in respect of this part of the defendant's appeal: *ibid.*, para.62.

Add a new note at the end of the paragraph: 33–065

NOTE 315a: This distinction derives some support from the complex *Blue Sky One Ltd v Mahan Air* [2010] EWHC 631 (Comm) where a whole raft of cases on recovery of damages by claimants with a limited interest were introduced by the defendants' counsel and commented upon by Beatson J. in an elaborate judgment. The case concerned the conversion by an Iranian airline, one of the defendants, of a number of aircraft which had been chartered to it. In reliance on the cases cited the defendants sought unsuccessfully to have the damages payable reduced on account of the claimants having a limited interest in the aircraft: see the discussion at *ibid.*, para.97 *et seq.* At the end of this discussion Beatson J. said (*ibid.*, para.115):

> "It is thus seen that the cases upon which the [defendants] have relied are not cases where damages were restricted because the claimants had a limited interest in the converted goods. The fundamental difference between them and the present case is that in the present case the [defendants] are not precluded from claiming the repayment of sums outstanding . . . "

NOTE 317: Add at the end of the note: Remoteness apart, the claimant has the   33–066
burden of proving that consequential loss has been suffered. This the claimant failed to do in *Checkprice (UK) Ltd v Revenue and Customs Commissioners* [2010] EWHC 682 (Admin) in respect of the conversion of cider for which there was an entitlement to compensatory damages: see the facts at paras 33–009B and 33–009C, above.

Add at the end of the paragraph: Yet after having considered in some detail the   33–067
above authorities of *Kuwait Airways* and *Strand Electric*, the trial judge was surely wrong in *Tanks and Vessels Industries Ltd v Devon Cider Co Ltd* [2009] EWHC 1360, Ch to refuse an award, either on a damages basis or a restitutionary basis, to the claimant company for loss of use of its industrial plant and equipment converted, being so persuaded by her drawing of some in this context irrelevant distinctions between conversion and the former detinue and between the claimant electing for redelivery and electing for damages: see the judgment at *ibid.*, paras 62 to 67.

Insert a new note after "of the goods," on line 5 of the paragraph: 33–074

NOTE 388a: This is also the position where there has been redelivery to the claimant before any action by him has been brought, as in *Kani v Barnet LBC*

[2010] EWCA Civ 818 where the claimant's cars were seized by the defendant borough council but eventually returned to him. He claimed that he could have sold the cars during the period of their detention before the market fell but was unable to prove this: see *ibid.*, para.31 *et seq.*

33–082   NOTE 427: Add at the end of the note: This interpretation is now to be made statutory: see para.11–031, above.

CHAPTER 34

TORTS AFFECTING LAND

			PARA.
☐	I.	DAMAGE	34–003
■		1. Normal measure	34–003
☐		2. Consequential losses	34–023
		3. Prospective loss	34–031
		4. Claimant with a limited interest	34–034
☐		5. Aggravation and mitigation; exemplary damages	34–040
☐	II.	OCCUPATION AND USER	34–042
■		1. Normal measure	34–044
☐		2. Consequential losses	34–052
		3. Prospective loss	34–053
☐		3A. The interrelation of these various measures of damages	34–058A
		4. Claimant with a limited interest	34–059
☐		5. Aggravation and mitigation; exemplary damages	34–062
☐		6. The statutory action	34–067

Insert a new note before "but separate" on line 4 of the paragraph:

34–001   NOTE 1a: This was so at first instance in *Network Rail Infrastructure Ltd v Conarken Group Ltd* [2010] EWHC 1852 (TCC), a claim in trespass and nuisance as well as negligence, but the Court of Appeal ([2011] EWCA Civ 644) dealt only with the negligence claim: facts at para.34–023A, below.

34–005   Insert in the text before the last short sentence of the paragraph: In the claim in *Bole v Huntsbuild Ltd* (2009) 127 Con. L.R. 154, CA for the defendant's breach of statutory duty under the Defective Premises Act 1972 by the construction of badly designed foundations for the claimant's house which rendered it uninhabitable, the Court of Appeal upheld the trial judge's award covering the cost of remedying all of the defects and damage to the house attributable to the badly designed foundations; this amounted to foreseeable loss well within the damage contemplated by the statute. The Court of Appeal would have nothing of the defendant's argument that the award should have been limited to covering only that which was necessary to render the house fit for habitation: *ibid.*, para.36 *et seq.*

34–006   Insert a new note at the end of the paragraph as it stands:

NOTE 25a: *Skandia* was distinguished in *Linklaters Business Services v Sir Robert McAlpine Ltd* [2010] EWHC 2931 (TCC), a contract case at para.26–011, above.

34–006   Add at the end of the paragraph: *Harrison v Shepherd Homes Ltd* [2012] EWCA Civ 904 was a claim under the Defective Premises Act 1972 by owners of houses on an estate built by the defendant which suffered significant cracking as a result of defective piling. At first instance the judge concluded that it was not reasonable to award the cost of reinstatement by the re-piling of the houses as this cost would exceed the value of the houses in their undamaged state. Instead, he awarded diminution in value together with the cost, appropriately discounted, of two sets of remedial works over the next 20 years. The defendant's appeal on the judge's calculation of the diminution in value and on whether there was double counting in awarding diminution in value and remedial costs as well was unsuccessful.

34–016   Insert a new note at the end of the heading immediately before this paragraph:

NOTE 76a: That the damages are generally the same in nuisance and in negligence is illustrated by *Network Rail Infrastructure Ltd v Conarken Group Ltd* [2010] EWHC 1852 (TCC) at first instance, the Court of Appeal ([2011] EWCA Civ 644) dealing only with negligence: facts at para.34–023A, below.

34–016   Add at the end of the paragraph: And when it came to the damages assessment in *Dobson v Thames Water Utilities Ltd* [2011] EWHC 3253 (TCC), the class action by claimants suffering over many years from smells from the defendant's works (facts at para.34–022A, below), the claimants with a proprietary interest in the land affected were held entitled to recover the cost of de-odourisers and fans purchased to overcome the nuisance: see the details at *ibid.*, para.1018.

34–019   NOTE 103: Insert at the beginning of the note: In *Berent v Family Mosaic Housing* [2012] EWCA Civ 961 the Court of Appeal confirmed that the general damages for having to live in a house structurally damaged were intended to provide modest, not generous, compensation: *ibid.*, paras 39 and 40.

34–019   Insert in the text at the end of the penultimate sentence of the paragraph: In *Barr v Biffa Waste Services Ltd* [2011] 4 All E.R. 1065 damages were claimed in nuisance by over 150 households on account of the smell from pre-treated waste coming from the defendant's landfill site. While the claims all failed as the defendant's user was held to be reasonable and therefore not a nuisance (*ibid.*, para.582) and, this apart, while practically all of the household claims would have failed as the smell was not shown to have exceeded a permissible threshold (*ibid.*, para.583), any household which could prove that for it the threshold had been exceeded would have been held entitled to £1,000 per annum for loss of enjoyment of the property (*ibid.*, para.584 as explained in paras 542 to 559), there being no diminution in value of any of the properties.

34–019   Add at the end of the paragraph: In *Simmons v Castle* [2012] EWCA Civ 1039, in addition to adopting the recommendation of the Jackson Report that the level of personal injury general damages should be increased by 10 per cent (the details of this development are set out at para.35–287A, below), the Court of Appeal, again following Jackson, declared that from April 1, 2013 the increase of 10 per cent should also apply to all torts causing suffering, inconvenience or distress (see *ibid.*, para.20 together with para.14). Nuisance is the only applicable tort, other than the tort of defamation, specifically mentioned by the Court of Appeal (*ibid.*, para.20); it is also specifically mentioned in the Jackson Report (recommendation 10). [In the judgment in the further hearing of *Simmons v Castle* [2012] EWCA Civ 1288, just out (for details see para.3–030, fn.172a, above), the Court of Appeal has extended its ruling to all civil claims and to all types of non-pecuniary loss: see the court's conclusion at *ibid.*, para.50.]

Insert new paragraphs after para.34–020:

In *Dobson v Thames Water Utilities Ltd* [2009] 3 All E.R. 319, CA it was   **34–020A**
emphasised by the Court of Appeal that it was damage to the land and not damage to the person that was the essence of recovery in nuisance. Interference with the claimant's enjoyment of his property is the gist of the claim here; it is the proprietary loss of amenity not the personal loss of amenity, as in personal injury claims, for which the damages are awarded. This was said in the context of a class action brought by some with a proprietary interest in land and some without (facts of the case are at para.34–022A, below) and explained why only the former were successful in the nuisance claim. From this it would seem to follow that, when land is owned in joint names by two or more, the nuisance award should be only for the total loss of the amenity of enjoyment of the land rather than for the personal loss of amenity of each joint owner.

Whereas in nuisance the damages for the non-pecuniary loss have tended to be   **34–020B**
assessed by reference to precedent and to the amounts awarded in preceding cases (as illustrated in the authorities at para.34–019 of the main work), when in the Dobson case it came to the damages assessment before Ramsey J. in *Dobson v Thames Water Utilities Ltd* [2011] EWHC 3253 (TCC), he preferred for the non-pecuniary loss to use an alternative method and, in the many claims before him, to go on the basis of the notional, as opposed to the actual, diminution in value due to the loss of amenity. He assessed percentage reductions in rental value year by year to take account of the loss of amenity caused by the nuisance, the percentages used by him running from 5 per cent down to 1.25 per cent: see *ibid.*, para.1019 *et seq.*, especially paras 1020 and 1032. (Ramsey J. in a later hearing of *Dobson*, at [2012] EWHC 986 (TCC), had also to deal with the awarding of interest: see for this paras 15–049 and 15–134A, above.) The same approach had been taken in *Lawrence v Fen Tigers Ltd* [2011] EWHC 360, QB so as to award as damages the notional diminution in the value of residential property resulting from a nuisance by the noise of racing cars from a nearby stadium and track: see at *ibid.*, paras 310 to 323. Here the court relied for this approach on what had been said by Waller L.J. (at para.33) in the earlier Court of Appeal hearing of *Dobson* (which see at para.34–020A, above).

34–020C   The question of whether there can be recovery in nuisance for personal injury appeared, somewhat tangentially, in *Jones v Ruth* [2012] 1 W.L.R. 1495, CA, another case of a dispute between neighbours in adjoining properties. The claimants were two women living together in a house adjacent to that of the defendant. The development of his property on which the defendant embarked caused excessive and persistent noise and vibration, took four years rather than one to complete, involved an invasion of the adjoining property to achieve a further storey for the defendant's own building, and all this with no consideration given to the two neighbouring women to whom the defendant acted throughout in a bullying and unpleasant manner; the details of the appalling behaviour are graphically listed by the trial judge in his findings on nuisance (see at *ibid.*, para.9). In the appeal to the Court of Appeal nuisance was hardly touched upon as the appeal turned on the question of harassment. One of the women claimants had suffered psychiatric injury causing her a loss of earnings for a number of years and the Court of Appeal held, departing from the trial judge, that she could recover for her lost earnings in her harassment claim and without the need to show negligence. As for nuisance, there had been no difficulty in allowing the claimants damages for loss of amenity and loss of enjoyment of their property, but the trial judge had refused recovery for the loss of earnings apparently on the basis that the law is that recovery for personal injury cannot arise out of nuisance, and the Court of Appeal, though citing this remark of the trial judge, did not comment on it: see *ibid.*, para.22. It is considered that the remark goes too wide and that, if the personal injury and its financial and other consequences are attributable to the enjoyment, or lack of enjoyment, of property, damages should be recoverable. It may be noted that the authorities appear to have accepted that damages for injury to health are allowable: see para.34–019 of the main work.

Insert a new paragraph after para.34–022:

34–022A   The interaction of damages for infringement of human rights and damages for nuisance was considered again by the Court of Appeal in *Dobson v Thames Water Utilities Ltd* [2009] 3 All E.R. 319, CA. The claimants who were occupiers of properties in the vicinity of the defendant's sewage treatment works complained that they were affected by odours and mosquitoes from the defendant's negligent operation of those works. A class action was brought, by occupiers with and occupiers without a proprietary interest alike, claiming common law damages for nuisance and damages for breach of Art.8 of the Human Rights Act, the defendant being a public authority. It was to be expected that only those with a proprietary interest succeeded in nuisance. As for a claim under Art.8 by one with a proprietary interest, which he had an entitlement to make, the Court of Appeal thought that his obtaining of an award for the nuisance would render it most unlikely that any further award for him under Art.8 would be held to be needed in order to achieve just satisfaction. As for the position of those without a proprietary interest they would be more likely to succeed in obtaining damages under an Art.8 claim. Nevertheless the award in nuisance to the head of a household who had a proprietary interest in the premises lived in would, in the court's view, be relevant in assessing whether damages were necessary to ensure just satisfaction to those living in the same household. *Dobson* in its human rights aspect is considered in the chapter on that topic, at para.43–027B, below.

Insert new paragraphs after para.34–023:

The paucity of authority on recovery of loss of profits where there has been   **34–023A**
damage to land received a boost in the Court of Appeal's decision in *Conarken Group Ltd v Network Rail Infrastructure Ltd* [2011] EWCA Civ 644. Road drivers employed by the defendants had inflicted damage to the railway tracks of Network Rail, the claimant, causing severe disruption of rail services, thereby disabling Network Rail from making the affected sections of track available to the companies operating the trains. Network Rail generates its revenue by making the rail network available to these companies for a fee. It is at the same time liable to make payments to these companies in respect of periods when the rail network is unavailable to them. Such payments are made under provisions in the contracts between Network Rail and the companies and represent a net loss of revenue for Network Rail. The Court of Appeal, affirming the judge below, held Network Rail entitled to claim this loss from the defendant tortfeasors.

It was argued by the defendants that a loss in the form of a liability to make   **34–023B**
these payments to the train operating companies was too remote to be recoverable and not within the scope of their duty. The defendants' liability should be limited to the immediate consequences of the physical damage and should not go beyond the cost of repairing the track and the loss of revenue attributable to the unavailability of the track. There should be no liability in respect of the compensation payments under the contracts with the train operating companies, payments which were calculated by reference to an agreed formula that took into account the effect of the disruptions on the public's confidence in the service and its preparedness to travel by rail, and which represented very substantial loss to the train operating companies going well into the future. This argument did not prevail. The defendants could undoubtedly foresee that financial damage would result from the loss of the use of the tracks and it did not matter, in relation to remoteness, that they did not know how the loss would be made up or the extent of the loss or the precise manner in which the loss would come about.

It was also argued by the defendants, and also unsuccessfully, that, since they   **34–023C**
were not parties to the contracts between Network Rail and the train operating companies, the contracts could not bind them to pay the compensation amounts set out in what was similar to a liquidated damages clause which should be confined in its effect to the contracting parties themselves. While it is true that a claimant cannot impose liabilities on a tortfeasor simply by making an agreement with others, it was not in dispute that here there was a genuine, careful and reasonable pre-estimate of the financial loss that the train operating companies would suffer from disruption of the rail services and that the compensation payments represented the best assessment that could be made of the commercial

damage done to them. It was therefore appropriate for the court to utilise the agreed compensation payments for the assessment of the damages payable to Network Rail.

34–040   Insert a new note at the end of the paragraph:

NOTE 224a: No aggravated damages were awarded in the nuisance case of *Lawrence v Fen Tigers Ltd* [2011] EWHC 360, QB (facts at para.34–020B, above) as the defendants' conduct was eventually considered not to have justified them: see the very lengthy examination of the evidence at *ibid.*, paras 247 to 299.

34–041   NOTE 234: Add at the end of the note: No exemplary damages were awarded in the nuisance case of *Lawrence v Fen Tigers Ltd* [2011] EWHC 360, QB (facts at para.34–020B, above) as motivation for profit on the part of the defendants was not made out: see at *ibid.*, paras 300 to 309.

34–042   NOTE 237: Add at the end of the note: See also the complicated case of *Ramzan v Brookwide Ltd* [2012] 1 All E.R. 903, CA at paras 34–058A to 34–058K, below.

34–044   NOTE 246: Add at the end of the note: Mesne profits for trespass by occupiers holding over after notice to vacate were awarded in *London Development Agency v Nidai* [2009] 2 P. & C.R. DG23.

34–044   Insert in the text before "If the rental" on the last line but three of the paragraph: *Ramzan v Brookwide Ltd* [2012] 1 All E.R. 903, CA (at paras 34–058A to 34–058K, below) is similar to *Horsford v Bird* (at para.34–044 of the main work) in that there was no mandatory injunction to restore the expropriated property to its rightful owner with the result that there was a claim for damages representing its value in addition to the claim for mesne profits. Indeed it was said at first instance in *Ramzan*, [2011] 2 All E.R. 38, that deliberate mis-appropriation of property was so rare that counsel had found no case of it other than *Horsford v Bird*.

34–044   Add at the end of the paragraph: The Court of Appeal in *Earlrose Golf & Leisure Ltd v Fair Acre Investments Ltd* [2009] EWCA Civ 1295 emphasised that the correct approach to determining rental value is by reference to comparables, and the master's award was substantially reduced by the court on account of his reliance on inappropriate and unsuitable rentals: see para.37 *et seq*. *Seeff v Ho* [2011] EWCA Civ 186 was a dispute between neighbouring householders where the defendants built an extension slightly encroaching over the claimants' property without decreasing its value and possibly—it is nowhere stated—without increasing the value of the defendants' property. The Court of Appeal moved up the trial judge's award of damages from £200 to £500 but the basis of this award is not made at all clear in the only reasoned judgment of Thomas L.J: see at *ibid.*, paras 44 to 46. Mesne profits were not mentioned.

Add at the end of the paragraph: Again in *Stadium Capital Holdings v St* **34–051** *Marylebone Properties Co Plc* [2010] EWCA Civ 952, where the trespass arose from the defendant's advertising hoarding intruding into the airspace of the claimant's land, the Court of Appeal accepted that the damages should be awarded on a restitutionary basis but regarded this as generally meaning a hypothetical licence fee for the trespasser's occupation of the land. The judge was considered wrong, in the circumstances of the case, to have thought in terms of awarding all of the defendant's gains; this amounted to an account of profits. The case was sent back for a reassessment which it fell to Vos J. to make in *Stadium Capital Holdings (No.2) Ltd v St Marylebone Properties Co Plc* [2011] EWHC 2856, Ch. On damages Vos J. started from the position that the parties were in agreement that a hypothetical licence fee was the appropriate way of going about the assessment (*ibid.*, para.56) and that what was in dispute concerned the factors to be taken into account in arriving at the hypothetical licence fee. Vos J. proceeded to conduct a useful review of the relevant authorities (*ibid.*, paras 57 to 68) and concluded that, in the light of the claimant's holding the trump card of being able to stop the defendant's retention of the hoarding in its place, the hypothetical licence fee should be half of the expected net revenue that the defendant would receive from a particular advertiser. A further case of an advertising hoarding encroaching on to the claimant's land went to the Court of Appeal, H.H. Judge Seymour below having awarded only nominal damages. The defendants in *Enfield London Borough Council v Outdoor Plus Ltd* [2012] EWCA Civ 608 did not own the land upon which the advertising hoarding was erected but had entered into a licence agreement with a Mr Shah entitling them to erect it on his land. The hoarding was duly erected on that land but inadvertently it was built with its steel supports extending over the boundary of Mr Shah's land on to waste land belonging to the claimant. This marginal invasion of the claimant's land did not come to light for several years. H.H. Judge Seymour had awarded nominal damages on the ground that, had the parties appreciated the position before erection, no trespass would have occurred as the hoarding would have been built wholly within Mr Shah's land. The Court of Appeal rightly saw this as the wrong approach to the damages question. What mattered was that the trespass had occurred and it was necessary to ascertain the value of the benefit to the defendant of that trespass, which was the function of the hypothetical negotiation (*ibid.*, para.47), the court being in no doubt that the hypothetical negotiation approach was the right one to adopt (*ibid.*, para.53). The court then turned to what, in place of nominal damages, should be awarded. Split ownership of the site used for an erection being unprecedented in the authorities, the Court of Appeal accepted the evidence of the joint expert in the case that it was likely that the licence fee would be split evenly between the parties, here the claimant and Mr Shah.

Insert new paragraphs after para.34–051:

Modern technology has produced in *Bocardo SA v Star Energy UK Onshore* **34–051A** *Ltd* [2011] 1 A.C. 380 a dramatic variant on the prolific 19th century cases of unauthorised mining (at para.34–045 of the main work), cases which started off this whole chapter of damages authorities. The defendant company in the construction of oil wells entered the substrata beneath the surface of the claimant company's land at 800 to 2,900 feet below ground level and, despite the fact that the entry was at such a very great depth, it was held to constitute a trespass. Yet the case does not take the law further on the damages front as the parties were agreed that damages assessed on user are based on the negotiated price for the grant of a licence, and because the main argument on quantum revolved around the assessment of compensation under statute. Lord Clarke set out at some length how he saw the law as having developed in this area: *ibid.*, paras 118 to 124; but there is nothing new in what he said. In particular, no mention is made of whether the damages at common law are to be regarded as compensatory or as restitutionary.

34–051B   Much more valuable is the Court of Appeal's decision in *Shi v Jiangsu Native Produce Import & Export Corp* [2010] EWCA Civ 1582 where the interrelation of compensatory damages and restitutionary damages in the context of mesne profits was again in issue. A claim for arrears of salary by an employee against the company employing him was met by a counterclaim of the company for mesne profits in respect of the employee's occupation of a house for over five years after his licence to occupy it rent-free as an employee of the company had been terminated by notice, after which termination the employee, as the trial judge held, became a trespasser.

34–051C   On his treatment of the counterclaim, which was by way of a cross-appeal, the trial judge was roundly reversed by the Court of Appeal. He had made no award by way of damages because he had assumed, wrongly, that the company's counterclaim was on a restitutionary basis. He then had made a nil award by way of restitution because of exceptional circumstances which he held, again wrongly, subjectively devalued the benefit to the employee of occupying the premises to the extent of eliminating it. These exceptional circumstances were that the employee was an employee of the company, had lived in the house rent-free, believed that he had a right to occupy it and may have had nowhere else to move to, and that the company had long delayed claiming possession and was a foreign company that had wound up its domestic operations.

34–051D   Dyson L.J., whose judgment was the only one to deal with the counterclaim and cross-appeal, pointed out that the counterclaim was clearly pleaded as a claim for damages and held that the company was entitled to damages by way of mesne profits based on the rental market value of the house because that amount represented the company's loss: *ibid.*, para.23. While this disposed of the company's cross-appeal, and in its favour, Dyson L.J. sought to indicate what should have been the decision of the trial judge had the counterclaim indeed been advanced on a restitutionary basis. Dyson L.J. rightly saw none of the factors listed by the trial judge as being exceptional circumstances, so that there was no basis for treating the value to the employee of the benefit of occupation as being less than the rental market value: *ibid.*, paras 25 and 26. The decisions in *Ministry of Defence v Ashman* and the similar *Ministry of Defence v Thompson* (at para.34–048 of the main work) were very much to the fore, both at first instance and in the Court of Appeal, and Dyson L.J. specifically referred to Hoffmann L.J.'s saying in the former case that the value of the right of occupation to a former licensee who has occupied at a concessionary rent is not in itself a special, or exceptional, circumstance though it may become one when taken in conjunction with the fact that the occupant has no choice but to stay in the premises until he or she is rehoused in cheaper accommodation: *ibid.*, para.25. That was not however the employee's position here; he could have moved to alternative accommodation had he been so minded.

34–051E This useful decision of the Court of Appeal thus accepts that it is now recognised that recovery for mesne profits may be on a damages basis or on a restitution basis and that whether the one route or the other is pursued lies in the election of the party claiming. In addition, it affords an illustration of the situation where recovery will be the same on either basis, and also an illustration of the situation where either recovery will be of rental market value because that constitutes the loss to the landowner and the benefit to the trespasser. The decision further indicates that there is only limited scope for reduction of the value of the benefit to the trespasser by way of subjective devaluation.

34–051F *Jones v Ruth* [2012] 1 W.L.R. 1495, CA involved a dispute between neighbouring occupiers where one of them was in the process of making alterations to his own building. Here the Court of Appeal corrected the trial judge's award where by trespass and nuisance the defendant had added an extra storey to his building (facts at para.34–020B, above). The trial judge awarded the amount by which the value of the defendant's property had been increased, the Court of Appeal unsurprisingly held this to be wrong and made its own award. Patten L.J. in the one reasoned judgment went along the now familiar route of the hypothetical negotiated licence and came up with one third of the increased value of the defendant's property: see his reasoning at *ibid.*, paras 39 to 41. Nothing was said of either mesne profits or restitutionary damages.

34–052 Insert in the text after "tipping soil" on line 10 of the paragraph: Where in *Ramzan v Brookwide Ltd* [2012] 1 All E.R. 903, CA the claimant, barred by the defendant's expropriation of his flying freehold from using the first floor of his restaurant had lost profits, recovery was allowed him for many years of restaurant profits. This curious and difficult case is given extended consideration at paras 34–058A to 34–058K, below.

34–055 Add at the end of the paragraph: So too in *HKRUK II (CHC) Ltd v Heaney* [2010] EWHC 2245, Ch, where again a right to light had been infringed, a mandatory injunction was awarded but a computation of damages was also made, the trial judge taking into account a number of factors to reach £225,000 as the amount that he considered right for the hypothetical licence between the dominant and servient owners.

Insert a new heading and new paragraphs after para.34–058:

3A. THE INTERRELATION OF THESE VARIOUS MEASURES OF DAMAGES

34–058A   The extremely complicated case of *Ramzan v Brookwide Ltd* is best considered in relation to all the measures of damages dealt with in paras 34–044 to 34–058 of the main work, that is to say, normal measure of damages, damages for consequential losses and damages for prospective loss. It needs to be examined both at first instance, [2011] 2 All E.R. 38, and in the Court of Appeal, [2012] 1 All E.R. 903, CA, the judgments in the Court of Appeal having appeared only the day before the cut-off date for this Supplement. Arden L.J. opened her leading judgment by calling it a remarkable case (*ibid.*, para.1) while Lloyd L.J. spoke of its unusual features (*ibid.*, para.90) and Tomlinson L.J. of its very unusual facts (*ibid.*, para.100). Nonetheless, it deserves very careful analysis in the light and context of the principles and authorities set out and discussed in the previous paragraphs of the main work.

34–058B   Two adjoining buildings belonged, the one to an individual who ran a restaurant in his building, and the other to a financially powerful company which was in the process of converting its building into several flats. By way of a so-called flying freehold the restaurateur owned a store room on the first floor of the company's building. Access to this store room was from, and only from, the first floor part of the restaurant, the store room also providing access to a fire escape which ended up at the back of the restaurateur's building. By trespass the company, acting in a high-handed and highly unpleasant manner, incorporated the store room into its building in order to provide extra space for the flats it was constructing, at the same time knocking down the fire escape. By these actions of the company the use of the first floor part of the restaurant was barred since there was no longer available to it a fire escape as was required by regulations.

34–058C   There is a further complication which should be mentioned although it need not detain us as the damages are only marginally affected by it. Some two years after the expropriation by the company the restaurateur transferred building and restaurant to his son. This was by way of gift. Accordingly, while the father had made a claim against the company on other matters concerned with the expropriation, it was the son who was the claimant against the company in the litigation with which we are concerned.

34–058D   The expropriated store room having for a good many years before the trial formed part of one of the flats constructed and let out by the defendant company in its building, it was highly unlikely that a mandatory injunction returning the store room to the claimant would be ordered. Indeed this was declined by the trial judge, Geraldine Andrews QC, and on this there was no appeal. The case therefore as to damages became one where the principles and authorities considered at paras 34–053 to 34–058 of the main work apply. The authorities here generally concern invasions of another's property as by infringement of a right to light or a right of way and damages tend to be based upon the fee that could have been extracted had permission been requested. However, with outright expropriation which the court is not prepared to reverse, a hypothetical licence fee does not seem appropriate and the Privy Council in *Horsford v Bird* [2006] UKPC 3 had already shown the way in such a case by awarding as damages the value of the expropriated land, *Horsford* being the only other known case, according to the trial judge in *Ramzan*, where there has been expropriation of property without a mandatory injunction for its return. And in addition *Horsford* held that there was a clear claim to mesne profits for the use of the land up until the time that judgment in the case gave the value of the land in lieu of an injunction.

By far the greatest loss to the claimant was the loss of profits from running the **34–058E** restaurant. This was clearly caused by the defendant's tort and, subject to proof, must be recoverable. It is worth noting that loss of profits, apart from loss of mesne profits stemming from the tort, relate to property other than the property directly affected by the tort, whether trespass, nuisance or other wrong. This is true not only of *Ramzan* but of such earlier cases as there are, which are collected at para.34–052 of the main work. Such losses can thus properly be categorised as consequential.

In the discussion in the main work it is pointed out that the authorities are **34–058F** moving towards allowing mesne profits, and also damages beyond mesne profits where there is no mandatory injunction, on either the compensatory or the restitutionary basis: see paras 34–044 to 34–051 and paras 34–053 to 34–058 respectively. Here if the claimant can show the defendant's gains to be greater than his losses as enumerated above, he can go down the restitutionary route. These two approaches to the awarding of damages being necessarily alternative, at some point the claimant must elect between the two.

Turning to the award of the trial judge, in relation to the three items of **34–058G** damages considered in the preceding paragraphs, she awarded, in rounded figures:

1. £55,000 as the store room's capital value and £23,000 in mesne profits;
2. £225,000 for nine years of restaurant profits;
3. £20,000 as the rent from the flat which incorporated the expropriated store room.

In addition, she awarded £72,000 for restoring the fire escape destroyed by the defendant and made awards of exemplary damages and of interest which are considered elsewhere in the Supplement. She further ordered that the sum for rent of the defendant's flat should be set off against the sum for mesne profits in order to avoid double recovery.

34–058H   The second item of damages awarded was obviously on a compensatory basis and the trial judge made it clear in her judgment that she regarded her award for the first item of damages as also being on a compensatory basis (see [2011] 2 All E.R. 38, Ch at paras 36, 41 and 42). In these circumstances it would seem that the right thing to do was simply to ignore the third item of damages as representing a restitutionary alternative to the other two items of damages rather than to award the third item of damages followed by a deduction of the amount of it from the mesne profits awarded in the first item of damages. The reason for this seemingly odd approach was that in the trial judge's earlier judgment on liability she had found the defendant to be a trustee of the expropriated property so that there was not only a claim in tort but also one for breach of trust, and it was for this breach of trust that the third item of damages was being awarded, although, it should be noted, it was exactly the same profits that were to be accounted for in the breach of trust claim as the trial judge would have awarded had she been awarding restitutionary damages. That such was the position helps to explain why the trial judge felt obliged to make the award for the profit from the flat and then deduct the amount awarded from her mesne profits award. This was an unfortunate complication which has not troubled any of the earlier cases in the field and hopefully will not have to be grappled with again in the future.

34–058I   While all three members of the Court of Appeal rightly paid tribute—their very words ([2012] 1 All E.R. 903, CA, paras 28, 90 and 100)—to the judgment of the trial judge, they nonetheless reduced her total award in a number of respects. They were content with the award of lost restaurant profits, (subject to a small reduction of six months' profit to allow time for the claimant son to re-establish the first floor part of the restaurant: see *ibid.*, para.41 together with para.34–058C, above) but when it came to the first item of damages—the capital value of, and the mesne profits from, the store room—the Court of Appeal made a massive reduction to the mesne profits and it is thought would have done the same with the capital value had it not been precluded both by the parties' experts at first instance having agreed £55,000 to be the capital value, which is why it was awarded by the trial judge ([2011] 2 All E.R. 38, paras 17 and 18) and by there being no appeal on the capital value issue ([2012] 1 All E.R. 903, CA, para.29). The reduction of the mesne profits figure was based essentially on the fact that, the trial judge's figure stemming from what the store room on its own was worth to the defendant (see [2011] 2 All E.R. 38, para.32), the award smacked of restitutionary damages rather than the compensatory damages —which of course included the lost restaurant profits—that the claimant was claiming. The parties now having agreed a comparatively small sum for the market value of the store room as a store room, the Court of Appeal's figure for mesne profits came out at just a little over £1,000: [2012] 1 All E.R. 903, CA, para.46.

Even this much-reduced figure the Court of Appeal was not prepared to allow **34–058J**
the claimant. This refusal could be misconceived. Arden L.J. and also Lloyd L.J.
said that since the claimant needed the store room for access to the fire escape he
could not let it out ([2012] 1 All E.R. 903, CA, paras 67 and 95 respectively).
This fails to take account of the host of authorities, appearing in the main work,
that it is irrelevant that the claimant would not, or could not, have let out or
otherwise used the property. Arden L.J. added here that she saw as the predominant element the reversal of the defendant's benefit from using the store
room, but this would amount to restitutionary damages and this was not how the
mesne profits damages were being claimed. Still the amount being so small, the
point is of little consequence in the context of the case. And it may be noted at
this point that the Court of Appeal was right to remove the trial judge's award for
the rebuilding of the fire escape. As Lloyd L.J. put it at *ibid.*, para.97, how could
the claimant claim to have lost the cost of rebuilding within the expropriated
property once he has recovered its capital value.

There remains the award of £20,000 made for breach of trust which, as we **34–058K**
have seen, is the same amount as the trial judge would have awarded had she
been awarding restitutionary damages. It was no longer possible to avoid double
recovery by a deduction of the £20,000 from the mesne profits awarded in the
first item of damages as the amount had fallen from £23,000 to a mere £1,000.
The Court of Appeal had therefore to turn to the award for lost restaurant profits
to make an appropriate adjustment ([2012] 1 All E.R. 903, CA, para.47). Had the
£20,000 award been for restitutionary damages it would have been quite easy to
eliminate it as inconsistent with the much larger compensatory award for lost
profits, but it took Arden L.J. through a lengthy analysis (*ibid.*, paras 49 to 64)
to reach the clearly correct conclusion that the claim for breach of trust and the
claim for loss of profit were also not cumulative but alternative and inconsistent
remedies, thereby removing the award for breach of trust from the scene. As said
at para.34–058H, above, it is to be hoped that this breach of trust complication
can now be put to rest and not appear again.

Insert a new note after "unscrupulous landlords" on line 2 of the **34–063**
paragraph:

NOTE 330a: The eviction was not by the landlord in *Islam v Yap* [2009]
EWHC 3603, QB; aggravated and exemplary damages were awarded as well as
damages based on the claimant's rental rate.

NOTE 367: Add at the end of the note: The Court of Appeal held the trial **34–071**
judge to be entirely right to refuse mitigation of the damages where the point was
not taken in the defence, in correspondence, at the trial, or indeed anywhere at
any time before the appeal: *Kalas v Farmer* [2010] H.L.R. 25, CA, p.420.

CHAPTER 35

TORTS CAUSING PERSONAL INJURY

			PARA.
I.		FORMS OF AWARD AND OF COMPENSATION	35–003
☐	1.	Interim awards	35–004
■	2.	Provisional awards	35–006
☐	3.	Periodical payments awards	35–008
II.		CERTAINTY OF LOSS	35–033
	1.	Changes before the decision of the court of first instance	35–036
	2.	Changes before the decision of the appeal court	35–045
	3.	Changes after the litigation has ended	35–054
■ III.		HEADS OF DAMAGE: FUNCTION AND INTERRELATION	35–055
	1.	Function	35–056
	2.	Interrelation	35–058
IV.		LOSS OF EARNING CAPACITY AND RELATED BENEFITS	35–061
■	(A)	GENERAL METHOD OF ASSESSMENT	35–065
	(B)	CALCULATION OF THE MULTIPLICAND AND OF THE MULTIPLIER	35–074
☐		1. Diminution in earnings: the basic factor for the multiplicand	35–074
☐		2. Earnings of different categories of person	35–078
☐		3. Adjustments for variation in annual earnings loss	35–094
		4. Period of years of claimant's disability: the basic factor for the multiplier	35–100
		5. Adjustments where life expectancy is cut down by the injury	35–103
■		6. The appropriate discount rate for the multiplier	35–117
■		7. Adjustments to the multiplier for contingencies	35–133
		8. No specific adjustments for unearned income	35–144
		9. No specific adjustments for inflation	35–146
		10. Adjustments for taxation	35–147
	(C)	THE DEDUCTIBILITY OF COLLATERAL BENEFITS	35–150
		1. Insurance moneys	35–151
		2. Wages, salary, sick pay	35–153
		3. Pensions	35–155
☐		4. Gratuitous payments privately conferred	35–160
		5. Monetary social security benefits	35–163
		6. Social security benefits other than monetary	35–183
V.		MEDICAL AND RELATED EXPENSES	35–185
	(A)	EXPENSES INCLUDED	35–185
■		1. Medical expenses	35–185
■		2. Related expenses	35–198
☐	(B)	GENERAL METHOD OF ASSESSMENT	35–212
	(C)	THE DEDUCTIBILITY OF COLLATERAL BENEFITS	35–224
		1. Insurance moneys	35–225
☐		2. Payments under obligation by private third parties other than insurers	35–226
☐		3. Payments made gratuitously by third parties	35–227
☐		4. Care provided gratuitously by relatives and others	35–228
		5. Monetary social security benefits	35–239
☐		6. Social security benefits other than monetary	35–247
VI.		NON-PECUNIARY DAMAGE	35–258
	1.	A conventional award	35–258
	2.	Heads of non-pecuniary damage	35–259
■	3.	Various aspects of non-pecuniary award	35–272

   4. Level of awards.. 35–279
VII. ENVOI: THE PARTICULAR CASE OF CLAIMS BY PARENTS ARISING OUT
   OF THE BIRTH OF THEIR CHILDREN.. 35–288
   1. Setting the scene 35–288
   2. Developments before *McFarlane v Tayside Health Board* 35–291
   3. The new thinking: *McFarlane v Tayside Health Board*.................................. 35–294
   4. The new thinking extended: *Rees v Darlington Memorial Hospital NHS Trust* ... 35–295
   5. The position today 35–300
   6. Addendum: issues of avoided loss... 35–307

NOTE 11: It may not always be possible to have an interim payment sufficient to acquire alternative accommodation, whether special or not, as in *Mabirizi v HSBC Insurance (UK) Ltd* [2011] EWCA Civ 1280, QB. **35–004**

NOTE 16: Add at the end of the note: The practice which developed has had to be modified to accommodate the periodical payments regime along the lines set out by the Court of Appeal in *Eeles v Cobham Hire Services Ltd* [2010] 1 W.L.R. 409, CA. **35–005**

Insert a new note before "More precisely" at the end of line 6 of the paragraph: **35–006**

NOTE 16a: In *Kotula v EDF Energy Networks (EDN) Plc* [2011] EWHC 1586, QB the claimant was awarded provisional damages allowing him to return for a further lump sum should his condition substantially worsen while retaining the right to seek, in the same eventuality, to have his periodical payments varied upwards. In *Woodward v Leeds Teaching Hospitals Trust* [2012] EWHC 2167, QB there was held to be a real risk of the claimant's condition deteriorating disastrously so as to allow an award of provisional damages in respect of part of her personal injury claim.

Insert a new note after "Supreme Court Act" (and before "1981") on line 7 of the paragraph: **35–006**

NOTE 16b: Now renamed the Senior Courts Act: see para.15–031, fn.111a, above.

NOTE 18: Insert before "Provisional damages" on line 4 of the note: By contrast, *Willson* was applied so as to allow a provisional award to be made in *Kotula v EDF Energy Networks (EDN) Plc* [2011] EWHC 1586, QB. **35–006**

NOTE 38: Add at the end of the note: In *Morton v Portal Ltd* [2010] EWHC 1804, QB there is a valuable consideration of the operation of the various matters and factors that a court is required to take into account in deciding whether or not to make a periodical payments order: see *ibid.*, paras 10 to 22. The claimant favoured periodical payments for his future care and the defendant had no objection to this. Walker J. rightly rejected the approach that, if a claimant of full age and capacity, which the claimant was, wished to have a periodical payments order, this was conclusive in its favour. The matter was for the court which must **35–015** be satisfied that a periodical payments order was in the claimant's best interests. Walker J. also rightly rejected the suggestion that, if the claimant and the defendant were agreed on a periodical payments order, a periodical payments order should follow; against this was the requirement that the court had to be satisfied that continuity of payment was secure. Nonetheless, independently of these considerations, Walker J. was satisfied that a periodical payments order was appropriate (see *ibid.*, para.22), in coming to which conclusion he expressed himself as further satisfied that the 25 per cent deduction for contributory negligence, which was a feature of the case, would not present too great a difficulty for the claimant: see *ibid.*, para.12.

35–030   NOTE 99: Add at the end of the note: In *Kotula v EDF Energy Networks (EDN) Plc* [2011] EWHC 1586, QB, the claimant, in addition to having the right, should his condition substantially worsen, to seek to have the periodical payments awarded him varied upwards, was awarded provisional damages allowing him, in the same eventuality, to return for a further lump sum.

35–055   Insert a new note at the end of the paragraph:

NOTE 197a: The Judicial Committee of the Privy Council, allowing the appeal in *Patel v Beenessreesingh* [2012] UKPC 18, saw the Court of Appeal of Mauritius as having got it wrong with every single head of damage.

35–065   Insert a new note before "Further adjustments" on the last line but three of the paragraph:

NOTE 255a: In many cases it will be necessary to have separate multiplicands and multipliers for the earnings which the claimant would have made but for the injury and the earnings which he can make after the injury. A good illustration is afforded by *XYZ v Portsmouth Hospitals NHS Trust* [2011] EWHC 243, QB (facts at para.8–077A, above) where there is dealt with separately the claimant's loss of future earnings (*ibid.*, para.42 *et seq.*) and his residual earning capacity (*ibid.*, para.221 *et seq.*).

35–070   Substitute for "their sixth edition in 2007" on line 7 of the paragraph: their seventh edition in 2011.

35–077   NOTE 320: Substitute for "[2009] 2 W.L.R. 351 CA" on line 3 of the note: [2009] A.C. 1339, CA

35–077   NOTE 320: Substitute for "[2009] 3 W.L.R. 167 HL" on line 5 of the note: [2009] A.C. 1339

35–078   NOTE 325: Substitute a comma for "and" on the last line, and add at the end, of the note: , *Appleton v El Safti* [2007] EWHC 631, QB, *Collett v Smith* [2009] EWCA Civ 583, *Clark v Maltby* [2010] EWHC 1201, QB and *XYZ v Portsmouth Hospitals NHS Trust* [2011] EWHC 243, QB.

NOTE 427: Add at the end of the note: and *Conner* further at para.35–139, **35–099**
fn.580, below.

Insert new paragraphs after para.35–132:

The Lord Chancellor's discount rate, set at 2.5 per cent in 2001 and still with   **35–132A**
us in 2012, does not apply in Guernsey, our Damages Act 1996 not extending to
the Channel Islands. Instead the common law stemming from *Wells v Wells*
[1999] 1 A.C. 345 applies and the Privy Council in *Simon v Helmot* [2012]
UKPC 5 has upheld the award of the Guernsey Court of Appeal to a young man
with very grave injuries, using a rate of 1.5 per cent for his earnings-related
losses, being his own earnings and his carers' earnings, and a rate of 0.5 per cent
for costs that were not earnings-related, presumably being such items as transport
costs and accommodation costs. This 0.5 per cent was arrived at by first taking
the 1.25 per cent rate of return then current in Guernsey on index-linked
securities, reducing this to 1 per cent for the incidence of tax, and reducing
further to 0.5 per cent on account of the extent that inflation was higher in
Guernsey than in the United Kingdom. The minus 1.5 per cent was then achieved
by taking the 0.5 per cent and reducing it by 2 per cent to mark the extent that
earnings inflation was higher than price inflation. The court was aware that today
the position is reversed, certainly in the United Kingdom, with price inflation
greater than earnings inflation, but their Lordships relied on the strong unchal-
lenged evidence that over the long term the annual average works out at 2 per
cent, though with considerable fluctuations from year to year: *ibid.*, paras 64
(Lady Hale), 84 (Lord Clarke) and 108 (Lord Dyson). Of course, once one is into
minus figures, it is inapt to speak of the rate as a discount rate and, while Lord
Dyson was content with "negative discount" though accepting that the term was
somewhat odd (*ibid.*, para 118), Lord Hope, who gave the leading judgment with
which the others agreed, preferred to describe the exercise simply as a process of
adjustment (*ibid.*, para.14).

This dramatic decision, while it does not apply to us who are hemmed in by   **35–132B**
the discount rate that the Lord Chancellor has decreed, does nonetheless indicate
that it is high time that he should set a new discount rate, and indeed should think
of setting two discount rates as it is clear that in *Simon v Helmot*, and most other
cases where the injuries are very grave, the great bulk of the damages for future
financial loss is in respect of the earnings-related losses. There was talk of this
happening soon after the Privy Council's decision was handed down early in
March of this year but nothing has yet appeared. A Government Consultation
Paper has now appeared, calling for responses by late October 2012. This hardly
seems necessary and simply leads to more delay.

NOTE 563: Substitute for "6th edn (2007)": 7th edn (2011).   **35–135**

NOTE 570: Substitute for "6th edn (2007)": 7th edn (2011).   **35–136**

35–139   Substitute for "is introduced in the latest and sixth" on line 2 of the paragraph: was introduced in the sixth and is repeated in the current, seventh.

35–139   NOTE 577: Substitute for "the 6th edition (2007)": the 7th edition (2011).

35–139   NOTE 578: Substitute for "the 6th edition (2007)": the 7th edition (2011).

35–139   NOTE 580: Add at the end of the note: As for *Conner v Bradman* itself, it is thought that by splitting the difference between the discount for the non-disabled and that for the disabled H.H. Judge Coulson QC may, for reasons which cannot be gone into here, have gone too far in favour of the defendant. In *Connery v PHS Group Ltd* [2011] EWHC 1685, QB where the claimant was disabled by the injury, H.H. Judge Platts said he was adopting the approach taken in *Conner v Bradman*. In *XYZ v Portsmouth Hospitals NHS Trust* [2011] EWHC 243, QB (facts at para.8–077A, above) the difference between the non-disabled and disabled discounts was again split in circumstances where the trial judge thought it was a borderline decision as to whether the claimant met in full the criteria for disability set out in Ogden: *ibid.*, paras 229 to 233. The correct application of the new Ogden discounts based on disability when it comes to assessing the degree of discount appropriate in a case of a disability which is only partial needs the attention of the Court of Appeal.

35–141   NOTE 587: Delete the second sentence of the note.

35–141   NOTE 590: Substitute for "the 6th edition (2007)": the 7th edition (2011).

35–185   Insert a new note before "The only condition" on line 7 of the paragraph:

NOTE 794a: While it is clear that credit must be given for expenditure which a claimant would have incurred if the injury had not happened and which he will no longer incur, it was sensibly held by Edwards-Stuart J. in *Sklair v Haycock* [2009] EWHC 3328, QB, in the absence of authority, that no deduction should be made in respect of gratuitous care that the claimant had been receiving before the injury except to the extent that expenditure had been incurred by the carer: see *ibid.*, paras 86 to 92.

35–188   Insert a new note before "principally because" on line 3 of the paragraph:

NOTE 807a: Where a settlement has been reached under which the tortfeasor does fund private care but only from a date somewhat into the future, it is improper and wrong for the NHS to withdraw nursing care from the patient claimant in advance of that date: *R. (on the application of Booker) v NHS Oldham* [2010] EWHC 2593 (Admin).

35–188   Add at the end of the paragraph: In *XYZ v Portsmouth Hospitals NHS Trust* [2011] EWHC 243, QB (facts at para.8–077A, above) Spencer J. said that he was satisfied, indeed sure, that the claimant would use private medical facilities and purchase private medication, so that the sums claimed were recoverable. Indeed he went further and held, although, as he said, there was no need for him to do so, that in the claimant's very unfortunate circumstances it was entirely reasonable for him to go private: see *ibid.*, paras 33 to 41. In *Woodward v Leeds Teaching Hospitals Trust* [2012] EWHC 2167, QB H.H. Judge Stuart Baker held that on all the evidence, while the claimant had for the years up to trial relied on the NHS for care, it was more likely than not that when she had the means, which a damages award would give her, she would have her medical treatment provided on a private basis (*ibid.*, para.56).

NOTES 857a, 857b, 857c and 857d: Substitute for [2009] LS Law Med. 229 **35–197** CA in each note: [2010] Q.B. 48, CA.

Insert a new note before "especially as" on the last line but 2 of the **35–197** paragraph:

NOTE 857dd: Edwards-Stuart J. accepted in *Sklair v Haycock* [2009] EWHC 3328, QB that *Peters* had changed the law: see *ibid.*, paras 78 and 79.

NOTE 916: Add at the end of the note: In *Whiten v St George's Healthcare* **35–206** *NHS Trust* [2011] EWHC 2066, QB the defendant argued unsuccessfully that, where the parents of the child claimant moved with him into the property acquired for him in order, naturally, to look after and care for him, there should be a deduction for the capital value of the property which the parents would have had in any event. Otherwise, it was said, the family would be living free of charge in the claimant's home. Swift J. said she found this a difficult issue (*ibid.*, para.464); her full discussion of it and of the authorities bearing on it (*ibid.*, paras 458 to 472) is valuable.

Add at the end of the paragraph: In the application for an interim payment in **35–206** *Oxborrow v West Sussex Hospitals NHS Trust* [2012] EWHC 1010, QB (facts at para.35–211, below) the defendant argued before Tugendhat J. that the claimant's accommodation needs could adequately be met by renting rather than purchasing. However, in the absence of any authorities going down the renting path (though a note of a judgment unreported on this issue was provided to the court after the case was concluded: see *ibid.*, para.49) and in view of the practical difficulties connected with the renting solution (*ibid.*, paras 11 and 12), Tugendhat J. saw no likelihood of the final judgment including an assessment of damages based on renting accommodation for the claimant (*ibid.*, para.30).

Add at the end of the paragraph: In *Oxborrow v West Sussex Hospitals NHS* **35–211** *Trust* [2012] EWHC 1010, QB the claimant was so catastrophically injured at birth that he was expected to live only to the age of 21. In these circumstances, in an application for an interim payment on account of damages to provide suitable accommodation for the claimant, his counsel argued that *Roberts v*

[153]

Johnstone should not apply in view of the multiplier being small on account of the shortness of the claimant's life and that the solution suggested in this paragraph (see the main work) should be adopted: *ibid.*, paras 9 and 44. Since Tugendhat J. was prepared to award the interim payment asked for—to get to this result a whole range of figures which it is difficult adequately to comprehend appear in the judgment at *ibid.*, paras 23 to 31—he was able to avoid taking a decision on counsel's argument. While he was not prepared to express a view, he said that he thought that there was considerable force in the argument: *ibid.*, para.47.

35–221   Add a note at the end of the paragraph:

NOTE 972a: In *Whiten v St George's Healthcare NHS Trust* [2011] EWHC 2066, QB there were computations for three care periods for the young claimant (*ibid.*, para.179 *et seq.*) but the annual sums arrived at were ordered to be paid by periodical payments.

35–223   NOTE 986: Add at the end of the note: *Smith v LC Window Fashions Ltd* [2009] EWHC 1532, QB has now followed *Crofts v Murton* and again applied Table 1 rather than Table 28, the trial judge adopting, in order to show that there was no double counting, the same unconvincing distinction between years of life remaining to the claimant and years by which the claimant's life has been reduced: see the judgment at paras 40 to 43. So too in *Whiten v St George's Healthcare NHS Trust* [2011] EWHC 2066, QB Swift J., after a useful, extended discussion of the arguments and authorities involved (*ibid.*, paras 87 to 104), applied Table 28 in preference to Table 1.

35–232   Add at the end of the paragraph: The Civil Law Reform Bill 2009 proposed substituting for a trust a personal obligation. However, the Bill's proposals on damages have all been abandoned as thought by the Government not to be vote-catching. The details of this particular proposal are at this paragraph in the First Supplement to the 18th edition.

Insert a new paragraph after para.35–232:

35–232A   The authorities dealt with so far have all concerned, naturally enough, care provided by family members. Now in *Drake v Foster Wheeler Ltd* [2011] 1 All E.R. 63, QB recovery has been allowed for the palliative care provided gratuitously by a charitable hospice foundation to a man dying from much earlier contact with asbestos. The man having died, the claim was by the estate, but since the estate was suing in respect of the damage suffered during the deceased's lifetime, the case is clearly relevant at this point. The trial judge rightly took the view that recovery for gratuitous care was not confined to care given by family members: see *ibid.*, para.31 *et seq.*

Add at the end of the paragraph: The Civil Law Reform Bill 2009 proposed **35–234** substituting for no recovery a limited recovery by the tortious gratuitous carer. However the Bill's proposals on damages have all been abandoned as thought by the Government not to be vote-catching. The details of this particular proposal are at this paragraph in the First Supplement to the 18th edition.

Add at the end of the paragraph: So too in *Manning v King's College Hospital* **35–236** *NHS Trust* [2008] EWHC 3008, QB the trial judge, after a very lengthy discussion of the authorities and the arguments of counsel (*ibid.*, paras 82 to 103), discounted by 20 per cent.

NOTE 1150a: Substitute: [2010] Q.B. 48, CA. **35–257**

NOTE 1232: Substitute for "9th edn (2008)": 10th edn (2010) [With a new **35–274** edition eventually coming out in late September, now substitute: 11th edn (2012)]

Insert a new note after "sex abuse" on line 8 of the paragraph: **35–277**

NOTE 1251a: Aggravated damages are now being awarded in personal injury claims for dreadful sex abuse without the need for a claim in assault: *BJM v Eyre* [2010] EWHC 2856, QB; *RAR v GGC* [2012] EWHC 2338, QB. The reason that the Court of Appeal did not award aggravated damages in the personal injury case of *C v Flintshire County Council* (in this paragraph in the main work) is because they do not seem to have been claimed.

Insert a new note before "entitled *Guidelines*" on line 2 of the paragraph: **35–280**

NOTE 1260a: The name of the Judicial Studies Board has now been changed, rather curiously, to the Judicial College. It is understood that its future publications will come out under the new name. [The new edition eventually coming out in late September does incorporate this new name, by way of *Judicial College Guidelines.*]

Substitute for "ninth edition of 2008" on line 6 of the paragraph: tenth edition **35–280** of 2010 [With a new edition eventually coming out in late September, now substitute: eleventh edition of 2012]

Insert a new note before "Its aim is explained" on line 6 of the paragraph: **35–280**

NOTE 1260b: An eleventh edition is due out in 2012 but it will not be in time for treatment in this Supplement. Whether it will incorporate in its figures the effect of the Court of Appeal's ruling that tortious damages for non-pecuniary loss are soon to be increased by 10 per cent (see *Simmons v Castle* at para.35–287A, below) is not known. [The new edition eventually coming out in late September refers to but does not incorporate the 10 per cent increase.]

35–280   Insert a new note after "is there" on line 10 of the paragraph:

NOTE 1260c: Very occasionally, as in *Woodward v Leeds Teaching Hospitals Trust* [2012] EWHC 2167, QB, the injury may not feature in the *Guidelines* because of its rarity (*ibid.*, para.180).

35–280   Insert a new note after "personal injury claims" in the last line but 2 of the paragraph:

NOTE 1261a: The *Guidelines* will not always pinpoint a figure, or a range of figures, so that the Court of Appeal in *Steele v Home Office* [2010] EWCA Civ 724, in reopening the trial judge's award for seven years of toothache endured in prison, made its assessment by reference only to the general framework of damages for personal injury: see *ibid.*, paras 44 to 52.

35–280   Insert a new note at the end of the paragraph:

NOTE 1261b: For awards without reference to the *Guidelines* to four children who had been subjected to sustained and serious sexual abuse throughout their childhood (awards primarily for the non-pecuniary loss but including sums for pecuniary loss), see *ABB v Milton Keynes Council* [2011] EWHC 2745, QB.

35–281   NOTE 1267: Add at the end of the note: In *Sadler v Filipiak* CA, October 10, 2011, unreported, where the claimant had suffered multiple injuries, the Court of Appeal varied the trial judge's award, after conducting a review of each of the individual amounts as assessed by him and pointing out that to be reasonable compensation for the totality of the injury the global aggregate need not be a sum of the parts.

35–287   Substitute for "ninth edition of 2008" on line 6 of the paragraph: tenth edition of 2010 [With a new edition eventually coming out in late September, now substitute: eleventh edition of 2012]

35–287   Substitute for "£206,750 to £257,750" on the last line but 3 of the paragraph: £212,500 to £265,000 [With a new edition eventually coming out in late September, now substitute: £232,000 to £288,500]

35–287   Substitute for "£180,000 to £257,750" on the last line but 2 of the paragraph: £185,000 to £265,000 [With a new edition eventually coming out in late September, now substitute: £201,500 to £288,500]

35–287   NOTE 1274: Substitute for "(2008)": (2010) [With a new edition eventually coming out in late September, now substitute: (2012)]

Insert a new paragraph after para.35–287:

35–287A   In *Simmons v Castle* [2012] EWCA Civ 1039 the Court of Appeal has declared that from April 1, 2013 the level of general damages for pain, suffering and loss of amenity should be increased by 10 per cent: *ibid.*, para.20. This adopts the recommendation made as one in the package of reforms appearing in the Jackson Report on Civil Litigation Costs, to the implementation of which recommendation the judiciary is committed: see *ibid.*, para.7. April 1, 2013 is the date on which legislation brings certain of the reforms proposed in Jackson into effect. [In the judgment in the further hearing of *Simmons v Castle* [2012] EWCA Civ 1288, just out (for details see para.3–030, fn.172a, above), the Court of Appeal has extended its ruling to all civil claims and to all types of non-pecuniary loss: see the court's conclusion at *ibid.*, para.50.]

			PARA.
I.	CLAIMS FOR THE BENEFIT OF THE DECEASED'S DEPENDANTS		36–003
	(A) The Statutory Action		36–004
☐	1. The entitled dependants		36–005
☐	2. The entitlement of the dependants		36–008
	(B) The Statutory Measure of Damages		36–017
■	1. Losses in respect of which damages are not recoverable or are recoverable only within limits		36–018
■	2. The value of the dependency		36–026
☐	3. The non-deductibility of collateral benefits		36–103
II.	CLAIMS SURVIVING THE DEATH FOR THE BENEFIT OF THE DECEASED'S ESTATE		36–118
■	1. Prospective losses of deceased		36–119
■	2. Accrued losses of deceased		36–124
☐	3. Losses for which the deceased could not have sued		36–132

36–007   Add at the end of the paragraph: The Civil Law Reform Bill 2009 sensibly proposed extending entitlement to any person who was being maintained by the deceased immediately before the death. However, the Bill's proposals on damages have all been abandoned as thought by the Government not to be vote-catching. The details of this particular proposal are at this paragraph in the First Supplement to the 18th edition.

36–019   NOTE 97: Add at the end of the note: The Court of Appeal's ruling in *Simmons v Castle* [2012] EWCA Civ 1039 that the level of general damages in all torts causing suffering, inconvenience or distress is to be increased by 10 per cent (for which see at, *inter alia*, para.37–001, fn.1a, below) would not seem to apply to bereavement damages since the level of these damages is controlled by the Lord Chancellor. [Now that the Court of Appeal has changed its initial ruling so as to apply to all civil claims (for which see, *inter alia*, para.37–001, fn.1a, below), it may be a nice question whether this overtakes the Lord Chancellor's power to vary the amount of bereavement damages that may be awarded.]

36–019   Add at the end of the paragraph: The Civil Law Reform Bill 2009 proposed to introduce new categories of entitled claimants, with a qualification as to the amount awarded to some of them. However the Bill's proposals on damages have all been abandoned as thought by the Government not to be vote-catching. The details of these particular proposals are at this paragraph in the First Supplement to the 18th edition.

NOTE 192: Substitute for "6th edition published in 2007": 7th edition published in 2011. **36–039**

Substitute for "sixth" on the last line but 3 of the paragraph: seventh. **36–053**

Substitute for "2007" on the last line but 2 of the paragraph: 2011 **36–053**

Substitute for "£536,100" on line 24 of the paragraph: £538,500. **36–055**

Substitute for "£571,500" on line 25 of the paragraph: £573,300. **36–055**

Delete from "In order" on line 27 of the paragraph to the end of the paragraph. **36–055**

NOTE 263: Substitute for "the current 6th" on line 1 of the note: the later editions. **36–055**

NOTE 263: Delete line 3 after the word "multiplier". **36–055**

NOTE 263: Substitute for "£585,900" and "pp.27–28" on the penultimate line: £588,000 and p.31. **36–055**

NOTE 263: Delete the last sentence. **36–055**

NOTE 264: Substitute for "p.24": p.25. **36–055**

NOTE 266: Substitute for "p.25": p.26. **36–055**

NOTE 267; Substitute for "pp.26 to 28": pp.27 to 28. **36–055**

NOTES 268, 269 and 270: Delete. **36–055**

NOTE 273: Substitute for "the current 6th edition of 2007": the later editions. **36–055**

Add at the end of the paragraph: Scotland has now legislatively abandoned *Cookson v Knowles* and adopted the true rule. Section 7(1)(d) of the Damages (Scotland) Act 2011 provides that **36–056**

"any multiplier applied by the court—
(i) is to run from the date of the interlocutor [*i.e.* judgment] awarding damages, and
(ii) is to apply only in respect of future loss of support".

Insert a new paragraph after para.36–066:

The Civil Law Reform Bill 2009 proposed that marriage, civil partnerships and other relationships are now to be taken into account. However the Bill's **36–066A** proposals on damages have all been abandoned as thought by the Government not to be vote-catching. The details of these particular proposals are at this paragraph in the First Supplement to the 18th edition.

Insert a new paragraph after para.36–068:

36–068A   The Civil Law Reform Bill 2009 made proposals as to the taking into account or not of the prospect of divorce, dissolution or breakdown in cohabiting relationships. However the Bill's proposals on damages have all been abandoned as thought by the Government not to be vote-catching. The details of these particular proposals are at this paragraph in the First Supplement to the 18th edition.

36–083   Insert a new note at the end of line 3 of the paragraph:

NOTE 397a: Where in *Devoy v William Doxford & Sons Ltd* [2009] EWHC 1598, QB the wife had before the death become disabled and had been looked after by the husband, both being at the time in their 60s, the cost of carers brought in to replace the husband was awarded, the position being similar to that in the equivalent case of *Feay v Barnwell*, cited to the court and at para.36–092 of the main work, where it was the husband who had died.

36–083   Add at the end of the paragraph: Nevertheless in *Devoy v William Doxford & Sons Ltd* [2009] EWHC 1598, QB a further award was made along these lines. This seems dubious, for the reasons given in the main work. It is significant that the trial judge recognised that there might be an overlap between such an award and the award for bereavement. See *ibid.*, para.79.

36–084   Insert a new note after "the father's death" on line 6 of the paragraph:

NOTE 406a: As in *Drake v Foster Wheeler Ltd* [2011] 1 All E.R. 63.

36–085   Insert a new note at the end of the paragraph:

NOTE 416a: In *Drake v Foster Wheeler Ltd* [2011] 1 All E.R. 63 the dependants included not only children but grandchildren and great grandchildren. The two daughters received smallish sums and the many others trifling sums each: see *ibid.*, para.52.

36–090   NOTE 447: Insert after "child (of £3,000)" on line 2 of the note: and *Manning v King's College Hospital NHS Trust* [2009] EWHC 3008, QB saw awards to the husband (£3,000) and to two children (£4,000).

36–100   NOTE 512: Add at the end of the note: A substantial award was possible in *Amin v Imran Khan & Partners* [2011] EWHC 2958, QB where the deceased son was from a Moslem family which was tight-knit and strongly supportive: *ibid.*, para.84 *et seq.*

Insert a new note after "loss of income" on the last line but two of the paragraph: **36–121**

NOTE 608a: Not applicable to the loss of death-in-service benefits to an employee who died soon after he had been unfairly dismissed, for which loss to the deceased the estate could recover: *Fox v British Airways Plc* Employment Appeal Tribunal, July 30, 2012, unreported.

Insert a new note before "a provision which" on the penultimate line of the paragraph: **36–121**

NOTE 608b: Commonwealth countries that still retain appeals to the Privy Council may not have effected such a legislative change so that the Privy Council from time to time may still have to consider an award to a deceased's estate for the lost years, as in *George v Eagle Air Services* [2009] UKPC 35, an appeal from the Court of Appeal of the Eastern Caribbean (St Lucia): see *ibid.*, para.6.

NOTE 612: Add at the end of the note: While loss of expectation of life as a separate head of damage has been legislatively removed from the English scene, Commonwealth countries that still retain appeals to the Privy Council may not have effected such a legislative change so that the Privy Council from time to time may still have to consider an award to a deceased's estate for loss of expectation of life, as in *George v Eagle Air Services Ltd* [2009] UKPC 35, an appeal from the Court of Appeal of the Eastern Caribbean (St Lucia): see *ibid.*, para.3. **36–123**

NOTE 614: Insert after the first sentence of the note: Also £5,085 was awarded to a wife and mother for family care and £4,604 for inability to continue household duties in *Manning v King's College Hospital NHS Trust* [2008] EWHC 3008, QB, a cancer case. In *Drake v Foster Wheeler Ltd* [2011] 1 All E.R. 63 £10,021 was awarded for care by a charitable hospice foundation. **36–125**

Insert a new note before "In *Watson v Wilmott*" on the last line but 11 of the paragraph: **36–126**

NOTE 622a: In *Amin v Imran Khan & Partners* [2011] EWHC 2958, QB, where the deceased had been clubbed to death in his prison cell by a fellow inmate and had survived barely conscious for a week, there was sufficient evidence of a period of intense conscious pain to make a small award of £5,000 possible: *ibid.*, para.84 *et seq.*

Add at the end of the paragraph: Similarly, where in *Manning v King's College Hospital NHS Trust* [2008] EWHC 3008, QB, after a negligent failure to detect tongue cancer, several years of what was described as appalling pain and suffering had been endured until the release of death, £65,000 was awarded, an amount in which the element of loss of amenity was included (*ibid.*, para.70). **36–126**

36–132   Add at the end of the paragraph: The attempt in *Watson v Cakebread Robey Ltd* [2009] EWHC 1695, QB of a living claimant expected very soon to die to recover his own funeral expenses by, as it were, stepping into the shoes of his estate was clearly a nonsense and rightly rejected (*ibid.*, paras 48 to 57).

CHAPTER 37

ASSAULT AND FALSE IMPRISONMENT

			PARA.
I.	ASSAULT		37–001
■	1.	Heads of damage	37–001
□	2.	Aggravation and mitigation	37–002
□	3.	Exemplary damages	37–010
II.	FALSE IMPRISONMENT		37–011
■	1.	Heads of damage	37–011
	2.	Remoteness of damage: continuation of the imprisonment by judicial order	37–016
■	3.	Aggravation and mitigation	37–017
□	4.	Exemplary damages	37–019

Insert a new note after the third sentence of the paragraph: **37–001**

NOTE 1a: In *Simmons v Castle* [2012] EWCA Civ 1039, in addition to adopting the recommendation of the Jackson Report that the level of personal injury general damages should be increased by 10 per cent (the details of this development are set out at para.35–287A, above), the Court of Appeal, again following Jackson, declared that from April 1, 2013 the increase of 10 per cent should also apply to all torts causing suffering, inconvenience or distress (see *ibid.*, para.20 together with para.14). Though not specifically mentioned by the Court of Appeal, or by Jackson, assault would be one of them. [In the judgment in the further hearing of *Simmons v Castle* EWCA Civ 1288, just out (for details see para.3–030, fn.172a, above), the Court of Appeal has extended its ruling to all civil claims and to all types of non-pecuniary loss: see the court's conclusion at *ibid.*, para.50.]

NOTE 4: Add at the end of the note: An even more horrific case is *AT, NT, ML,* **37–001** *AK v Dulghieru* [2009] EWHC 225, QB where four young women, after being induced by fraud to come from Moldova to the United Kingdom, were coerced into unwanted and constant sexual activity, were kept apart and had their and their families' safety threatened, suffered chronic post traumatic stress disorder and were falsely imprisoned for two months or more. The basic damages awarded by Treacy J. to the four of them—he awarded, as we shall see, aggravated and exemplary damages in addition—ranged from £125,000 down to £82,000.

Add at the end of the paragraph: One of the four claimants in *AT, NT, ML, AK* **37–003** *v Dulghieru* [2009] EWHC 225, QB (facts at para.37–001, fn.4, above) was awarded £35,000, and the other three £30,000 each, by way of aggravated damages, Treacy J. considering the defendants' conduct to be "so appalling, so malevolent, and so utterly contemptuous" of the claimants' rights (*ibid.*, para.62) as to justify such an award. This was in addition to the basic awards to the four, but here there was, as well as assault by way of coerced sexual activity, substantial psychological harm and false imprisonment.

37–006   NOTE 22: Add at the end of the note: Separate awards of aggravated damages were also made in *AT, NT, ML, AK v Dulghieru* [2009] EWHC 225, QB: see para.37–003, above. It seems that the Court of Appeal in *Richardson v Howie* is, fortunately, being generally ignored. It is true that in *AB v Nugent Care Society* [2010] EWHC 1005, QB an award for sexual assault of a child was stated to be for the shame and distress and psychological effects of the abuse with no mention of aggravation but undoubtedly an element of aggravation featured in the award; there were cited both this text (para.37–001) and *Richardson v Howie* (at para.37–004 of the main work): see the discussion in *AB* at paras 87 to 94.

Insert a new paragraph after para.37–009:

37–009A   After the Court of Appeal decision in *Co-operative Group (CWS) Ltd v Pritchard* [2012] Q.B. 320, CA (for which see para.5–005A, above) there must be doubt as to whether there survives the possibility of reducing the damages for non-pecuniary loss on account of provocation by the victim of the assault making the insult suffered by him or her the less. In his extended judgment Aikens L.J. at *ibid.*, para.40 *et seq.* went through what was said in *Lane v Holloway* and in *Murphy v Cullane* (which are dealt with at paras 37–008 and 37–009 respectively of the main work), and ended up, at *ibid.*, para.62, rejecting the remarks in those cases that damages can be reduced for contributory negligence. Yet in *Lane*, as distinct from *Murphy*, Lord Denning M.R., who was in both cases, spoke only of the effect of provocation and did not refer to the defence of contributory negligence at all as Aikens L.J. specifically recognised at *ibid.*, para.41. Since then the Court of Appeal was dealing only with contributory negligence, could it not be said that provocation can still be introduced for the purpose of damages reduction? It is thought that this should be possible. But we shall have to wait and see.

37–010   Add at the end of the paragraph: An illustration of the use of the second common law category is now provided by *AT, NT, ML, AK v Dulghieru* [2009] EWHC 225, QB (facts at para.37–001, fn.4, above) where four claimants were awarded £60,000, to be divided equally between them, by way of exemplary damages, this being in addition to the basic awards and the aggravated damages awards made to the four (see para.37–001, fn.4 and para.37–003 respectively, above). There was here, as well as assault by way of coerced sexual activity, substantial psychological harm and false imprisonment.

Add a new note at the end of the paragraph: **37–011**

NOTE 48a: Where there is no loss, only nominal damages are awarded, as happened in all four of the claims against the Secretary of State for the Home Department listed at para.10–002, fn.3, above.

NOTE 50: Add at the end of the note: In *Iqbal v The Prison Officers'*   **37–012** *Association* [2010] Q.B. 732, CA in the circumstances of the claimant being confined to his small prison cell in the course of a day without being let out for exercise and other activities within the prison generally, the Court of Appeal found the *Thompson* guidance on the amount of damages of no real assistance and, had there been held to be false imprisonment which there was not, would have made a relatively modest award of £120 for the six hours of false imprisonment: *ibid.*, para.44 *et seq.* This would have been in place of the trial judge's award of nominal damages.

NOTE 53: Add at the end of the note: In *Simmons v Castle* [2012] EWCA Civ   **37–012** 1039, in addition to adopting the recommendation of the Jackson Report that the level of personal injury general damages should be increased by 10 per cent (the details of this development are set out at para.35–287A, above), the Court of Appeal, again following Jackson, declared that from April 1, 2013 the increase of 10 per cent should also apply to all torts causing suffering, inconvenience or distress (see *ibid.*, para.20 together with para.14). Though not specifically mentioned by the Court of Appeal, or by Jackson, false imprisonment would be one of them. [In the judgment in the further hearing of *Simmons v Castle* [2012] EWCA Civ 1288, just out (for details see para.3–030, fn.172a, above), the Court of Appeal has extended its ruling to all civil claims and to all types of non-pecuniary loss: see the court's conclusion at *ibid.*, para.50.]

Add at the end of the paragraph: Thus the global approach was utilised in *R.*   **37–012** *(on the application of Mehari) v Secretary of State for the Home Department* [2010] EWHC 636 (Admin) and £4,000 was awarded for a week's unlawful detention of an asylum seeker who was a woman of good character: *ibid.*, paras 32 to 39. In *Takitota v Attorney General* [2009] UKPC 11, where the claimant had been incarcerated for over eight years in appalling prison conditions and the Court of Appeal of The Bahamas had not adopted the global approach but had multiplied the daily amount by as many days as are in eight years, the Privy Council said that this would not do and sent the case back for a reassessment. For a false imprisonment lasting for over three weeks in *R. (on the application of MK (Algeria)) v Secretary of State for the Home Department* [2010] EWCA Civ 980 the Court of Appeal increased the trial judge's award of £8,500 to £17,500; this included £5,000 of aggravated damages. Yet far larger amounts were the awards made to the four claimants in *AT, NT, ML, AK v Dulghieru* [2009] EWHC 225, QB (facts and amounts at para.37–001, fn.4, above), awards which, as we shall see, were supplemented by awards of aggravated and exemplary damages, but in *Dulghieru* there was assault by way of coerced sexual activity and substantial psychological harm as well as false imprisonment. Awards of non-pecuniary damages for wrongful arrest and false imprisonment keep appearing as in *Okoro v The Commissioner of Police of the Metropolis* [2011] EWHC 3, QB (arrest and a few hours' imprisonment causing physical injury: £13,000 awarded) and *R. (on the application of NAB) v Secretary of State for the Home Department* [2011] EWHC 1191 (Admin) (improper immigration detention, with neither aggravated nor exemplary nor vindicatory damages and no contributory negligence or failure to mitigate: £6,150 awarded).

Insert a new paragraph after para.37–013:

37–013A   However, the Supreme Court in the false imprisonment case of *R. (on the application of Lumba (Congo)) v Secretary of State for the Home Department* [2012] 1 A.C. 245 has now, by a majority of six to three, held that it was inappropriate there to award vindicatory damages. The Secretary of State for the Home Department was held liable for the false imprisonment of foreign national prisoners pending their deportation as she had applied an unpublished policy which was unlawful when exercising her power to detain them but, since they would have been detained in any event if she had applied the lawful published policy, they had suffered no loss so that compensatory damages were out of the question. While it was accepted that they were entitled to nominal damages, false imprisonment being a tort actionable *per se*, they sought, unsuccessfully, vindicatory damages not in order to clear their reputation, a reputation which they did not have, but because of infringement of a right, that is, the right to liberty. The minority of three was persuaded by this but, fortunately, not the majority. It is thought that vindicatory damages may, indeed should, still be available in cases of false imprisonment where, as in the related case of defamation (see para. 39–032 of the main work), the claimant's reputation is at stake. See further on this paras 42–009A and 42–009B, below.

37–018   Insert in the text before "The award of" on the last line but 6 of the paragraph: Similarly, on the unusual facts of *Ahmed v Shafique* [2009] EWHC 618, QB, where the defendants who were in business with the claimant procured his false arrest leading to his detention for 15 hours, the award of £2,000 general damages was supplemented by another £2,000 of aggravated damages to compensate for the humiliation of the arrest and the trauma suffered as a result of it by a man of good character.

37–018   Insert in the text before "It was also" on the last line but 2 of the paragraph: In *R. (on the application of MK (Algeria)) v Secretary of State for the Home Department*, [2010] EWCA Civ 980 an award of £17,500 for false imprisonment only, an unlawful detention of an asylum seeker lasting for over three weeks, included aggravated damages of £5,000, the Court of Appeal saying that the case was pre-eminently one for aggravated damages as the secretary of state had acted in a high-handed manner. Later cases also involving the false imprisonment of asylum seekers have been heard in the Employment Appeal Tribunal, *R. (on the* *application of J) v Secretary of State for the Home Department* [2011] EWHC 3073 (Admin), where the award of aggravated damages was reduced, *R. (on the application of M) v Secretary of State for the Home Department* [2011] EWHC 3667 (Admin), where the award was split between basic damages and aggravated damages, *AM v Secretary of State for the Home Department*, County Court, March 13, 2012, unreported, where no aggravated damagers were awarded, and *R. (on the application of N) v Secretary of State for the Home Department* [2012] EWHC 1031 (Admin), where aggravated damages were not in issue. Much larger amounts than in all these cases were awarded to the four claimants in *AT, NT, ML, AK v Dulghieru* [2009] EWHC 225, QB (facts at para.37–001, fn.4, above) by way of aggravated damages (amounts at para.37–003, above), but in *Dulghieru* there was assault by way of coerced sexual activity and substantial psychological harm as well as false imprisonment.

NOTE 93: Add at the end of the note: But see, at para.3–011, fn.47, above, the **37–018** concerns expressed in *Commissioner of Police of the Metropolis v Shaw* [2012] I.C.R. 464, [2012] I.R.L.R. 291 over having separate awards.

Insert in the text before "with false imprisonment" on line 8 of the paragraph: **37–019** and an illustration of the use of the second common law category is now provided by *AT, NT, ML, AK v Dulghieru* [2009] EWHC 225, QB (facts and amounts at para.37–001, fn.4 and para.37–010 respectively, above).

CHAPTER 38

MALICIOUS INSTITUTION OF LEGAL PROCEEDINGS

		PARA.
I.	TYPES OF ACTIONABLE DAMAGE	38–002
II.	PARTICULAR TORTS	38–004
■	1. Malicious criminal prosecutions	38–004
	2. Malicious bankruptcy and company liquidation proceedings	38–008
■ III.	AGGRAVATION AND MITIGATION	38–012
☐ IV.	EXEMPLARY DAMAGES	38–014

38–004   Insert a new note at the end of the paragraph:

NOTE 16a: The claimant in *Clifford v The Chief Constable of the Hertfordshire Constabulary* [2011] EWHC 815, QB, who was wrongly charged with child pornography offences leading to his arrest and unsuccessful prosecution, was awarded damages both for the resulting psychological damage (*ibid.*, paras 58 to 61) and for the immense distress suffered (*ibid.*, paras 62 and 63), £10,000 for each.

38–005   NOTE 22: Add at the end of the note: In *Simmons v Castle* [2012] EWCA Civ 1039, in addition to adopting the recommendation of the Jackson Report that the level of personal injury general damages should be increased by 10 per cent (the details of this development are set out at para.35–287A, above), the Court of Appeal, again following Jackson, declared that from April 1, 2013 the increase of 10 per cent should also apply to all torts causing suffering, inconvenience or distress (see *ibid.*, para.20 together with para.14). Though not specifically mentioned by the Court of Appeal, or by Jackson, malicious prosecution would be one of them. [In the judgment in the further hearing of *Simmons v Castle* [2012] EWCA Civ 1288, just out (for details see para.3–030, fn.172a, above), the Court of Appeal has extended its ruling to all civil claims and to all types of non-pecuniary loss: see the court's conclusion at *ibid.*, para.50.]

38–005   Insert a new note at the end of the paragraph:

NOTE 22a: £20,000 was awarded in *Clifford v The Chief Constable of the Hertfordshire Constabulary* [2011] EWHC 815, QB: see the case at para.38–004, fn.16a, above.

38–012   NOTE 46: Add at the end of the note: No aggravated damages as such were awarded in *Clifford v The Chief Constable of the Hertfordshire Constabulary* [2011] EWHC 815, QB (facts at para.38–004, fn.16a, above): *ibid.*, para.64.

NOTE 52: Add at the end of the note: But see, at para.3–011, fn.47, above, the   **38–013**
concerns expressed in *Commissioner of Police of the Metropolis v Shaw* [2012]
I.C.R. 464, [2012] I.R.L.R. 291 over having separate awards.

Insert a new note at the end of the paragraph: **38–014**

NOTE 60a: No exemplary damages were awarded in *Clifford v The Chief
Constable of the Hertfordshire Constabulary* [2011] EWHC 815, QB (facts at
para.38–004, fn.16a, above): *ibid.*, para.65.

CHAPTER 39

DEFAMATION

			PARA.
I.		SLANDERS ACTIONABLE ONLY ON PROOF OF SPECIAL DAMAGE	39–002
	1.	Meaning of special damage	39–002
	2.	Remoteness of special damage	39–010
	3.	Pleading and proof of special damage	39–020
	4.	Additional general damages	39–022
II.		SLANDERS ACTIONABLE *PER SE* AND LIBEL	39–023
■	1.	Level of awards	39–023
□	2.	Heads of damage	39–029
	3.	Remoteness of damage	39–035
	4.	Pleading and proof of damage	39–036
■	5.	Aggravation and mitigation: relevance of the conduct, character and circumstances of the parties	39–039
	6.	Vindicatory damages: the effect of the judge's comments in his judgment	39–070
	7.	Exemplary damages	39–073

39–027   Insert a new note after the first sentence of the paragraph:

NOTE 144a: In *KC v MGN Ltd* [2012] EWHC 483, QB it was stated that the ceiling of £200,000 would now be £256,000: *ibid.*, para.26. After reviewing all the authorities on amounts awarded, Bean J. came to a figure of £150,000 in relation to a false accusation of raping a young girl, a figure that was subject to an amends offer discount (at para.39–055, below).

Insert a new paragraph after para.39–028:

39–028A   In *Simmons v Castle* [2012] EWCA Civ 1039, in addition to adopting the recommendation of the Jackson Report that the level of personal injury general damages should be increased by 10 per cent (the details of this development are set out at para.35–287A, above), the Court of Appeal, again following Jackson, declared that from April 1, 2013 the increase of 10 per cent should also apply to all torts causing suffering, inconvenience or distress (see *ibid.*, para.20 together with para.14). Defamation is the only applicable tort, other than the tort of nuisance, specifically mentioned by the Court of Appeal (*ibid.*, para.20); it is also specifically mentioned in the Jackson Report (recommendation 65(i)). [In the judgment in the further hearing of *Simmons v Castle* [2012] EWCA Civ 1288, just out (for details see para.3–030, fn.172a, above), the Court of Appeal has extended its ruling to all civil claims and to all types of non-pecuniary loss: see the court's conclusion at *ibid.*, para.50.]

NOTE 174: Add at the end of the note: Only injured feelings featured in the **39–031** modest damages award in *Clynes v O'Connor* [2011] EWHC 1201, QB, a rather trivial case.

Add at the end of the paragraph: By contrast, in *Metropolitan International* **39–031** *Schools Ltd v Designtechnica Corp* [2010] EWHC 2411, QB (facts at para. 39–032, below) it was held that there could be no award for injured feelings, the claimant being a company and not an individual, and damages were awarded primarily for vindication.

Insert a new note before "being in" in the penultimate line of the **39–032** paragraph:

NOTE 179a: Vindication was also central in *Al-Amoudi v Kifle* [2011] EWHC 2037, QB since the claimant, an international businessman of huge wealth who had suffered a most appalling libel suggesting links to murder, terrorism and even the killing of his daughter, was not interested in the finances of a probably unenforceable award but in showing to the world that his reputation was secure: see *ibid.*, para.45. The award came to £175,000.

Add at the end of the paragraph: A libel on the internet, suggesting that the **39–032** learning courses for adult students run by the claimant company were a scam, led in *Metropolitan International Schools Ltd v Designtechnica Corp* [2010] EWHC 2411, QB, to a £50,000 award of damages. This was primarily for vindication (see *ibid.*, para.35), there being no provable loss of business and no injury to feelings as the claimant was a company. Vindication had also been the object of the claimant in *Hays Plc v Hartley* [2010] EWHC 1068, QB (see *ibid.*, para.44), but the claim failed. So too in *Farrall v Kordowski* [2011] EWHC 2140, QB, where defamatory statements about a young solicitor claimant had been published anonymously on the defendant's website, Lloyd Jones J. considered that, there being neither retraction nor apology, the vindicatory purpose of damages was much in play.

Insert in the text before the last sentence of the paragraph: Thus, where in **39–034** *Cambridge v Makin* [2011] EWHC 12, QB there was a libel of the claimant in her profession, that of public service interpreter, a libel of some seriousness as it was published to her professional colleagues, and the claimant believed but could not prove that she had lost professional engagements, Tugendhat J., while commenting that it was very rare in libel actions for a claimant to be able to prove pecuniary loss, classified as special damage, added that "where a libel is likely to cause significant loss of earnings, that can be taken into account in the assessment of general damages": *ibid.*, para.229. Similarly in *Metropolitan International Schools Ltd v Designtechnica Corp* [2010] EWHC 2411, QB (facts at para.39–032, above) Tugendhat J. was satisfied that the claimant company, while unable to prove a specific loss of business, had suffered actual damage in the form of students not taking courses (*ibid.*, para.32) and he will have factored this into his £50,000 award which primarily constituted vindicatory damages.

39–034   NOTE 195: Add at the end of the note: *Thornton v Telegraph Media Group Ltd* [2011] EWHC 1884, QB where the claimant, a journalist and academic, was libelled in a book review, which libel struck at her professional reputation, illustrates recovery for financial loss, and such loss appears to have been a major feature of the award of £65,000.

39–039   Insert a new note after "to defamation" on the last line of the paragraph:

NOTE 209a: See, at para.3–011, fn.47, above, the concerns expressed in *Commissioner of Police of the Metropolis v Shaw* [2012] I.C.R. 464, [2012] I.R.L.R. 291 over having separate awards.

39–043   Insert a new note before "but there are" on line 2 of the paragraph:

NOTE 218a: On his employment as a company's chief executive officer being terminated by one of the company's directors, the defendant in *Cooper v Turrell* [2011] EWHC 3269, QB embarked on an internet campaign accusing the company and director of dishonesty and criminal conduct and, with the use of confidential information that he had recorded, publishing damaging statements about the director's health and fitness for his job. Malice was easily proved by the two claimants and Tugendhat J. saw as aggravating factors—the director was claiming aggravated damages—the defendant's awareness that he was publishing false information, his targeting of people whose good opinion was important to the director, and the fact that his actions had taken the form of an internet campaign. Tugendhat J. awarded £30,000 to the company for the libel and to the director £50,000, the higher award reflecting the unavailability to corporations of damages for injury to feelings.

39–046   Add at the end of the paragraph: And coming to modern times, in *Cairns v Modi* [2012] EWHC 756, QB, where a professional cricketer had been falsely accused of match fixing, what Bean J. called "the sustained and aggressive assertion of the plea of justification at the trial" was aggravation sufficient to increase the damages by a factor of 20 per cent, moving his award up from £75,000 to £90,000: *ibid.*, paras 136 and 137. No specific reference to malice was made.

39–055   NOTE 269: Add at the end of the note: In *Bowman v MGN Ltd* [2010] EWHC 895, QB, a case of a libel described by Eady J. as amounting to a bit of celebrity gossip, where there was an early apology, a willingness to remove the offending words immediately and a very prompt reliance on the offer of amends regime, the discount was 50 per cent. In *KC v MGN Ltd* [2012] EWHC 483, QB, where the apology was reasonably prompt, clear and unqualified, and given prominence in the defendant's newspaper (*ibid.*, para.44), the discount was again 50 per cent.

While recognising that an unqualified offer of amends should give the tortfeasor a healthy discount, Bean J. said that it should not be so great as to induce equanimity in potential libellers through the knowledge that they can easily buy themselves out of trouble with an apology (*ibid.*, para.46). No case has allowed a discount in excess of 50 per cent.

NOTE 344: Add at the end of the note: Compensation received from a third **39–068** party was taken into account in reduction of the damages in *Cambridge v Makin* [2011] EWHC 12, QB (facts at para.39–034 above): *ibid.*, para.235.

CHAPTER 40

ECONOMIC TORTS

			PARA.
	I.	INDUCEMENT OF BREACH OF CONTRACT	40–004
	II.	INTIMIDATION: THIRD PARTY ASPECTS	40–009
	III.	INJURIOUS FALSEHOOD	40–011
■		1. Injurious falsehoods other than passing off	40–011
□		2. Passing off	40–018
□	IV.	UNLAWFUL INTERFERENCE WITH ECONOMIC INTERESTS	40–021
□	V.	CONSPIRACY	40–022
■	VI.	BREACH OF CONFIDENTIAL INFORMATION	40–027
□	VII.	INFRINGEMENT OF RIGHTS IN INTELLECTUAL PROPERTY	40–031
□		1. Infringement of trade marks	40–033
■		2. Infringement of patents	40–036
■		3. Infringement of copyright and design right	40–042

40–003   Insert a new note at the end of the paragraph:

NOTE 5a: In *Simmons v Castle* [2012] EWCA Civ 1039, in addition to adopting the recommendation of the Jackson Report that the level of personal injury general damages should be increased by 10 per cent (the details of this development are set out at para.35–287A, above), the Court of Appeal, again following Jackson, declared that from April 1, 2013 the increase of 10 per cent should also apply to all torts causing suffering, inconvenience or distress (see *ibid.*, para.20 together with para.14). While not specifically mentioned by the Court of Appeal, or by Jackson, economic torts, to the extent that they generate recovery for non-pecuniary loss, would be included. [In the judgment in the further hearing of *Simmons v Castle* [2012] EWCA Civ 1288, just out (for details see para.3–030, fn.172a, above), the Court of Appeal has extended its ruling to all civil claims and to all types of non-pecuniary loss: see the court's conclusion at *ibid.*, para.50.]

40–013   NOTE 56: Add at the end of the note: Tugendhat J. held in *Tesla Motors Ltd v B.B.C.* [2011] EWHC 2760, QB that, where the claimant relied on the probability of damage under s.3, particulars must be given of the nature of the alleged probable damage and the grounds relied on for saying that the damage was probable. Otherwise the claim must be struck out.

40–019   Insert a new note before "The principal" on line 3 of the paragraph:

NOTE 91a: There is now *Fearns v Anglo-Dutch Paint & Chemical Co Ltd* [2010] EWHC 1708, Ch where it was common ground that damages in respect of the defendant's unlawful sales should be calculated on the basis that the claimant would have made equivalent sales (*ibid.*, para.33) and the claimant also recovered for the loss of his network of distributors but was unable to claim for the collapse of his business as he was unable to prove that this was caused by the defendant's unlawful activities.

Add a new note at the end of the paragraph: **40–021**

NOTE 100a: The claimant in *Fearns v Anglo-Dutch Paint & Chemical Co Ltd* [2010] EWHC 1708, Ch failed to establish that this tort had been committed (*ibid.*, para.15) so that any need to calculate damages fell away, but it would appear that the damages, if available, would have followed the same lines as those awarded in the successful claims for passing off and infringement of trade marks dealt with at para.40–033, fn.153 and para.40–034, fn.156, below.

Add at the end of the paragraph: In the highly complicated *National Grid* **40–024** *Electricity Transmission Plc v McKenzie* [2009] EWHC 1817, Ch the claimant company was held entitled to substantial damages in conspiracy, among other wrongs, against one of its employees and one of its independent contractors who were milking it of its funds by corrupt practices. And where in *Noble Resources SA v Gross* [2009] EWHC 1435 (Comm) losses on unauthorised speculative trading in aluminium futures were made, and concealed, by two employees of the claimant companies, it was accepted that damages for conspiracy (there were also claims in deceit and for breach of the contract of employment) were at large and not limited to the loss that could be strictly proved, thereby allowing an award of damages in many millions: see *ibid.*, paras 222 to 227.

Insert a new note after the second sentence of the paragraph: **40–027**

NOTE 136a: Arnold J. said in *Force India Formula One Team Ltd v 1 Malaysia Racing Team SDN BHD* [2012] EWHC 616, Ch (*ibid.*, paras 388 and 407) that the Court of Appeal decided in *Kitechnology BV v Unicor GmbH Plastmaschinen* [1995] F.S.R. 765 that breach of confidence was not a tort, being actionable only in equity. There is no doubt that initially liability was only in equity but things may be changing. What Evans L.J. said in *Kitechnology* about breach of confidence was more of a proposition than a decision (*ibid.*, pp.777–778) and there are pointers in a different direction. Some time ago Lord Denning M.R. in *Seager v Copydex (No.2)* [1969] 1 W.L.R. 809, CA took as an analogy for damages for wrongful use of confidential information damages for conversion (*ibid.*, 813A) and more recently in *Douglas v Hello!* [2001] Q.B. 967, CA, which was concerned with privacy, Sedley L.J. twice referred to "the tort of breach of confidence" (*ibid.*, paras 117 and 123).

Insert a new paragraph after para.40–030:

40-030A   The confidential information taken in *JN Dairies Ltd v Johal Dairies Ltd* [2010] EWHC 1689, Ch was again customer information, being by way of invoices showing customer names and prices. The claimant chose not to claim damages for actual loss of profits and instead sought to claim damages based on the value of the information taken from it, putting forward a calculation based on what it alleged to be the market value of the information on a sale between a willing buyer and a willing seller. The defendant applied for a strike out on the basis that such a measure of damages was only available to a claimant who would not have used the information to earn profits but would have exploited it by licensing others to do so. The judge, without deciding between the competing arguments, was content to allow the case to proceed to trial on the ground that it was at least arguable that an assessment of damages based on the value of the information taken should be available to a manufacturing claimant who was in difficulties in proving the exact extent of its actual financial loss.

40-030B   A further case, also at first instance, is *Force India Formula One Team Ltd v 1 Malaysia Racing Team SDN BHD* [2012] EWHC 616, Ch. The claimant, operating a Formula 1 racing team, sued a series of defendants on account of the use, by one of the defendants initially employed by the claimant as designer, of some parts of the claimant's model in designs for another defendant which also operated a Formula 1 racing team. This was a misuse of confidential information. Maintaining that he could not find a clear, accurate and comprehensive statement of the principles applicable to the assessment of damages for breach of confidence (*ibid.*, para.374), Arnold J. in an elaborate judgment embarked upon an extended consideration of the relevant principles (*ibid.*, paras 375 to 394) and upon a survey of a whole series of authorities (*ibid.*, paras 395 to 423), leading him to a general conclusion which is thought to fit with what is set out in the main work and which is as follows. Where the claimant cannot prove that financial loss has been suffered by way of lost manufacturing profits, lost licence fees or lost moneys from disposal of the confidential information, recovery will be of such sum as would be negotiated between a willing licensor and a willing licensee for permission to use the confidential information in the manner in which it has been misused (*ibid.*, para.424). This is effectively an application of the so-called user principle, producing what Arnold J. calls negotiating damages: see *ibid.*, paras 383 and 385 to 387.

40-030C   It may be noted that Arnold J. points out that, while confidential information is not strictly intellectual property, it has been suggested that the European Union Directive directed to the harmonisation of the rules on the enforcement of intellectual property rights, which Directive has been brought into force in English law and contains a provision on damages (for details see para.40-032A, below), applies to breach of confidential information (*ibid.*, para.378). Then in his lengthy consideration of what are appropriate damages for breach of confidential information he pays no further attention to the damages provision of the Directive, simply saying in his general conclusions that his approach to the damages to be awarded is consistent with the damages provision of the Directive (*ibid.*, para.424). This accords with our view, set out in detail in relation to a copyright case at paras 40–032A to F, below, that the damages provision adds nothing to English law as it stands.

Insert a new note after the first sentence of the paragraph: **40–031**

NOTE 144a: Rights in intellectual property may be infringed outside the bounds of these statutory torts, as in *Double Communications Ltd v News Corp International Ltd* [2011] EWHC 961, QB where the defendant had licensed a board game of its invention to be promoted and marketed by the claimant licensee and had then withdrawn the licence in breach of contract. Damages for loss of the profits that would have been made from sales of the game over the three-year licence period fell to be assessed and the resolution of this question by Eady J. turned on a detailed consideration by him of the facts and the evidence. It would seem, however, from what is said by him at *ibid.*, paras 4 to 5 together with para.99 that he considered that the principle in the very old case of *Armory v Delamirie*, recently resurrected, which eases the claimant's passage on proof (see paras 8–083 and 33–049 of the main work) applied. As explained at para.8–002D, above, that this is so is dubious.

Insert new paragraphs after para.40–032:

While as a rule damages do not feature in European Union Directives, a clear   **40–032A**
exception appears in a measure directed to the harmonisation of the rules on the enforcement of intellectual property rights. This is Directive 2004/48/EC, Art.13 of which is entitled "Damages" and which article has been implemented in the UK by means of reg.3, entitled Assessment of Damages, of the Intellectual Property (Enforcement, etc.) Regulations 2006 (SI 2006/1028). Yet scant attention has been paid to these provisions in the English cases and, though the Regulations have been in force since April 29, 2006, not until 2010 in *Experience Hendrix LLC v Times Newspapers Ltd* [2010] EWHC 1986, Ch do the Directive and Regulations appear to have been relied upon. The explanation for this could well be that the position under the Directive and Regulations is seen as being no different from the position at common law. Certainly, Sir William Blackburne in his judgment in the *Experience Hendrix* case, which concerned copyright or an extension thereto, moved between Directive and Regulations on the one hand and English authorities and statute on the other. This suggests that he must have been of much the same view.

The details of Art.13 and reg.3 need to be referred to—this being a Supplement   **40–032B**
they are not set out here *in extenso*—in order to appreciate the proposition that they introduce no variant to English law as it stood before they appeared on the scene. At the start it should be noted that the damages provisions of the Directive and Regulations apply only to those who are intentionally or negligently infringing; others, who may be called innocent infringers, are left to the domestic law

untrammelled by the Directive and Regulations: see the interrelation of Art.13.1 and 13.2 of the Directive, the equivalent relation of regs 3(1) and (2) with reg.3(3) of the Regulations, and para.68 of Sir William Blackburne's judgment in *Experience Hendrix*, the one case which is known to have applied the Directive.

40–032C   Turning to the intentional or negligent infringer, that is to say in the words of the Directive one who "knowingly, or with reasonable grounds to know, engaged in an infringing activity", it is first provided that the damages are to take into account all the financial loss that the injured party has suffered, which simply represents the pre-Directive English law. Lost profits are specifically mentioned in the Directive and the Regulations and these would be either profits made by use of the intellectual property, be it trade mark, patent or copyright, or by licence of the intellectual property: see Art.13.1(a) of the Directive and reg.3(2)(a)(i) of the Regulations.

40–032D   There may also be recovery for loss other than economic, such as the moral prejudice caused by the infringement: see Art.13.1(a) of the Directive and reg.3(2)(a)(ii) of the Regulations. This would appear to be equivalent to English law's allowance of damages for injury to feelings in intentional torts where the defendant's behaviour is flagrant, outrageous or similarly unacceptable, damages which are brought in by statute in copyright cases. Such damages are said in the Directive to be available only in appropriate cases and it is thought that appropriate cases should comprise only situations where the infringer's conduct is deliberate, indeed flagrant. Certainly, no such damages were considered appropriate to award under the Directive by Sir William Blackburne in *Experience Hendrix* where he found the defendant to have infringed negligently rather than deliberately: see [2010] EWHC 1986, Ch, paras 73 to 76.

40–032E   In addition, recovery is provided for unfair profits made by the infringer or, instead, for a notional licence fee or royalty where no profit would have been made by use or by licence of the intellectual property: see Art.13.1(a) and (b) of the Directive and reg.3(2)(a)(i) and (b) of the Regulations. These are two forms of restitutionary damages which today should also be available under English common law.

40–032F   In summary, under Directive and Regulations recovery of damages is allowed for lost profits, for licence fees or royalties, for moral prejudice, for profits made by the defendant, and these are all available under English law as compensatory damages, aggravated damages and restitutionary damages as the paragraphs which follow in the main work show.

40–033   NOTE 153: Add at the end of the note: Thus no distinction was made between the claims for passing off and for infringement of trade marks in *Fearns v Anglo-*

Dutch Paint & Chemical Co Ltd [2010] EWHC 1708, Ch, both being treated together along the same lines: see para.80.

NOTE 156: Add at the end of the note: Similar is *Fearns v Anglo-Dutch Paint*   **40–034**
& Chemical Co Ltd [2010] EWHC 1708, Ch, where it was common ground that damages in respect of the defendant's unlawful sales should be calculated on the basis that the claimant would have made equivalent sales: *ibid.*, para.33. However, the claimant was unable to prove that the collapse of his business was caused by the defendant's unlawful activities although he recovered for the loss of his network of distributors.

Add at the end of the paragraph: The claimant in *National Guild of Removers*   **40–034**
& Storers Ltd v Jones [2011] EWPCC 4 was a trade association the members of which were allowed to use its trade marks as part of their advertising. There was provision where a member ceased his membership for a hire charge. The use by the defendants of the trade marks once they had ceased to be members constituted a trade mark infringement, for which infringement damages had to be assessed. The trial judge pointed out that Knox J.'s concern (for which see the main work at this paragraph) about employing the user basis of damages for trade mark cases because of the lack of the proprietary element that existed with patents no longer ran as the Trade Marks Act 1994 now provided that a trade mark is a property right (*ibid.*, para.11). Beyond this he expressed the view that the user basis was appropriate for all trade mark cases even if the trade mark would not have been hired out by its owner (*ibid.*, para.14) although he said nothing about the award in such cases being essentially restitutionary. He added that he did not have to decide if he were right on this since the possibility of hiring out existed in *National Guild* (*ibid.*, para.15).

Add at the end of the paragraph: As for *Fabio Perini SPA v LPC Group Plc*   **40–038**
[2012] EWHC 911, Ch, where the claimant's patent of a method of selling paper rolls had been infringed, the calculation of the damages proved very complex and Norris J.'s elaborate and lengthy judgment requires study. An interesting feature of his decision on damages is his use of loss of a chance, both in its causation and its assessment aspects, of making sales, arriving at a 65 per cent chance in relation to some sales and a 25 per cent chance in relation to others: see *ibid.*, paras 166 and 167.

Add at the end of the paragraph: On the other hand, in *Experience Hendrix*   **40–044**
LLC v Times Newspapers Ltd [2010] EWHC 1986, Ch which concerned not copyright but rights in performance (also covered by the 1988 Act), being rights to performance and recording of a concert (full facts at para.8–002B, above), damages were awarded on the loss of profits basis because the claimants planned to exploit their performance rights and also because the licence approach faced formidable difficulties in assessment: *ibid.*, para.133 *et seq.* It should be noted that *Experience Hendrix* was decided under a European Union Directive and the Regulations implementing it rather than under English common law and statute

but this made no difference to the result: see the discussion at paras 40–032A to 40–032F, above.

Insert a new paragraph after para.40–044:

40–044A   The claim may be for loss of profits and a reasonable royalty combined. This was so in *The Magic Seeder Co Ltd v Hamble Distribution Ltd* [2012] EWPCC 9 where a number of the defendant's infringing sales lost sales to the claimant, giving rise to recovery of lost profits, and the remaining infringing sales of the defendant, in excess of the sales the claimant would have made, attracted a reasonable royalty.

40–047   Insert a new note after "additional damages" on the last line but two of the paragraph:

NOTE 250a: It was proposed in the Civil Law Reform Bill 2009, because of the uncertainty over the meaning and ambit of the term "additional damages", to replace it with a reference to aggravated and restitutionary damages. However the Bill's proposals on damages have all been abandoned as thought by the Government not to be vote-catching. The details of this particular proposal are at this paragraph in the First Supplement to the 18th edition. In any event the courts seem to have worked out for themselves that aggravated damages and restitutionary damages are what the term "additional damages" encompasses as what is said at paras 40–048 to 40–050 of the main work shows.

40–050   Insert a new note after "aggravation of damages" at the end of line 14 of the paragraph:

NOTE 285a: The Civil Law Reform Bill 2009 proposed that the additional damages of the statute should be available in claims "whether brought by an individual or a body". But aggravated damages should be available only to individuals. It is therefore fortunate that this proposal has gone together with all the others on damages, abandoned by the Government as not vote-catching. The impropriety of the proposal for aggravated damages is discussed in para.40–051 of the First Supplement to the 18th edition.

40–050   NOTE 290: Insert after the first sentence of the note: Nor was there in *Experience Hendrix LLC v Times Newspapers Ltd* [2010] EWHC 1986, Ch, which concerned not copyright but rights in performance, for infringement of which there is a similar provision for additional damages in the 1988 Act: see *ibid.*, paras 73 to 76 and the case at para.40–032A *et seq.*, above. Also in *Harrison v Harrison* [2010] F.S.R. 25, p.604 the infringement of copyright did not attract an award of additional damages: see the judge's analysis, legal and factual, at para.38 *et seq.*

Add at the end of the paragraph: Whereas the courts have found the criteria for **40–050** the assessment of additional damages somewhat uncertain, with a variety of views being put forward in the cases, once the damages come to be seen as aggravated or restitutionary damages, the criteria which have been established for such damages should apply and uncertainty be at an end.

CHAPTER 41

MISREPRESENTATION

PARA.
I. FRAUDULENT MISREPRESENTATION: DECEIT 41–002
   1. The tortious measure of damages.. 41–002
■ 2. Heads of damage.. 41–007
   3. Exemplary damages... 41–040
II. NEGLIGENT MISREPRESENTATION.. 41–041
   1. Liability at common law and under statute 41–041
   2. The tortious measure of damages... 41–043
■ 3. Heads of damage.. 41–049
III. INNOCENT MISREPRESENTATION 41–060

41–007   NOTE 28: Add at the end of the note: Also in *Noble Resources SA v Gross* [2009] EWHC 1435 (Comm), where losses on unauthorised speculative trading in aluminium futures were made, and concealed, by two employees of the claimant companies, it was accepted that damages in deceit (there were also claims in conspiracy and for breach of the contract of employment) went beyond recovery for foreseeable loss, thereby allowing an award of damages in many millions: see *ibid.*, paras 222 to 227.

41–014   Insert a new note at the end of the paragraph:

NOTE 61a: By contrast, in *Invertec Ltd v De Mol Holding BV* [2009] EWHC 2471, Ch the claimant company, which had been induced to purchase the entire share capital of another company by fraudulent representations as to its value and solvency, was held not to have been locked into continuing to hold the shares bought. While the claimant was entitled to recover in damages its entire purchase consideration as, but for the fraud, it would not have bought valueless share capital, it could not recover the loans that it had made to the company in order to keep it trading, loans which were now lost to it by reason of the company's insolvency. The decision to keep the company trading was a commercial one and a gamble which did not pay off; also, it could not be regarded as a step taken in mitigation. The company was not locked into its shareholding, having two exit routes; it could have rescinded the contract or it could have allowed the company to go into administration or liquidation. See *ibid.*, para.378 *et seq.*

41–025   NOTE 111: Substitute for [2006] EWHC 2973 Ch. on line 1 of the note: [2009] 1 Lloyd's Rep. 601, CA.

Insert a new note before "but the principles" on line 5 of the paragraph: **41–026**

NOTE 112a: See now *Butler-Creagh v Hersham* [2011] EWHC 2525, QB where value transferred less contract price was awarded. A company had been induced to buy a large property for £25 million by fraudulent misrepresentations as to its value and to the cost of its development. Without the assistance of a resale price, the property having been retained, there was difficulty in reaching a figure for value (*ibid.*, para.104 *et seq.*). Value was taken at the time of contract following the normal rule. The judge saw no reason to adopt a later date, as the House of Lords has allowed in the context of share sales (see para.41–014 in the main work), the defence having contended for the date of completion (*ibid.*, para.103).

NOTE 127: Add at the end of the note: For the recovery of a whole series of   **41–028** consequential losses, with *Doyle v Olby* cited, see *Kinch v Rosling* [2009] EWHC 286, QB. Limited consequential losses, by way of various expenditures, were allowed in *Butler-Creagh v Hersham* [2011] EWHC 2525, QB (*ibid.*, para.110 *et seq.*) where the property purchased was retained rather than resold (facts at para.41–026, fn.112a, above).

Add at the end of the paragraph: In contrast to *Downs v Chappell* no limits   **41–028** were placed on the recovery of consequential losses in *Nationwide Building Society v Dunlop Haywards* [2010] 1 W.L.R. 258 where a valuer had fraudulently given a massive overvaluation of commercial property on the security of which the claimants were lending. Christopher Clarke J. detailed a whole series of such losses for which he had no hesitation in allowing recovery (*ibid.*, paras 10 to 34), including the cost of the time of management and staff in investigating the fraud, an item of loss which had already been accepted in deceit and in other intentional torts (see paras 40–024 and 41–023 of the main work).

NOTE 140: Insert before "See also at" on the last line but 4 of the note: The   **41–029** Court of Appeal has affirmed the trial judge's decision to allow recovery as damages of the legal and other costs, giving a detailed analysis of the law and the facts covering causation and reasonableness: *Dadourian Group International Inc v Simms* [2009] 1 Lloyd's Rep. 601, CA, paras 109 to 148.

Insert a new paragraph after para.41–033:

Loss of profits featured in, indeed dominated, *Parabola Investments Ltd v*   **41–033A** *Browallia Cal Ltd* [2011] Q.B. 477, CA. We have already seen, at para.8–029 above, where the facts of the case are given, that the defendant's argument that the profits the claimant would have made from its trading fund were too speculative to be recoverable was not accepted. The defendant also argued that the claimant's loss fell to be assessed as at the date of discovery of the fraud so that the profits that would have been made from then on to the date of trial were not recoverable. The Court of Appeal, and Flaux J. below, disagreed, holding that discovery of the fraud did not provide a cut-off point. The effects of the fraud continued after its discovery because the claimant no longer had the amount by which its trading fund had been depleted, so that it was locked into a disadvantageous situation just as the House of Lords had held the claimant to have been in the deceit case of *Smith New Court* (see at para.41–014 of the main work). It was also said that damages for loss of profits from an alternative investment were capable of being recovered in an action of deceit just as they had been in *East v Maurer* (see at para.41–029 of the main work) where the deceit concerned the sale of a business. As for the defendant's further contention that the claim was for damages for delay in the payment of damages, this was shown to be false and rejected. On this see *Parabola* at para.41 *et seq.* but the whole of Toulson L.J.'s judgment—his brethren simply concurred—deserves attention.

41–039   Add at the end of the paragraph: And in *Kinch v Rosling* [2009] EWHC 286, QB the claimant was awarded £10,000 on account of the humiliation, distress and anxiety suffered as a consequence of the bankruptcy forced on him by reason of an advanced fee fraud of which he was the victim: see *ibid.*, para.18.

41–039   Insert a new note at the end of the paragraph (as changed):

NOTE 190a: In *Simmons v Castle* [2012] EWCA Civ 1039, in addition to adopting the recommendation of the Jackson Report that the level of personal injury general damages should be increased by 10 per cent (the details of this development are set out at para.35–287A, above), the Court of Appeal, again following Jackson, declared that from April 1, 2013 the increase of 10 per cent should also apply to all torts causing suffering, inconvenience or distress (see *ibid.*, para.20 together with para.14). Though not specifically mentioned by the Court of Appeal, or by Jackson, deceit would be one of them. [In the judgment in the further hearing of *Simmons v Castle* [2012] EWCA Civ 1288, just out (for details see para.3–030, fn.172a, above), the Court of Appeal has extended its ruling to all civil claims and to all types of non-pecuniary loss: see the court's conclusion at *ibid.*, para.50.]

Insert new paragraphs after para.41–057:

41–057A   Illustrating this basic rule, and adding to the paucity of authority, there is *Scullion v Bank of Scotland Plc* [2011] P.N.L.R. 5, p.68. It is true that the decision has now been reversed by the Court of Appeal, [2011] 1 W.L.R. 3212, CA, but this was only on the issue of liability, holding there to be no duty of care in the particular circumstances. Nevertheless, Lord Neuberger M.R., who gave the only reasoned judgment, did think it necessary to point out where the trial judge had gone wrong on the damages he awarded as his approach to damages might otherwise be relied on in other cases.

41–057B   The claimant wished to enter the buy-to-let housing market. He bought a flat with the intention of letting it at a rental which would be more than sufficient to pay the mortgage, and also the outgoings, on the flat, thus making the transaction self-financing. The defendants had produced a valuation report for the claimant's mortgage lender upon which they knew or should have known that the claimant would rely in making his purchase. In their report the defendants had negligently overstated both the capital value of the flat and the rental income that could be achieved from it. As a result the claimant was able first to let the flat only at a lower rent than anticipated and then to sell it, on a falling market, for less than he had paid for it.

His claim for the difference between the price he paid and the amount for which he sold failed because he had not in fact paid more for the flat than its true value at the time of purchase. His loss was due entirely to the subsequent fall in the market and for this loss, on a direct application of *SAAMCO* (see para.29–065 of the main work), he could not recover. While there was no appeal by the claimant on this, it is clear that the Court of Appeal would have agreed with the trial judge's rejection of the claimant's attempt to obtain the difference between his purchase price and his later sale price. **41–057C**

His claim in connection with the misrepresentation as to rental income succeeded, the loss being the claimant's liability to make good the shortfall on his mortgage, arising from the inadequate rental payments, from his own resources. However, Lord Neuberger M.R., with whose judgment the other members of the Court of Appeal simply agreed, considered that the trial judge's approach came close to treating the negligent statement as a warranty and he spelt out a more limited recovery: for the details see his judgment at paras 64 to 68. **41–057D**

Insert a new note at the end of the paragraph: **41–059**

NOTE 306a: In *Simmons v Castle* [2012] EWCA Civ 1039, in addition to adopting the recommendation of the Jackson Report that the level of personal injury general damages should be increased by 10 per cent (the details of this development are set out at para.35–287A, above), the Court of Appeal, again following Jackson, declared that from April 1, 2013 the increase of 10 per cent should also apply to all torts causing suffering, inconvenience or distress (see *ibid.*, para.20 together with para.14. Today this should include negligent misrepresentation). [In the judgment in the further hearing of *Simmons v Castle* [2012] EWCA Civ 1288, just out (for details see para.3–030, fn.172a, above), the Court of Appeal has extended its ruling to all civil claims and to all types of non-pecuniary loss: see the court's conclusion at *ibid.*, para.50.]

CHAPTER 42

INVASION OF PRIVACY AND MISFEASANCE IN PUBLIC OFFICE

			PARA.
I.		INVASION OF PRIVACY	42–002
■	1.	Heads of damage	42–003
■	2.	Aggravation and mitigation	42–013
	3.	Exemplary damages	42–015
II.		MISFEASANCE IN PUBLIC OFFICE	42–018
■	1.	Heads of damage	42–019
■	2.	Aggravation and mitigation	42–023
□	3.	Exemplary damages	42–025

42–007   Insert a new note at the end of the paragraph:

NOTE 19a: Tugendhat J. too appears to favour higher damages in privacy cases: see his comment at para.114 of *Spelman v Express Newspapers* [2012] EWHC 355, QB, a human rights and injunction case.

Insert new paragraphs after para. 42–009:

42–009A   The Supreme Court has now established, by a six to three majority in *R. (on the application of Lumba (Congo)) v Secretary of State for the Home Department* [2012] 1 A.C. 245, that the infringement of a right does not lead in our law to an entitlement to vindicatory damages. The leading speech on the damages issues in *Lumba* was that of Lord Dyson, with whom on the issues of damages all of the other Justices in the majority agreed. He dealt with the matter in some detail (*ibid.*, paras 97 to 101), citing, and stating his agreement with what is said in para.42–009 of the main work. He rightly regarded the Caribbean cases in the Privy Council as special, being limited to claims involving the infringement of constitutional rights. He pointed out that the implications of allowing vindicatory damages in the case before the court would be far reaching and lead to undesirable uncertainty, he asked rhetorically where it would all end if the court granted the claimed vindicatory damages against the state for false imprisonment, and he boldly concluded that he saw "no justification for letting such an unruly horse loose on our law": all this at *ibid.*, para.101.

42–009B   It seems that vindicatory damages will now be confined to defamation where they began, being intended to make manifest that the claimant's reputation is unsullied. They may also occasionally make an appearance in false imprisonment which, as has been said, can affect reputation as well as liberty. Indeed the claims in *Lumba* itself were for false imprisonment but in that case there was no call for vindicatory damages for the protection of reputation as the claimants had no reputation to protect: see the facts at para.37–013A, above and the cogent comments of Lord Kerr at *ibid.*, para.256.

Thus Nicola Davies J., in arriving at £15,000 for her award of damages in *AAA v Associated Newspapers Ltd* [2012] EWHC 2103, QB, was wrong to take into account Eady J.'s support in *Mosley* of vindicatory damages in privacy cases: *ibid.*, paras 126 and 127. What Eady J. said there on vindicatory damages and privacy (see para.42–008 of the main work) has been overtaken by the Supreme Court's decision in *Lumba*, above. **42–009C**

NOTE 30: Add at the end of the note: In *Simmons v Castle* [2012] EWCA Civ 1039, in addition to adopting the recommendation of the Jackson Report that the level of personal injury general damages should be increased by 10 per cent (the details of this development are set out at para.35–287A, above), the Court of Appeal, again following Jackson, declared that from April 1, 2013 the increase of 10 per cent should also apply to all torts causing suffering, inconvenience or distress (see *ibid.*, para.20 together with para.14). Though not specifically mentioned by the Court of Appeal, breach of privacy will be a relevant tort. This is underlined by the fact that breach of privacy specifically features in the Jackson Report as a relevant tort (recommendation 65(i)). [In the judgment in the further hearing of *Simmons v Castle* [2012] EWCA Civ 1288, just out (for details see para.3–030, fn.172a, above), the Court of Appeal has extended its ruling to all civil claims and to all types of non-pecuniary loss: see the court's conclusion at *ibid.*, para.50.] **42–010**

NOTE 37: Add at the end of the note: But note, at para.3–011, fn.47, above, the concerns expressed in *Commissioner of Police of the Metropolis v Shaw* [2012] I.C.R. 464, [2012] I.R.L.R. 291 over having separate awards. **42–013**

Add at the end of the paragraph: The libel awards made in *Cooper v Turrell* [2011] EWHC 3269, QB to both the individual and corporate claimants (facts at para.39–043, above) were supplemented by further awards for what was referred to as the misuse of private information (*ibid.*, para.107), being in line with breach of confidential information but being, it is thought, nearer to the law of privacy. This is said because the cases relied on for the damages award by counsel and listed by Tugendhat J. in his judgment (*ibid.*, para.92) all concerned awards for loss of privacy while Tugendhat J. also said that, because of the seriousness of the damage, the privacy case of *Mosley* (see para.42–007 of the main work) was a more appropriate guide for him than the earlier privacy cases (*ibid.*, para.106). In the result, while he awarded £10,000 to the corporate claimant, he awarded £30,000 to the individual claimant, adding that it would have been £40,000 had compensation for the individual's distress not already been included in the libel award; double counting had to be avoided (*ibid.*, para.107). **42–013**

42–022   NOTE 71: Add at the end of the note:

While the claim in *Clifford v The Chief Constable of the Hertfordshire Constabulary* [2011] EWHC 815, QB (facts at para.38–004, fn.16a, above) was for malicious prosecution and misfeasance in public office, the damages awarded, all for non-pecuniary loss, were given under the malicious prosecution head.

42–022   Insert a new note at the end of the paragraph:

NOTE 72a: In *Simmons v Castle* [2012] EWCA Civ 1039, in addition to adopting the recommendation of the Jackson Report that the level of personal injury general damages should be increased by 10 per cent (the details of this development are set out at para.35–287A, above), the Court of Appeal, again following Jackson, declared that from April 1, 2013 the increase of 10 per cent should also apply to all torts causing suffering, inconvenience or distress (see *ibid.*, para.20 together with para.14). Though not specifically mentioned by the Court of Appeal, or by Jackson, misfeasance in public office would be one of them. [In the judgment in the further hearing of *Simmons v Castle* [2012] EWCA Civ 1288, just out (for details see para.3–030, fn.172a, above), the Court of Appeal has extended its ruling to all civil claims and to all types of non-pecuniary loss: see the court's conclusion at *ibid.*, para.50.]

42–023   Insert a new note after the first sentence of the paragraph:

NOTE 72a: The judge in *Amin v Imran Khan & Partners* [2011] EWHC 2958, QB was wrong to give aggravated damages on pecuniary loss arising from misfeasance in public office: see *ibid.*, paras 104 to 107.

42–026   Insert a new note after "close the matter." on lines 3 and 4 of the paragraph:

NOTE 81a: Exemplary damages would undoubtedly have been awarded for this tort in *Muuse v Secretary of State for the Home Department* [2010] EWCA Civ 453 had the Court of Appeal felt able to uphold the trial judge's finding of misfeasance in public office. Instead, exemplary damages were awarded for false imprisonment, which tort was indeed admitted: see the facts at para.11–018, above.

BOOK THREE
HUMAN RIGHTS

CHAPTER 43

DAMAGES UNDER THE HUMAN RIGHTS ACT

			PARA.
■	1.	Introduction	43–001
■	2.	Scope of the cause of action	43–007
■	3.	Criteria for decision whether to award damages	43–020
	4.	The court's approach to determining quantum	43–032
□	5.	Particular aspects of quantum	43–041
■	6.	Damages under particular convention articles	43–054

Insert a new note at the end of the paragraph: **43–005**

NOTE 13a: See further the fuller discussion of "just satisfaction" at paras 43–023 and 43–024 of the main work.

Insert a new note at the end of the paragraph: **43–006**

NOTE 19a: See further paras 43–024A and 43–024B, below and the consideration of *R. (Sturnham) v Parole Board* [2012] 3 W.L.R. 476 where the Court of Appeal contrasted a violation of the convention with a breach of a public law right where there is generally no right to damages.

Add at the end of the paragraph: Lord Scott's *obiter dictum* was considered by **43–014** the Supreme Court in *Rabone v Pennine Care NHS Trust* [2012] 2 A.C. 72 and, echoing the views expressed above, the Supreme Court rejected the notion that a close family member could not be a victim for the purposes of the substantive obligations owed under Art.2. Lord Dyson said (at para.46) that the ECtHR has repeatedly stated that family members of a deceased can bring claims in their own right, citing *Yasa v Turkey* (1999) 28 E.H.R.R. 408 at para.64, *Edwards v United Kingdom* (2002) 35 E.H.R.R. 19 at para.106, *Renolde v France* (2009) 48 E.H.R.R. 42 at para.69 and *Kats v Ukraine* (2010) 51 E.H.R.R. 44 at para.94.

Add at the end of the paragraph: In *Rabone v Pennine Care NHS Trust* [2012] **43–019** 2 A.C. 72, where the trial judge had refused to extend the one-year time limit for bringing the claim under the HRA, this decision was reversed by the Supreme Court which, rejecting the basis upon which the judge and the Court of Appeal had refused to extend time (namely that the claim was doomed to failure on other grounds), exercised the discretion afresh. The Supreme Court affirmed the relevant principles: the court has a wide discretion in determining whether it is equitable to extend time in the particular circumstances of any case and it will often be appropriate to take into account factors of the type set out in s.33 of the Limitation Act 1980: the length and reasons for the delay in issuing proceedings; the extent to which, having regard to the delay, the evidence is likely to be less cogent than if proceedings had been issued in time; and the conduct of the public authority after the right of claim arose, including the extent (if any) to which it responded to reasonable requests for information for the purpose of ascertaining the facts. However, the Supreme Court warned against any attempt to re-write the words of s.7(5)(b) of the HRA as if it contained the language of s.33(3) of the Limitation Act 1980. In extending time to allow the claim, reliance was placed upon the fact that, although the claimants were aware of the HRA in general terms and the possibility of bringing a claim, and could have issued proceedings within one year, they had acted reasonably in not so doing as they were awaiting a report on the death of their daughter from the defendant trust pursuant to their formal complaint made within five months of her death.

43–020   Add at the end of the paragraph: This was applied by HHJ Pelling QC in *Pennington v Parole Board* [2010] EWHC 78 (Admin) where, in assessing damages for breach of Art.5(4) ECHR, the court held that the assessment should be by reference to past decisions of the ECtHR rather than by reference to domestic scales. Where there was a three-month delay in the Board informing the claimant that he was to be released on licence, the court awarded damages of £1,750.

Insert new paragraphs after para.43–024:

43–024A   In the English courts, important and valuable contributions to the search for principle and the identification of a principle to distinguish between cases where damages should be awarded and where a finding of breach should be regarded as sufficient just satisfaction has been provided by the Court of Appeal in *R. (Sturnham) v Parole Board* [2012] 3 W.L.R. 476. This case included a claim for damages under s.8 HRA for breach of Art.5.4 where the defendant's consideration of the release of the claimant, who had been convicted of manslaughter and sentenced to an indeterminate term of imprisonment for public protection, was wrongly delayed by six months. The decision then reached was actually to refuse his release, so the delay did not result in the claimant being incarcerated for longer than he should have been. The trial judge awarded the claimant damages of £300, but this was overturned by the Court of Appeal. Giving the judgment of the court, Laws L.J. contrasted the position in English law where damages for breach of a private law wrong are generally a matter of entitlement and breach of a public law wrong where damages are not generally recoverable. Applying a similar distinction to claims for damages under Art.5 (but there seems no reason why this should not apply to any claim for damage under s.8), he said at para.15:

> "Now, the distinct territory of section 8 is marked by the fact that the defendant is a public authority and the wrong is a violation of the Convention. Depending on the

facts this territory is often a closer neighbour to our public than to our private law. That circumstance brings into focus a distinction of some significance in the search for principle. It is between cases where the violation of the Convention right has an outcome for the claimant which constitutes or is akin to a private wrong, such as trespass to the person, and cases where the violation has no such consequence."

In applying this principle, Laws L.J. drew support from the judgment of Lord Bingham in *Greenfield's case* [2005] 1 W.L.R. 673; see further para.43–024. As also observed by Laws L.J., the distinction between cases where the violation amounts to a private law wrong and those where it does not is reflected in some of the Strasbourg cases: see, for example, *Migon v Poland* (Application No 24244/94), *Nikolova v Bulgaria* (2001) 31 E.H.R.R. 3 and *Niedbala v Poland* (2000) 33 E.H.R.R. 1137, para.88.

Drawing together the Strasbourg and English jurisprudence, Laws L.J. **43–024B** expressed the principles to be applied as follows (*Sturnham* at para.22):

"(1) Damages are only to be awarded where that is necessary to afford just satisfaction under section 8(3) of the 1998 Act. (2) In an article 5.4 delay case the Convention right will ordinarily be vindicated and just satisfaction ordinarily achieved by a declaration. The focus of the Convention and of the court is on the protection of the right rather than compensation of the claimant. (3) But if the violation involves an outcome for the claimant in the nature of a trespass to the person, just satisfaction is likely to require an award of damages. The paradigm of such a case arises where the claimant's detention is extended by reason of the delay. Another case might be where the delay occasions a diagnosable illness in the claimant. (4) Other cases where the outcome or consequence of the delay is stress and anxiety, but no more, will not generally attract compensation in the absence of some special feature or features by which the claimant's suffering is materially aggravated."

Insert new paragraphs after para.43–027:

The relationship between s.8 HRA and Art.5(4) ECHR was considered by **43–027A** Saunders J. in *Degainis v Secretary of State for Justice* [2010] EWHC 137 (Admin). The claimant brought judicial review proceedings for breach of Art.5(4) in regard to the state's failure to provide him with a prompt review of his release. The Secretary of State admitted breach and apologised. The claimant submitted that this entitled him to damages pursuant to Art.5(5) which provides:

"Everyone who has been the victim of arrest or detention in contravention of the provisions of this article shall have an enforceable right to compensation."

Saunders J. rejected a submission that compensation in Art.5(5) is restricted in its meaning to money, saying: "I can see no basis for so limiting its meaning. Decisions of the European Court do not support the construction suggested by the Claimant." He observed that, in *Nikolova v Bulgaria* (2001) 31 E.H.R.R. 3, no award was made for breach of Art.5(4) whereas, if the construction of Art.5(5) proposed on behalf of the claimant were correct, namely that compensation only meant money, then the court would have to award damages in every case because that article gives the victim of a breach of Art.5(4) an enforceable right to them. See further *R. (Sturnham) v Parole Board* [2012] 3 W.L.R. 476, CA, considered at paras 43–024A and 43–024B, above.

43–027B   An interesting approach to the question of just satisfaction and whether to make an award of damages was adopted by the Court of Appeal in *Dobson v Thames Water Utilities Ltd* [2009] 3 All E.R. 319, CA. The claimants were occupiers of properties adversely affected by sewage treatment works operated by the defendant. Some of the claimants had a proprietary interest in the properties in question, making them eligible to claim damages for nuisance, but others did not. In addition to liability in negligence and nuisance, the defendant was in breach of the claimants' rights under Art.8 ECHR. The court held that where a public authority had been found to have acted unlawfully, the court could grant such relief or remedy as it considered just and appropriate. No award of damages was to be made unless, taking account of all the circumstances including any other relief or remedy granted in relation to the same act, the court was satisfied that the award was necessary to afford just satisfaction under Art.41 of the Convention. It further held that an award of damages in nuisance to a person or persons with a proprietary interest in a property would be relevant to the question whether an award of damages was necessary to afford just satisfaction under Art.8 to a person who lived in the same household but had no proprietary interest in the property. As the judge had held, the availability of other remedies was relevant to the issue of whether damages were necessary to afford just satisfaction under s.8(3) of the 1998 Act. Under that provision, all circumstances had to be taken into account. Despite the fact that damages for private nuisance were awarded as damage to "land", it was highly improbable, if not inconceivable, that Strasbourg would think it appropriate or just or necessary to award a further sum on top for breach of Art.8. Accordingly the award of damages at common law to a property owner would normally constitute just satisfaction to the owner for the purposes of s.8(3) of the 1998 Act and no additional award of compensation under that Act would normally be necessary. In so holding, the court considered a preliminary question raised for its decision, namely "Do, or might, damages for nuisance confer a sufficient remedy on those with a legal right to occupy such as to disentitle those living in the same household without such a legal right to a separate remedy under Article 8 and/or the Human Rights Act 1998?" Answering this question, and considering the claim of Thomas Bannister who lived with his parents in one of the properties, Waller L.J. said, at *ibid.*, paras 46 and 47:

> " . . . [W]e do not think it is possible to say until the case has been tried out whether it is just and appropriate and necessary to award some damages to Thomas Bannister if he is to have just satisfaction. For the reasons given, it may very well be that a declaration is sufficient in his case, but it will depend on the judge's findings in relation to his parents and to any particular consideration affecting Thomas. Even if it is thought that necessity be shown, the fact of any award to his parents, and its amount will be relevant as to quantum. It should be noted that in any event damages if awarded on such issues are not substantial.

We would accordingly reverse the judge on Issue 9. We would go no further than to state, by way of formal answer to the issue, that an award of damages in nuisance to a person or persons with a proprietary interest in a property will be relevant to the question whether an award of damages is necessary to afford just satisfaction under Article 8 to a person who lives in the same household but has no proprietary interest in the property."

The making of an award of damages pursuant to domestic law was similarly **43–027C** held to be relevant to whether an award of damages is necessary to give just satisfaction under Art.41 in *Rabone v Pennine Care NHS Trust* [2010] EWCA Civ 698, an action arising out of the death of a mental patient which included a claim under Art.2 ECHR. The Court of Appeal held that where an applicant brought a claim in his domestic court in respect of matters which formed the basis of the Convention claim and succeeded, that success might deprive him of the status of victim under Art.34 of the Convention. To ascertain whether the settlement or award of the domestic court had that consequence, it was necessary to consider all the circumstances of the domestic litigation and to determine whether it afforded effective redress for the Convention breach. In particular, it was necessary to consider (a) whether liability for the offending conduct had been either accepted by the state authority or found proven by the court; (b) the adequacy of any compensation awarded by the domestic court. If the compensation awarded fell substantially short of the pecuniary losses suffered by the applicant, that was a factor pointing against treating the domestic award as effective redress. The finding of the Court of Appeal that on the facts, the claimants had already obtained effective redress, in so far as the law could afford redress for a loss which lay beyond the reach of financial compensation and were accordingly not victims within Art.34 and therefore not entitled to pursue a claim under s.7 of the 1998 Act was reversed by the Supreme Court on appeal ([2012] 2 A.C. 72). It was held that settlement of the claim for damages for negligence did not prevent the claim for damages under s.7 HRA and Art.2 because English law damages for bereavement were available only for the loss of a child under the age of 18, and the deceased had been over 18 years of age, so the claims did not overlap.

Add at the end of the paragraph: Essentially the same distinction was applied **43–029** by the Court of Appeal in *R. (Sturnham) v Parole Board* [2012] 3 W.L.R. 476 where it was held, in relation to a breach of Art.5, that damages would not ordinarily be awarded unless the violation also amounted to breach of a private law right: see paras 43–023A and 43–023B, above.

Add at the end of the paragraph: The *Van Colle* approach to causation was **43–042** explicitly adopted and applied by Mackay J. in *Savage v South Essex Partnership NHS Foundation Trust* [2010] EWHC 865, QB where he said that the claimant only had to show that the deceased had lost a substantial chance of survival as a result of the trust's actions.

43–045   Substitute the table of awards below for the current table

Case Name	Date	Reference: Doc No.	Articles Breached	Nature of breach	Damages
DINCHEV v BULGARIA	22/01/09	AG0003337	6	The applicant was the alleged victim of a crime when shot in the face by a gas pistol, and his rights under Art.6 were breached when the case against the alleged perpetrator was dismissed after excessive delay.	€3,000
KUVALEHDET v FINLAND	10/02/09	AG0003352	10	The applicants were journalists who were ordered to pay damages for reporting on pending criminal proceedings which was found to be a serious breach of the freedom of the press.	€5,000
ROZSA v HUNGARY	28/04/09	AG0003381	6	The applicants were shareholders in a company which unlawfully liquidated and sought compensation for loss in the value of their shares in consequence of the unlawful liquidation. In breach of Art.6, the domestic court held that the applicants had no locus standi.	€2,000
DOGAN SORGUC v TURKEY	23/06/09	AG0003400	10	The applicant was convicted of defamation and this conviction was held to be a breach of his right to freedom of expression.	€3,500
MARIAPORI v FINLAND	06/07/10	AG0003587	10	The applicant was convicted of defamation and this conviction was held to be a breach of her right to freedom of expression.	€6,000
CIORAP v MOLDOVA (NO. 3)	20/07/10	AG0003622	3	The applicant was subjected to inhuman treatment as a result of being held for two weeks in substandard conditions and being denied hospital treatment for eight days, which aggravated his pre-existing medical condition.	€4,000

43–050   Add at the end of the paragraph: See further *Savage v South Essex Partnership NHS Foundation Trust* [2010] EWHC 865, QB where Mackay J. held that the test was whether the deceased had lost a "substantial chance" of survival in consequence of the breach of Art.2.

Insert new paragraphs after para.43–059:

43–059A   The leading case on the award of damages under Art.2 is now *Rabone v Pennine Care NHS Trust* [2012] 2 A.C. 72 in which the Supreme Court allowed the claimants' appeals against the refusal of the lower courts to award damages arising out of the death of their 24-year-old daughter who was a voluntary psychiatric patient at the defendant's hospital, and who committed suicide when on a home visit. The court held that, whilst in general in cases involving medical (clinical) negligence there is no operational duty, an exception applies to psychiatric patients detained in hospital, and no distinction is to be drawn between voluntary patients and those compulsorily detained when, very often, this is a matter of form rather than substance, the hospital having the power to intervene and prevent a patient from leaving where there is a real and immediate risk. In this case, the defendant not only owed the deceased an operational duty, but was in breach of that duty in failing to do all that it reasonably could have been expected to do to prevent the deceased's suicide. It was further held that family members (here, the deceased's parents) were entitled to bring claims in their own right under the HRA as victims of the breach of Art.2. Whilst, had the deceased been under 18, the claimants' remedy would have been damages for bereavement under the Fatal Accidents Act, here there was no domestic remedy and damages were awardable under the HRA. The Supreme Court decided that, this being a bad case of breach of Art.2, an award of damages was merited which was "well above the lower range of damages awarded to victims of a breach of article 2" and decided that the sum of £5,000 was appropriate for each claimant.

In principle, there seems no reason why this should not be extended to all **43–059B** "victims" who are family members and similarly bereaved by a death: siblings and grandparents for example. Indeed, there is no reason why those victims should not have a valid claim under the HRA where the deceased is under 18 and the domestic remedy is confined to the deceased's parents. The restricting factor will be the need to establish the "operational duty" which is generally only applied to those detained by the state, such as prisoners, immigrants kept in administrative detention, psychiatric patients either compulsorily detained or who are voluntary patients with the threat of compulsory detention hanging over their heads, and military conscripts.

Insert a new note at the end of the paragraph: **43–060**

NOTE 171a: For a case where the *Osman* test was found to be satisfied and damages were awarded for breach of Art.2, see *Savage v South Essex Partnership NHS Foundation Trust* [2010] EWHC 865, QB.

NOTE 172: Add at the end of the note: This causation test was applied by **43–061** Mackay J. when the case came back before the court for further determination: see [2010] EWHC 865, QB and para.43–042, above.

Insert a new paragraph after para.43–069:

In *R. (Sturnham) v Parole Board* [2012] 3 W.L.R. 476, the Court of Appeal **43–069A** gave consideration to the principles upon which the courts should award damages for breach of Art.5, stating that damages should not ordinarily be awarded unless the violation involves breach of a private law right, for example a trespass to the person. See further paras 43–024A and 43–024B, above.

Insert a new heading and new paragraphs after para.43–091:

(6) *Article 10: Right to Freedom of Expression*

43–092   Article 10 provides:

> "1. Everyone has the right to freedom of expression. This right shall include freedom to hold opinions and to receive and impart information and ideas without interference by public authority and regardless of frontiers. This Article shall not prevent States from requiring the licensing of broadcasting, television or cinema enterprises.
>
> 2. The exercise of these freedoms, since it carries with it duties and responsibilities, may be subject to such formalities, conditions, restrictions or penalties as are prescribed by law and are necessary in a democratic society, in the interests of national security, territorial integrity or public safety, for the prevention of disorder or crime, for the protection of health or morals, for the protection of the reputation or rights of others, for preventing the disclosure of information received in confidence, or for maintaining the authority and impartiality of the judiciary"

There have been a number of cases recently where the applicant has complained that a finding against him or her of defamation combined with an award of damages in the domestic court constitutes a breach of the applicant's rights to freedom of expression under Art.10. One of the questions that the ECtHR will consider in relation to such applications is the proportionality of the award of damages in the domestic court. Thus, in *Sorguc v Turkey* (Lawtel Case ref AG0003400), June 23, 2009, the ECtHR held that the amount of compensation awarded by the domestic court must "bear a reasonable relationship of proportionality to the . . . [moral] . . . injury . . . suffered" by the respondent in question, applying *Tolstoy Miloslavsky v United Kingdom* (July 13, 1995) and *Steel and Morris v United Kingdom* where the court held that the damages awarded, although relatively moderate by contemporary standards, were "very substantial when compared to the modest incomes and resources of the . . . applicants . . . " and, as such, were in breach of the Convention. It is in response to decisions such as these that English courts have significantly reduced the quantum of damages awarded for defamation, in the knowledge that excessive awards in comparison to the income and resources of the defendant against whom the award of compensation for defamation is being made will or may amount to a breach of that defendant's human right.

43–093   An interesting application of Art.10 came in the decision of the ECtHR in *Aquilina v Malta* (Application No.28040/08, June 14, 2011) where the applicant journalists had been found by the Maltese courts to have defamed a lawyer by reporting that he had been found to have been in contempt of court in failing to turn up to a hearing to represent his client on a charge of bigamy. The domestic courts had not been satisfied that the evidence in fact supported the allegation, particularly in the absence of anything to that effect on the court record. In finding a breach of Art.10, the ECtHR effectively acted as a final court of appeal, finding that the decision of the Maltese Courts was unsupportable in the light of the evidence which had been presented and that therefore

"in taking their decisions the domestic courts overstepped their margin of appreciation and the judgments against the applicants and the ensuing award of damages were disproportionate to the legitimate aim pursued. It follows that the interference with the applicants' exercise of their right to freedom of expression cannot be regarded as necessary in a democratic society for the protection of the reputation and rights of others."

This decision appears to suggest that the ECtHR, in enforcing a right considered to be as valuable as that protected by Art.10, may step into the arena and consider the evidential justification for a finding of defamation. So far as the damages were concerned, the applicants had, perhaps surprisingly, failed to claim as damages from the Maltese State the amounts that they had been ordered to pay in damages themselves to the lawyer—sums which the ECtHR acknowledged would have been awardable had they been claimed. Apart from that, the ECtHR found that the finding of a violation of Art.10 was not, by itself, just satisfaction, and awarded the applicants €4,000 together with €2,995 for the costs and expenses incurred before the domestic courts and €4,500 for those incurred before the ECtHR.

BOOK FOUR
PROCEDURE

CHAPTER 44

THE STATEMENT OF CASE

		PARA.
1.	The claim form	44–002
■ 2.	Particulars of claim	44–004
	(1) General and special damage	44–007
	(2) Exemplary damages	44–025
	(3) Aggravated damages	44–026
	(4) Aggravated damages	44–027
	(5) Periodical payments	44–028
	(6) Interest	44–031
	(7) The amount claimed	44–033
3.	Defence	44–034

Add at the end of the paragraph: Rix L.J.'s role as champion of the properly **44–004** pleaded case may be seen once again in thankful execution in *Jones v Environcom Ltd* [2012] P.N.L.R. 5, p.119. Refusing the appellant permission to amend the particulars of claim in third party proceedings in order to introduce an entirely new point of law on appeal and dismissing the proposed amendment for lack of particularisation, Rix L.J. said, at *ibid.*, para.20:

> "The importance of a proper pleading becomes the clearer when consideration is given to questions of scope of duty, causation and remoteness:"

All are of course central to the formulation of loss. A proper pleading in each respect can only be to the benefit of everyone.

CHAPTER 45

THE TRIAL

			PARA.
I.		PROOF	45–001
	1.	Burden of proof	45–001
☐	2.	Evidence	45–007
II.		JUDGMENT	45–015
☐	1.	Province of judge and jury: law and fact	45–015
■	2.	Assessment of damages	45–018

Insert a new paragraph after para.45–014:

45–014A   The Court of Appeal's decision in *Parabola Investments Ltd v Browallia Cal Ltd* [2011] Q.B. 477, CA provides an interesting example of the court's pragmatism in the proof of special damage. The second claimant was a company set up for the purpose of trading in stocks, shares and derivatives. The second defendant was a well established financial institution trading on the London Stock Exchange by whom the third defendant was employed as a senior futures broker. The claimant was induced to continue trading in so-called Stock Exchange Electronic Trading Service (SETS) by the third defendant's repeated false assurances that the trading was profitable whereas it was in truth disastrously loss-making from an early stage. The trial judge accepted the claimant's contention that, but for the third defendant's deceit, it would have made profits at a rate of 50 per cent per annum. On appeal, the second defendant argued that the judge's award of lost profit at the rate of 50 per cent was unsustainable because the claimant had failed to prove that a specific amount of profits would have been earned by a particular date. Highlighting what he referred to as the central flaw in the appellants' submissions, Toulson L.J. observed that some claims for consequential loss were capable of being established with precision whereas other forms of consequential loss were not capable of similarly precise calculation because they involved the attempted measurement of things which would or might have happened (or might not have happened) but for the defendant's wrongful conduct. In such a situation the law did not require a claimant to perform the impossible. Toulson L.J. continued, at *ibid.*, para.24:

> "It is true that by the nature of things the judge could not find as a fact that the amount of lost profit .... was more likely than not to have been the specific figure which he awarded but that is not to the point .... No method of assessment could be perfect, but the method of measurement accepted by the judge as a basis for estimating the lost profit was rational and supported by the opinion of an expert who impressed him."

In the right factual context, absent evidence sufficient to establish loss on balance of probability, special damage is thus seemingly capable of proof by inference derived from expert opinion, the only safeguards to the operation of proof by inference being the quality of the expertise and the rationality of the ensuing award.

Insert a new note at the end of the first sentence of the paragraph: **45–015**

NOTE 69a: For an interesting if ultimately jejune discussion on the aptness of trial by judge alone in defamation proceedings see *Fiddes v Channel Four Television Corp* [2010] 1 W.L.R. 2245, CA.

Insert a new paragraph after para.45–025:

The complication of contributory negligence put in a further appearance in   **45–025A**
Morton v Portal Ltd [2010] EWHC 1804, QB where the claimant's negligence served to reduce the damages recoverable by 25 per cent. The case contains a valuable consideration of the operation of the factors that a court is required to take into account in deciding whether or not to make a periodical payments order. The claimant favoured periodical payments for his future care to which the defendant had no objection. Walker J. nevertheless rejected the approach that, if a claimant of full age and capacity, which the particular claimant was, wished to have a periodical payments order, that was conclusive in its favour. The matter was for the court which must be satisfied that a periodical payments order was in the claimant's best interests. Walker J. also rejected the suggestion that, if the claimant and the defendant were agreed on a periodical payments order, a periodical payments order should follow; precluding an assumption in favour of such an order was the court's need to be satisfied that continuity of payment was secure. Nonetheless, independently of these considerations, Walker J. was persuaded that a periodical payments order was appropriate (see *ibid.*, para.22), in coming to which conclusion he expressed himself as further satisfied that the 25 per cent deduction for contributory negligence would not present too great a difficulty for the claimant (see *ibid.*, para.12). Whether or not Walker J.'s interpretation of the Court's supervisory jurisdiction in periodical payment cases is strictly consistent with the Court of Appeal's deference to the claimant's wishes, manifest in such cases as *Rowe v Dolman* [2008] EWCA Civ 1040, remains to be seen. Given the fact that the claimant in the instant case did not lack capacity, Walker J.'s determination to subordinate the claimant's wishes (and for that matter the wishes of the opposing party) to the outcome of his own assessment might be said to requisition for the court an unwarranted power to override a competent adult claimant's freedom of choice, a right which, save in the context of children and protected parties, the courts do not generally possess. For a further commentary on *Morton v Portal Ltd* see para.35–015, fn.38, above.

45–035   Add at the end of the paragraph: Two recent cases on the thorny subject of security of continuity of payment call for comment. In *Bennett v Stephens & Zenith Insurance Co* [2012] EWHC 1, QB; [2012] EWHC 58, QB, in which at a much earlier stage in the litigation doubt had been expressed as to the security of the defendant's insurer, the periodical payments order stipulated that the payments should be made by the insurer "or, if and to the extent that they are not paid by [them] within 7 days of the due date, by the Motor Insurers' Bureau". A separate security order provided that pursuant to the Uninsured Drivers' Agreement dated August 13, 1999, the MIB would be obliged to pay any sums in any judgment in the claim which remained unsatisfied for seven days. In determining that the continuity of payment under the orders was reasonably secure, Tugendhat J. held that, although the MIB was not a party to the litigation, it, or an equivalent body, was likely to subsist for the lifetime of the order, and that the 1999 Agreement was likely to be replaced by agreements to similar effect thereby enabling the claimant to retain accrued rights against the MIB. The MIB, which does not seem to have been consulted before the orders were approved, took issue with the judge's approach, submitting that the orders should not bind it to make payment in the event of the insurer's default because payment was the insurer's responsibility. After hearing further argument, Tugendhat J. held that he had not meant the MIB to remain liable to the claimant whatever might happen in the future. What he had decided was that the continuity of payment was reasonably secure as a result of the claimant's right to have recourse to the MIB or an equivalent body. The periodical payments order was not to be read as binding on the MIB but only on the insurer. The judge observed that, when drafting similar orders in the future, those preparing the draft should consider adopting a form of words which would not cause comparable concerns to the MIB. In the less analytical decision of *Boreham v Burton* [2012] EWHC 930, QB, H.H. Judge McKenna, sitting as a judge of the High Court, was also required to satisfy himself that the continuity of periodical payments proposed in settlement of the claimant's claim was reasonably secure. It seems that, while there were two major insurers behind the defendants, the defendants' counsel had raised doubt as to whether the two insurers would be secure because the accident giving rise to the claim had occurred in 1998 before the coming into force of the Financial Services and Markets Act 2000 and, pursuant to it, the Financial Services Compensation Scheme. The argument put on behalf of the claimant which the judge accepted was that the insurers were covered by the Financial Services Compensation Scheme even though the liability pre-dated the Scheme's establishment. On the reading of the relevant transitional provisions presented to the court, that conclusion seems unimpeachable.

45–036   Insert a new note at the end of the first sentence of the paragraph:

NOTE 118a: Combining periodical payments with provisional damages, in *Kotula v EDF Energy Networks (EPN) Plc* [2011] EWHC 1546, QB, in which the parties had agreed a settlement comprising a gross lump sum payment of £2.5

million and staged periodical payments for future care and case management linked to the ASHE 6115 earnings index but could not agree the consequences of any future deterioration in the claimant's medical condition, Irwin J. gave the claimant, a T6 paraplegic, permission to treat the lump sum award as provisional and granted him the right to seek to vary his otherwise agreed periodical payments if, in due course, he came to develop serious consequences as a result of acquired syringomyelia, a well known complication of spinal injury.

Insert a new note at the end of the paragraph: **45–036**

NOTE 118b: On October 1, 2011 amendments to CPR Pt 36 came into effect intended to clarify the meaning of the phrases "more advantageous" and "at least as advantageous" in relation to any money claim or money element of a claim where the court is required to determine whether a judgment equals or betters an offer to settle. A new rule numbered 36.14(1A) provides:

> "For the purposes of paragraph (1), in relation to any money claim or money element of a claim, 'more advantageous' means better in money terms by any amount, however small, and 'at least as advantageous' shall be construed accordingly:"

Thus the test is a direct monetary comparison. A Part 36 Offer is bettered if the eventual award exceeds it by as little as £1. Though commendably straightforward, the concept of direct monetary comparison is not easily applied to the complexities of settlement offers incorporating periodical payments. It can presumably be applied where a periodical payment offer is for a lower or higher annual sum than the court's eventual award. It may or may not be easily applied where the difference between offer and award is as to timing or indexation. It is of no help where the overall benefits of a mixed award are to be held against a similarly mixed but unequal Part 36 Offer. The safe conclusion is that the clarification barely changes the costs dynamic of complex offers. In relation of those, the parties must look to the trial judge's discretion.

Insert a new note at the end of the paragraph: **45–037**

NOTE 119a: Some of the more acute practical problems arising from the operation of CPR Pt 36 in periodical payment cases are now beginning to emerge. In *Pankhurst v White* [2010] EWHC 311, QB MacDuff J. awarded the claimant agreed periodical payments of £260,000 per annum plus a lump sum of £2.317 million, representing an equivalent capital value of around £6.1 million. The result was that, while the claimant failed to beat a Part 36 offer made by the defendant in 2008, he exceeded his own Part 36 offer made two years earlier. The claimant therefore sought the fruits of CPR Pt 36 for the period of two years until his offer was bettered by the defendant. Concluding that an enhanced consequences order in the form of increased interest was appropriate, MacDuff J. decided that it would be wrong to make an award of interest enhanced or otherwise in respect of those damages which were awarded for future losses and future expenditure. Enhanced interest was only appropriate upon past losses and not upon future losses. MacDuff J.'s conclusion is plainly correct. The court's power pursuant to CPR Pt 36 is to enhance the rate of interest recoverable. It is not to render heads of claim which would not otherwise attract an award of interest amenable to the recovery of interest. Furthermore, since the purpose of interest is to compensate the claimant for being kept out of his money, the only part of an award of which a claimant can be said to have been deprived is past loss. Such was clearly the view of Tugendhat J. when resolving a similar debate in the subsequent case of *Andrews v Aylott* [2010] P.I.Q.R. P13, p.241. While strictly a dispute as to the meaning of an earlier order of the court, the discussion in *Andrews* nevertheless extended to consideration of the elements of an award to which enhanced interest should attach pursuant to CPR Pt 36. Tugendhat J. concluded that, if he had to decide the point, he would respectfully be inclined to agree with MacDuff J.'s analysis in *Pankhurst v White* (see Tugendhat J.'s reasoning at *ibid.*, para.37). Tugendhat J. went on to hold that the word "interest" appearing in the court order under review was to be interpreted in its usual sense, namely as a sum which reflected the loss to the claimant equivalent to the actual or notional cost of being kept out of the monetary compensation. Interest was therefore not something to be applied to a payment to be made in the future, when payment of that sum would not have been delayed (see *ibid.*, para.52).

45–039　　Add at the end of the paragraph: Eady J.'s championing of the virtues of certainty and finality in *Adan v Securicor Custodial Services Ltd* [2005] P.I.Q.R. P6, p.79, sits uncomfortably with his decision in *Cook v Cook* [2011] EWHC 1638, QB. In *Cook*, the claimant, who was 10 years old at the date of the hearing before Eady J., claimed damages for very serious brain injuries sustained in part in a road traffic accident in 2001 when her mother was 28 weeks pregnant and in part through the negligent failure of the claimant's GP in 2004 to diagnose raised intra-cranial pressure. Applying to postpone quantification of the claimant's claims from the age of 16 onwards, it was argued for the claimant that because the claimant's long-term prognosis was unclear it would be unjust to assess her likely long-term losses at that time, the court and the parties being in a far better position to assess the long-term outcome and, correspondingly, the claimant's needs in adult life following a reassessment at or after her 16th birthday in 2017. Conceding that to adjourn any part of the assessment was a very exceptional course, Eady J. nevertheless resorted to CPR r.3.1(2) and ordered that the exercise of quantifying the claimant's long-term losses be postponed until there was solid evidence available. With due respect to the judge's laudable concern to avoid injustice, this was surely an erroneous exercise of judicial discretion. In truth, there was nothing exceptional about the claimant's claim or the problems of quantification to which it gave rise. Uncertainty inevitably surrounds the quantification of loss for any claimant with a significant life expectancy whose future losses fall to be assessed during their minority. Quantification is often necessarily approximate, for example where an infant claimant's uninjured future earning capacity has to be determined. With the assistance of appropriate expert evidence and the added consolation of variable periodical payments, the courts have proved perfectly capable of quantifying future loss without notorious injustice to anyone. If, by parity of reasoning, Eady J.'s approach were extended to comparable cases (of which there would be many) the quantification of damages risks disintegrating into a series of intermittent partial assessments, no doubt coupled with orders for the equivalent of interim payments, at the price of finality and certainty and immeasurably increased cost. That is surely not the direction of travel intended by the authors of CPR r.3.1(2). The decision is wrong in principle and should not be followed.

Add at the end of the paragraph: Another example of separate awards is *RAR*   **45–041**
v GGC [2012] EWHC 2338, QB. In a commendably clear breakdown of the sums awarded for serial physical and sexual abuse inflicted upon the claimant by her stepfather when the claimant was a minor, Nicola Davies J. awarded the claimant general damages for pain, suffering and loss of amenity in the sum of £70,000 and a further sum of £10,000 by way of aggravated damages, having first satisfied herself that awarding the latter would not represent double recovery.

Insert a new paragraph after para.45–057:

Given this historical lineage, the rationale for the quantification of aggravated   **45–057A**
damages tersely enunciated by Eady J. in the recent defamation case of *Bere-zovsky v Russian Television and Radio Broadcasting Co* [2010] EWHC 476, QB is anomalous and confusing. Asserting that in *Broome v Cassell & Co Ltd* [1972] A.C. 1027 both Lord Hailsham and Lord Reid had been of the opinion that any joint tortfeasor would only be liable for what he referred to as the lowest common denominator, Eady J. contended that the lowest common denominator approach was likely to be preferred by a modern appellate court. The assertion that Lord Reid had agreed with Lord Hailsham as to the applicability of the lowest sum principle to aggravated damages is to misread Lord Reid's careful opinion. While it is correct to say that Lord Hailsham's strictly obiter attempt to extend the lowest sum principle to aggravated damages received a somewhat indirect measure of support from Lord Diplock, such an extension of the principle was not endorsed by Lord Reid. To the contrary, in the part of his speech relied on by Eady J. (at *ibid.*, para.1090D–E) Lord Reid was referring exclusively to punitive (and thus exemplary) damages. He was not there addressing compensation for injury to feelings as such at all. Indeed, in the paragraph immediately preceding that relied on by Eady J. (at *ibid.*, para.1090C) Lord Reid indicated that, for compensatory damages, which of course include aggravated damages, it is the highest common factor that is appropriate (see further para.45–057 of the main work). Furthermore, Lord Hailsham's attempt to extend the lowest sum principle was firmly rejected by Lord Denning M.R. in *Hayward v Thompson* [1982] Q.B. 47, CA (at 62F), a case also taken into account by Eady J. In addition to its obfuscation of precedent, Eady J.'s bold proposition that the lowest sum principle is likely to be preferred by a modern appellate court can be challenged on the

further ground that it insufficiently acknowledges the conceptual distinction between exemplary and aggravated awards. In the case of aggravated damages, the injury for which compensation is payable is the aggregate injury inflicted by the combined act of both malicious and unmalicious tortfeasors. Aggregation in this sense permits no diminution in the liability of those liable in common for the overall injury. To introduce such a reduction would in effect be to demutualise the liability or to disaggregate the harm. Nor does Eady J.'s citation of Art.10 of the European Convention on Human Rights provide a convincing justification for his abandonment of the earlier authorities.

Insert a new heading and a new paragraph after para.45–060:

45–061   **(e) Where not all the defendants, or not all the claimants, are before the court and exemplary damages are claimed.** In the important case of *R. (on the application of Lumba (Congo)) v Secretary of State for the Home Department* [2012] 1 A.C. 245, the Court of Appeal upheld the first instance judge's decision that, on the facts, the threshold for an award of exemplary damages had not been reached, adding by way of further reason for declining to award exemplary damages that, where there is more than one victim of a tortfeasor's conduct, one award of damages should be made which award should be shared between the victims rather than a series of separate awards for each individual victim. Where, as in the instant case, the number of potential claimants was large and they were not all before the court, it was not appropriate to make an award of exemplary damages at all. In the Supreme Court, Lord Dyson, giving what may be treated as the majority speech, said the Court of Appeal was right to regard this as a reason for making no such award. He went on, at *ibid.*, para.168:

> "There is yet one further point. It is unsatisfactory and unfair to award exemplary damages where the basis for the claim is a number of serious allegations against named officials and Government Ministers of arbitrary and outrageous use of executive power and those persons have not been heard and their answers to the allegations have not been tested in evidence."

CHAPTER 46

APPEALS

		PARA.
I.	APPEALS FROM AN AWARD OF DAMAGES BY A JURY	46–002
	1. Powers available to the appellate court	46–003
	2. Grounds for granting a new trial: misleading and misconduct of the jury	46–007
	3. Grounds for reassessing the damages: miscalculation by the jury	46–018
II.	APPEALS FROM AN AWARD OF DAMAGES BY A JUDGE	46–024
	1. Power to reassess the damages	46–024
	2. Grounds for reassessing the damages	46–025

Insert new paragraphs after para.46–027:

The disturbing facts of *Ministry of Defence v Fletcher* [2010] I.R.L.R. 25, gave **46–027A**
rise to errors of law which served to vitiate awards of aggravated and exemplary
damages. For conduct on the part of the claimant's employer found to have been
both discriminatory and victimising, the claimant was awarded aggravated damages of £20,000 and exemplary damages in the sum of £50,000. Amidst the
behaviour which the Employment Tribunal took into account when awarding
aggravated damages was the objectionable manner in which the Ministry of
Defence had conducted its defence of the tribunal proceedings. On the Ministry
of Defence's appeal, the Employment Appeal Tribunal accepted that the Employment Tribunal had erred in law to the extent that it had taken into account as a
basis for an award of aggravated damages the contention that the Ministry's
conduct of its defence had created a media circus. Reflecting that error of law and
at the same time stripping away a degree of double counting, the Employment
Appeal Tribunal reduced the award of aggravated damages from £20,000 to
£8,000. Acknowledging a further error of law affecting the award of exemplary
damages, the Employment Appeal Tribunal overturned the entire award. For a
further discussion of *Ministry of Defence v Fletcher* see para.46–041, below.

The Court of Appeal's decision in *Beechwood Birmingham Ltd v Hoyer Group* **46–027B**
UK Ltd [2011] Q.B. 357, CA is another example of an error of law vitiating an
award, in this case an award of general damages. The claimant was a substantial
company of motor dealers with many vehicles at its disposal. A car belonging to
the claimant which had been allocated to one of its members of staff for his
personal use was damaged as a result of the negligence of the defendant's
employee. Rather than reallocating to himself a similar car from the claimant's
stock, the claimant's employee hired a replacement vehicle. At first instance, the
judge held that the resort to outside hire had been unreasonable and he therefore

declined to make any award of special damages for vehicle hire charges. However, by way of general damages for loss of use of the damaged vehicle during repair, the judge awarded the claimant the sum of £12,000 based on the spot hire rate for a comparable car. Allowing the defendant's appeal, the Court of Appeal held that while general damages were in principle recoverable for loss of use, they should reflect such sum as reasonably compensated the victim of the tort for the nature and extent of the financial loss suffered as a result of the neutering of the damaged asset employed in the business and the redeployment of another such asset. In the circumstances it was appropriate to base any award for loss of use not on the cost of outside hire but on the interest and capital employed and any depreciation sustained over the period of repair in respect of a vehicle of the type damaged in the accident. The judge's award of £12,000 was set aside, the parties being left to agree a suitable figure for loss of use which the court could award in substitution.

46–027C   The remarkable and important case of *Ramzan v Brookwide Ltd* [2012] 1 All E.R. 903, CA comprises amongst many other things an example of an award of damages overturned for error of law. The defendant company misappropriated a store room belonging at the time of the misappropriation to the claimant's father, from whose trustee in bankruptcy the claimant subsequently acquired the room, which was physically located on the first floor of an adjoining building owned by the defendant. Following a liability trial in 2008, the defendant was found to be liable to the claimant in damages, including exemplary damages, for the continuing infringement of his rights to enjoy the store room. In 2010 damages were assessed. Commenting that there was little guidance as to the assessment of exemplary damages, but nevertheless seizing upon the defendant's unrelenting lack of contrition for its wrongful conduct and the enormity of the defendant's means, the judge concluded that the appropriate figure to award was £60,000. The defendant appealed. Holding that the judge had fallen into error by failing to consider the impact of the fact that the claimant had become owner of the store room only after the defendant's incorporation of the room into a flat and that she could therefore interfere with the judge's award, for criteria relevant to computation Arden L.J. concentrated on the defendant's conduct in its expropriation of the property having taken place before it had been acquired by the claimant from his father (*ibid.*, para.78) and on the expropriation having had a deleterious effect on the health both of the claimant and of his father (*ibid.*, paras 78 to 80). These surely are matters that go to compensation by way of aggravated damages, which were here not allowed, and not to punishment by way of exemplary damages. Nor are convincing Arden L.J.'s statements that there is no scope for exemplary damages where an account of profits is claimed (*ibid.*, para.81), that the fact of making an exemplary award should largely be sufficient in itself (*ibid.*, para.82) and that there is little guidance on the quantification of exemplary damages (*ibid.*, para.82). Based upon these considerations, and primarily on account of the claimant's not being the owner of the property at the time of the tort (see *ibid.*, para.83 *in init.*) Arden L.J. decided to reduce from £60,000 to £20,000 (*ibid.*, para.83 *in med.*) Geraldine Alexander QC's careful award in a case which she had described as one of the worst of its kind ([2011] 2 All E.R. 38, para.69). It is not apparent from the respective judgments if paras 11–033 to 11–044 of this work were brought to the attention of the court either at first instance or on appeal. Had they been, abundant guidance on the quantification of exemplary damages would have been available. While the judge's figure was a little out of line with the reported awards, it is difficult to conclude that, had the guidance been followed in the Court of Appeal, a reduction of two-thirds would have resulted.

Add at the end of the paragraph: *Grand v Gill* [2011] 1 W.L.R. 2253, CA is to **46–028** be classified as an appeal on grounds of error of law where the damages were increased. The Court of Appeal overturned the first instance judge's decision to the effect that the internal plaster of the claimant's flat was a mere decorative finish and therefore did not form part of the structure of the demise for the purposes of quantifying general damages for breach of the covenant for quiet enjoyment. Determining that internal plaster did indeed form part of the structure of the building which the defendant was obliged to keep in repair, the Court of Appeal increased the judge's award of general damages from £600 to £1,275 to reflect the discomfort and inconvenience caused by the disrepair to the plaster.

Add at the end of the paragraph: Similar is *Smithurst v Selant Construction* **46–029** *Services Ltd* [2012] Med L.R. 258, CA, a personal injury claim in which the court was required to quantify damages for a disc prolapse attributable to the defendant employer's breach of duty. While holding that the judge had erred in law by treating issues as to whether the claimant would have suffered from a similar disc prolapse in the future and, if so, when, as ones of causation rather than ones of the assessment of the claimant's damages, the Court of Appeal nevertheless concluded that the judge's decision to the effect that the claimant would have suffered a similar injury within two years of the material accident was an entirely permissible one.

Insert a new paragraph after para.46–040:

The following recent cases are of relevance. In *Ministry of Defence v Fletcher* **46–041** [2010] I.R.L.R. 25, the hopefully exceptional underlying facts did not deter the Employment Appeal Tribunal from overturning an award of aggravated damages on grounds of double counting and perversity. When a serving soldier, the applicant had been subjected to conduct by her employer which was found to have been discrimination, harassment and systematic victimisation. For that conduct the Employment Tribunal awarded the applicant £30,000 for injury to feelings, aggravated damages in the sum of £20,000 and exemplary damages quantified at £50,000. Allowing the Ministry of Defence's appeal, the Employment Appeal Tribunal concluded that the award of aggravated damages over-lapped with matters which the Employment Tribunal had taken into account in their award for injury to feelings. Having regard to the element of double recovery, the totality of the award for non-pecuniary loss, the Judicial Studies Board guidelines in personal injury cases and decisions of the appellate courts, not only was the award of aggravated damages in the sum of £20,000 reached in error of law, it was also perversely high. The appropriate award in respect of aggravated damages was £8,000. In respect of exemplary damages, the Employment Appeal Tribunal held that the conduct for which the original award had been made, deplorable though it was found to be, did not cross the high threshold justifying an award of exemplary damages. The Employment Tribunal had therefore erred in law making such an award. The Employment Appeal Tribunal nevertheless troubled to observe that, if an award of exemplary damages was appropriate, it should have been no higher than £7,500. In addition to being legally erroneous, the Tribunal's valuation was therefore also excessive. In *Huntley v Simmons* [2010] Med L.R. 83, CA the claimant sought to challenge the trial judge's conclusion that the head injury for which he had claimed general damages fell near but not above the boundary between the second and third of the Judicial Studies Board's brackets for severe brain injuries. Rejecting the claimant's criticisms of the judge's methodology, Waller L.J. concluded that the judge had pitched the claimant at exactly the right point in the scale. The judge had furthermore cross checked against the authorities to see whether they confirmed his choice of bracket. The judge was not required to conduct a detailed analysis of the competing authorities cited by each party particularly where each side was suggesting that one rather than another of the decisions was closer to their case (see *ibid.*, para.44). In *Milner v Carnival Plc* [2010] 3 All E.R. 701, the Court of Appeal took the opportunity to extend the concept of tariffs to compensation for ruined holidays. Holding to be excessive and disproportionate the trial judge's award of £7,500 per claimant for distress and inconvenience arising from the disastrous outcome of a once in a lifetime Atlantic cruise, the Court of Appeal replaced the judge's awards with their own more modest valuations. For distress and disappointment, the Court of Appeal substituted figures of £4,000 for the male claimant and £4,500 for his wife. Ward L.J. observed that there must be some consistency with the level of damages awarded in other fields, the obvious point of comparison being with the assessment of general damages in personal injury cases where psychiatric injury had been suffered. However it was to be borne in mind that physical inconvenience and disappointment were ephemeral and distress fell within a category less serious and different from recognisable psychiatric injury (see *ibid.*, paras 57 and 58). In *Steele v The Home Office* [2010] EWCA Civ 724, the claimant, a Category A prisoner, brought proceedings against the Home Office for the Prison Service's failure to provide him with adequate dental care. That failure had resulted in the claimant suffering from toothache over a period of almost seven years. The judge at first instance awarded the claimant general damages of £45,000, by any standards a very considerable sum. On appeal, Smith L.J. concluded that the trial judge's award was out of line with awards in other types of case by a substantial margin. Accepting the trial judge's description of the pain and suffering which the claimant had endured, Smith L.J. substituted her own reduced valuation of £25,000.

Insert a new paragraph after para.46–041:

Simmons v Castle [2012] EWCA Civ 1039 is not an entirely erroneous **46–042** estimate case but is of such importance that it is necessary to bring it to the attention of practitioners and it is convenient to do so within a general discussion of appeals. In *Simmons*, in which the Court of Appeal was asked merely to rubber stamp the compromise of an appeal in a modest personal injury claim, because of the reform of civil costs brought about by the Legal Aid Sentencing and Punishment of Offenders Act 2012 which comes imminently into force, the Court of Appeal opportunistically promulgated a declaration uplifting awards of general damages. To address the imminent changes in the rules governing the recovery of success fees in cases funded pursuant to conditional fee agreements, with effect from April 1, 2013, the proper level of award for general damages for pain, suffering and loss of amenity, nuisance, defamation and all other torts which cause suffering, inconvenience or distress to the individual will be 10 per cent higher than previously. This uplift is said to take effect for all cases decided after April 1, 2013, irrespective of when the tort giving rise to the claim was committed or the litigation seeking the recovery of damages for that tort was commenced and irrespective of the manner in which the claim is funded. Thus the insurers of liable defendants will be required to meet liabilities computed at 110 per cent out of insurance premiums based on 100 per cent. Furthermore, while the 10 per cent uplift in general damages has been introduced to compensate for the loss of the success fee payable under the old style conditional fee arrangement, claimants litigating under old style conditional fee agreements and claimants with no conditional fee agreement of any kind are also to benefit from the enlargement of damages. Given the implications for the insurance market, it is perhaps a little surprising that this exercise of uplifting was carried out under the pretext of an appeal which had been compromised, and without first giving interested parties the opportunity to address the court. That omission has since been rectified by a further hearing at which insurers, the Association of Personal Injury Lawyers and the Personal Injuries Bar Association were represented. Judgment following that renewed hearing is eagerly awaited. [Hot on to the press, on October 10 the Court of Appeal handed down its further judgment in *Simmons v Castle* [2012] EWCA Civ 1288 holding that the 10 per cent increase in general damages should be denied to those claimants with conditional fee agreements entered into before April 1, 2013 who are still entitled to recover success fees from defendants, but otherwise allowed the increase, as before, in all cases decided after that date. A further feature of the Court of Appeal's mature reflections is that the increase is extended to claims in contract: see para.3–030, fn.172a, above].